ALLDATA 2017

The Third International Conference on Big Data, Small Data, Linked Data and Open Data

KESA 2017

The International Workshop on Knowledge Extraction and Semantic Annotation

April 23 - 27, 2017

Venice, Italy

ALLDATA 2017 Editors

Venkat N. Gudivada, East Carolina University, USA
Sandjai Bhulai, Vrije Universiteit Amsterdam, the Netherlands
Maria Pia di Buono, University of Zagreb, Croatia

Printed from e-media with permission by:

Curran Associates, Inc.
57 Morehouse Lane
Red Hook, NY 12571

Some format issues inherent in the e-media version may also appear in this print version.

Printed by Curran Associates, Inc. (2017)

International Academy, Research, and Industry Association (IARIA)
412 Derby Way
Wilmington, DE 19810

Phone: (408) 893-6407
Fax: (408) 527-6351

petre@iaria.org

Additional copies of this publication are available from:

Curran Associates, Inc.
57 Morehouse Lane
Red Hook, NY 12571 USA
Phone: 845-758-0400
Fax: 845-758-2633
Email: curran@proceedings.com
Web: www.proceedings.com

TABLE OF CONTENTS

ALLDATA 2017

Forward

The Third International Conference on Big Data, Small Data, Linked Data and Open Data (ALLDATA 2017), held between April 23-27, 2017 in Venice, Italy, followed a series of events bridging the concepts and the communities devoted to each of data categories for a better understanding of data semantics and their use, by taking advantage from the development of Semantic Web, Deep Web, Internet, non-SQL and SQL structures, progresses in data processing, and the new tendency for acceptance of open environments.

The volume and the complexity of available information overwhelm human and computing resources. Several approaches, technologies and tools are dealing with different types of data when searching, mining, learning and managing existing and increasingly growing information. From understanding Small data, the academia and industry recently embraced Big data, Linked data, and Open data. Each of these concepts carries specific foundations, algorithms and techniques, and is suitable and successful for different kinds of application. While approaching each concept from a silo point of view allows a better understanding (and potential optimization), no application or service can be developed without considering all data types mentioned above.

The conference had the following tracks:

- Big data
- Linked data
- Open data
- Challenges in processing Big Data and applications

The conference also featured the following workshop:

- **KESA 2017, The International Workshop on Knowledge Extraction and Semantic Annotation**

We take here the opportunity to warmly thank all the members of the ALLDATA 2017 technical program committee, as well as all the reviewers. The creation of such a high quality conference program would not have been possible without their involvement. We also kindly thank all the authors that dedicated much of their time and effort to contribute to ALLDATA 2017. We truly believe that, thanks to all these efforts, the final conference program consisted of top quality contributions.

We also gratefully thank the members of the ALLDATA 2017 organizing committee for their help in handling the logistics and for their work that made this professional meeting a success.

We hope that ALLDATA 2017 was a successful international forum for the exchange of ideas and results between academia and industry and to promote further progress of different types of data. We also hope that Venice, Italy provided a pleasant environment during the conference and everyone saved some time to enjoy the unique charm of the city.

ALLDATA 2017 Committee

ALLDATA Steering Committee

Venkat N. Gudivada, East Carolina University, USA
Sandjai Bhulai, Vrije Universiteit Amsterdam, the Netherlands
Jerzy Grzymala-Busse, University of Kansas, USA
Fabrice Mourlin, Université Paris-Est Créteil Val de Marne, France
Andrzej Skowron, Warsaw University, Poland

ALLDATA Industry/Research Advisory Committee

Stephane Puechmorel, ENAC, France
Cyril Onwubiko, Research Series Ltd., London, UK
Loganathan Ponnambalam, Institute of High Performance Computing, A*STAR, Singapore
Hanmin Jung [정 한 민], Korea Institute of Science and Technology Information, South Korea

ALLDATA 2017
Committee

ALLDATA Steering Committee

Venkat N. Gudivada, East Carolina University, USA
Sandjai Bhulai, Vrije Universiteit Amsterdam, the Netherlands
Jerzy Grzymala-Busse, University of Kansas, USA
Fabrice Mourlin, Université Paris-Est Créteil Val de Marne, France
Andrzej Skowron, Warsaw University, Poland

ALLDATA Industry/Research Advisory Committee

Stephane Puechmorel, ENAC, France
Cyril Onwubiko, Research Series Ltd., London, UK
Loganathan Ponnambalam, Institute of High Performance Computing, A*STAR, Singapore
Hanmin Jung [정한민], Korea Institute of Science and Technology Information, South Korea

ALLDATA 2017 Technical Program Committee

Rajeev Agrawal, North Carolina A&T State University, USA
Maurizio Atzori, University of Cagliari, Italy
Akhilesh Bajaj, University of Tulsa, USA
Sandjai Bhulai, Vrije Universiteit Amsterdam, Netherlands
Peter T. Breuer, Birmingham City University, UK / Hecusys LLC, Atlanta, USA
Rachid Chelouah, EISTI, France
Yue Chen, Florida State University, USA
Roger H. L. Chiang, University of Cincinnati, USA
Esma Nur Cinicioglu, Istanbul University, Turkey
Carmela Comito, National Research Council of Italy (CNR) - Institute for High Performance Computing and Networking, Italy
Cinzia Daraio, Sapienza University of Rome, Italy
Maria Cristina De Cola, IRCCS Centro Neurolesi "Bonino-Pulejo", Messina, Italy
Süleyman Eken, Kocaeli University, Turkey
Mounîm A. El Yacoubi, Telecom SudParis, France
Nadia Essoussi, University of Carthage, Tunisia
Denise Beatriz Ferrari, Instituto Tecnológico de Aeronáutica, São José dos Campos - SP, Brazil
Paola Festa, University of Napoli FEDERICO II, Italy
Fausto Pedro Garcia Márquez, University of Castilla-La Mancha, Spain
Jerzy Grzymala-Busse, University of Kansas, USA
Venkat N. Gudivada, East Carolina University, USA
Didem Gürdür, KTH Royal Institute of Technology, Stockholm, Sweden

Tzung-Pei Hong, National University of Kaohsiung, Taiwan
Wen-Chi Hou, Southern Illinois University, USA
Hanmin Jung, Korea Institute of Science and Technology Information, South Korea
David Kaeli, Northeastern University, USA
Sokratis K. Katsikas, Norwegian University of Science & Technology (NTNU), Norway
Rasib Khan, Northern Kentucky University, USA
Dimitris Kontokostas, University of Leipzig, Germany
Alexander P. Kuleshov, Skolkovo Institute of Science and Technology (Skoltech), Russia
Alexander Lazovik, University of Groningen, Netherlands
Jerry Chun-Wei Lin, Harbin Institute of Technology Shenzhen Graduate School, Chinas
Iryna Lishchuk, Institut für Rechtsinformatik - Leibniz Universität Hannover
Angelica Lo Duca, Institute of Informatics and Telematics, National Research Council (IIT-CNR), Italy
Wencan Luo, University of Pittsburgh, USA
Armando B. Mendes, Universidade dos Açores, Portugal
Haralambos Mouratidis, University of Brighton, UK
Fabrice Mourlin, Université Paris-Est Créteil Val de Marne, France
Hidemoto Nakada, National Institute of Advanced Industrial Science and Technology (AIST), Japan
Florence Nicol, Ecole Nationale de l'Aviation Civile, France
Sadegh Nobari, Innopolis University, Russia
Cyril Onwubiko, Research Series Ltd., London, UK
Ren-Hao Pan, Yuan Ze University, Taiwan
Luca Pappalardo, University of Pisa, Germany
Loganathan Ponnambalam, Institute of High Performance Computing, A*STAR, Singapore
Stephane Puechmorel, ENAC, France
Valderi Reis Quietinho Leithardt, Federal Institute Education of Santa Catarina - Campus Camboriu, Brazil
Zbigniew W. Ras, University of North Carolina, USA
Yehezkel Resheff, Hebrew University, Jerusalem, Israel
Paolo Romano, University of Lisbon / INESC-ID, Portugal
Ryan Rossi, Palo Alto Research Center, USA
Jedrzej Rybicki, Supercomputing Center Juelich, Germany
Suzanne Michelle Shontz, University of Kansas, USA
Andrzej Skowron, Warsaw University, Poland
Srivathsan Srinivasagopalan, Visa Inc., USA
Bela Stantic, Griffith University, Australia
Uta Störl, University of Applied Sciences Darmstadt, Germany
Chrisa Tsinaraki, European Commission - Joint Research Centre, Italy
Stefanos Vrochidis, ITI-CERTH, Greece
Hironori Washizaki, Waseda University, Japan
Ouri Wolfson, University of Illinois, USA
Feng Yan, University of Nevada, Reno, USA
Feng George Yu, Youngstown State University, USA

Fouad Zablith, American University of Beirut, Lebanon
Qiang Zhu, University of Michigan, USA

KESA 2017 IARIA Advisory

Dumitru Roman, SINDEF/University of Oslo, Norway

KESA 2017 Chairs

Maria Pia di Buono, University of Salerno, Italy
Annibale Elia, University of Salerno, Italy
Johanna Monti, University of Naples 'L'Orientale', Italy
James C.N. Yang, National Dong Hwa University, Taiwan

KESA 2017 Technical Program Committee

Afrand Agah, West Chester University of Pennsylvania, USA
Rodrigo Agerri, University of the Basque Country (UPV/EHU), Spain
Ahmet Aker, University of Sheffield, UK
Flora Amato, University of Naples, Italy
Mehran Asadi, Lincoln University, USA
Se-Hak Chun, Seoul National University of Science and Technology, South Korea
Bojana Dalbelo-Bašić, University of Zagreb, Croatia
Maaike de Boer, TNO and Radboud University, Netherlands
Maria Pia di Buono, Faculty of Electrical Engineering and Computing, University of Zagreb, Croatia
Antoine Doucet, University of La Rochelle, France
Goran Glavaš, University of Mannheim, Germany
Zhisheng Huang, VU University Amsterdam, Netherlands
Chih-Cheng Hung, Kennesaw State University, USA
Cheonshik Kim, Sejong University, Republic of Korea
Hyunsung Kim, Kyungil University, South Korea
Kristina Kocijan, University of Zagreb, Croatia
Giuseppe Laquidara, X23 Ltd., Italy
Shuai Li, University of Insubria, Italy
Antonino Mazzeo, University of Naples, Italy
Johanna Monti, University of Naples 'L'Orientale', Italy
Thiago Pardo, University of São Paulo, Brazil
Francesca Parisi, Università della Calabria, Rende, Italy
Jan Radimsky, University of South Bohemia, Czech Republic
Lukas Ruf, Consecom AG, Switzerland
Max Silberztein, University de Franche-Comté, France
Jan Šnajder, University of Zagreb, Croatia
Gary Weckman, Ohio University, USA

Ching-Nung Yang, National Dong Hwa University, Taiwan

Copyright Information

For your reference, this is the text governing the copyright release for material published by IARIA.

The copyright release is a transfer of publication rights, which allows IARIA and its partners to drive the dissemination of the published material. This allows IARIA to give articles increased visibility via distribution, inclusion in libraries, and arrangements for submission to indexes.

I, the undersigned, declare that the article is original, and that I represent the authors of this article in the copyright release matters. If this work has been done as work-for-hire, I have obtained all necessary clearances to execute a copyright release. I hereby irrevocably transfer exclusive copyright for this material to IARIA. I give IARIA permission or reproduce the work in any media format such as, but not limited to, print, digital, or electronic. I give IARIA permission to distribute the materials without restriction to any institutions or individuals. I give IARIA permission to submit the work for inclusion in article repositories as IARIA sees fit.

I, the undersigned, declare that to the best of my knowledge, the article is does not contain libelous or otherwise unlawful contents or invading the right of privacy or infringing on a proprietary right.

Following the copyright release, any circulated version of the article must bear the copyright notice and any header and footer information that IARIA applies to the published article.

IARIA grants royalty-free permission to the authors to disseminate the work, under the above provisions, for any academic, commercial, or industrial use. IARIA grants royalty-free permission to any individuals or institutions to make the article available electronically, online, or in print.

IARIA acknowledges that rights to any algorithm, process, procedure, apparatus, or articles of manufacture remain with the authors and their employers.

I, the undersigned, understand that IARIA will not be liable, in contract, tort (including, without limitation, negligence), pre-contract or other representations (other than fraudulent misrepresentations) or otherwise in connection with the publication of my work.

Exception to the above is made for work-for-hire performed while employed by the government. In that case, copyright to the material remains with the said government. The rightful owners (authors and government entity) grant unlimited and unrestricted permission to IARIA, IARIA's contractors, and IARIA's partners to further distribute the work.

Flexible Management of Data Nodes for Hadoop Distributed File System

Wooseok Ryu
Dept. of Healthcare Management
Catholic University of Pusan
Busan, Republic of Korea
e-mail: wsryu@cup.ac.kr

***Abstract*—Hadoop Distributed File System (HDFS) is a file system, which stores big data in a distributed manner. Although HDFS cluster provides a great scalability, it requires numerous dedicated data nodes, which makes it difficult for a small business enterprise to construct a big data system. This paper presents a novel mechanism for flexible management of data nodes in the HDFS cluster. A block replication scheme is also presented to ensure availability of data. Using the proposed scheme, storage capacity of HDFS cluster can be dynamically increased by using existing hardware systems.**

Keywords-Hadoop; HDFS; flexibility; node management.

I. INTRODUCTION

A big data system makes it possible to identify meaningful information by extracting and analyzing massive data created in the enterprise. Currently, Apache Hadoop [1] is one of the most popular open source distributed framework for big data analytics. In the Hadoop, Hadoop Distributed File System (HDFS) is provided to ensure reliability and high availability of data storage under distributed computing environment. The MapReduce framework is also used to provide parallel processing of big data stored in HDFS. Due to its scalability and fault tolerance, Hadoop system can process huge volume of data on a large-scaled cluster with 10,000 processing cores [2].

Among the various applications, health care is a very promising field for big data analytics [3]. Hospitals also demand big data analysis to improve quality of care and to establish management innovation strategy [4]. However, relatively small business domains, such as small-and-medium sized hospitals, have difficulty in adopting a big data system despite the potential for data analysis because of its high cost. As an alternative way, we can consider using existing systems used for daily business to minimize adoption cost for constructing a Hadoop cluster. These systems are normally used for routine work, joining them into the Hadoop cluster should be carefully investigated.

This paper discusses a cluster management technique for flexible management of data nodes in Hadoop. Data nodes in the original Hadoop are dedicated systems for the cluster and cannot be casually added to or removed from the cluster. This paper first analyzes node commission and de-commission mechanism of Hadoop and proposes a flexible management mechanism for the cluster, which allows existing systems to be added to or removed from the cluster dynamically. Using the proposed mechanism, existing systems used for daily work during business hours can be redirected to the Hadoop cluster out of hours, which maximizes system utilization. The rest of this paper is organized as follows. Section II describes the flexible management mechanism for Hadoop. A block replication for ensuring availability of data is presented in Section III. Section IV concludes the paper.

II. FLEXIBLE MANAGEMENT MECHANISM

A. *Node Management in HDFS*

A HDFS cluster consists of one name node which manages namespace of the file system and a number of data nodes that store user data. When the HDFS starts, a namenode daemon in the name node starts, followed by starting each datanode daemon in the data node. The HDFS can add a new data node to the cluster or remove an old data node from the cluster without stopping all services, named commissioning and decommissioning, respectively.

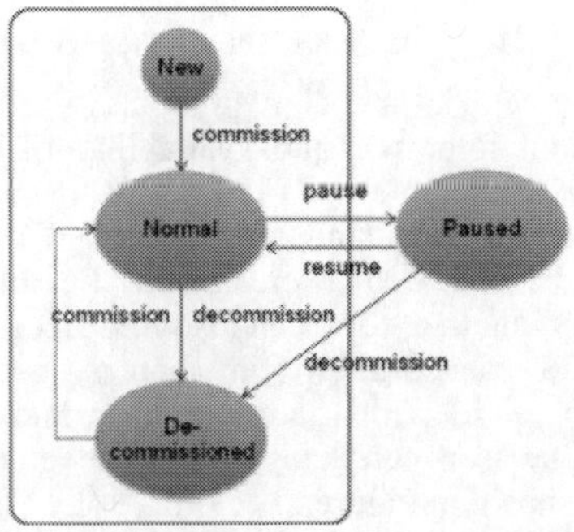

Figure 1. State transition diagram for a data node.

A boxed area of Figure 1 shows a state transition diagram for a data node in the original HDFS. When a new data node is about to join the cluster, a commissioning procedure is called to the node and the state of the node is changed to normal. After then, the node can store data blocks as requested by the name node. A normal node can be removed from the cluster via decommissioning procedure when the node is decrepit or malfunctioning. When the procedure is being executed, all data blocks stored in the node are moved to other normal nodes followed by the removal from the cluster. Note that a dotted line depicted in Figure 1 indicates that a decommissioned node could be commissioned again, however it is not practical because it required additional network overloads for the repeated copy of data blocks.

B. Flexible Data Node Management Mechanism

Providing flexibility for the Hadoop file system implies that nodes in the Hadoop cluster can be temporarily removed from the cluster and can re-join the cluster at any time. It is different from previous commission and decommission mechanisms because a decommissioned node is assumed to be permanently removed from the cluster.

This paper proposes an additional state named *paused* as depicted in Figure 1. The paused node maintains data blocks and can join the cluster again [5]. This means that a paused node has temporarily left from the cluster but the node will be rejoined when the system becomes available for analysis. The paused node can be used to other work, e.g. everyday business. The node rejoins the cluster when the node becomes idle. The pause procedure is as follows.

- A data node requests to name node via ssh which executes a script in the name node. The script adds the node descriptor to *dfs.host.pause* property in *hdfs-site.xml*.
- Refresh data nodes by calling *dfsadmin –refresh Nodes*, which removes data nodes from the cluster.
- Kill a *datanode* daemon running in the data node.

Paused nodes need to be managed in the name node because the paused nodes cannot be considered as target nodes for block reallocation which is executed by *HDFS balancer* daemon. This is achieved by *dfs.host.pause* property, which stores descriptors of paused nodes. The resume procedure for rejoining the cluster is similar to the commissioning procedure. However, data blocks of the resumed node should be checked for consistency since the data might be removed from the cluster while paused.

III. BLOCK REPLICATION SCHEME

Hadoop replicates each data block to separated nodes to provide fault tolerance and availability of accessing data. Default value of replication level is 3 [1]. When a block of certain node is unavailable, another copy from another node can be accessed. However, in the flexible management mechanism, another copy can also be inaccessible since any node can be paused at any time. To mitigate this problem, this paper divides distributed nodes into two types of clusters; one is a core cluster and the other is a flexible cluster as shown in Figure 2.

Data nodes in the core cluster is as same as the typical Hadoop cluster, which stores data blocks and used for analytical processes at all times. On the other hand, data nodes in the flexible cluster can be used for both daily business and data storage triggered by pause and resume mechanism discussed in Section 2. In this system, at least one replica should be stored in data nodes in the core cluster to guarantee minimum availability of data. For example, one replica is stored in the core cluster and two replicas are stored in any nodes in the flexible clusters. When all data nodes in the flexible clusters are paused, the core cluster with one replica can be used for Hadoop processing. If all data nodes are normal, extended data storage with improved processing power will be provided.

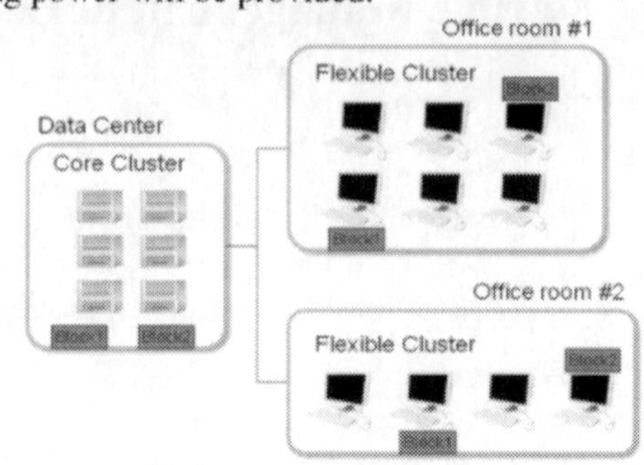

Figure 2. Block replication in the flexible cluster

The number of data nodes in flexible clusters and overall storage capacity are not linearly correlated since it is bounded by replication factor. Assuming each data node has the same storage capacity and the minimum replication factor for core cluster is 1, the maximum utilization can be achieved when the number of data nodes in the flexible cluster becomes twice the number of data nodes in the core cluster.

IV. CONCLUSION

This paper discussed a node addition and deletion mechanism of the HDFS and proposed a flexible node management mechanism which enables dynamic management of the Hadoop cluster. A block replication scheme is also presented to ensure minimum availability under flexible node clusters. Using the proposed mechanism, scale of the Hadoop cluster can be dynamically changed as the cluster can utilize existing systems, which implies that small business domains can efficiently construct a big data processing system without much cost. As a future work, evaluating the performance of this mechanism needs to be performed on a real business environment.

ACKNOWLEDGMENT

This work was supported by the National Research Foundation of Korea(NRF) grant funded by the Korea government(MSIP) (No. NRF-2016R1C1B1012364).

REFERENCES

[1] Apache Hadoop, http://hadoop.apache.org/, retrieved: Mar, 2017.

[2] C. W. Lee, K. Y. Hsieh, S. Y. Hsieh, and HC Hsiao, "A Dynamic data placement strategy for hadoop in heterogeneous environments," Big Data Research, 2014, vol. 1, pp.14–22, 2014.

[3] W. Raghupathi and V. Raghupathi, "Big data analytics in healthcare: promise and potential," Health Information Science and Systems, vol. 2, article 3, pp. 1–10, 2014.

[4] R . Miniati, et al. "Hospital-based expert model for health technology procurement planning in hospitals." Engineering in Medicine and Biology Society, IEEE, 2014, pp. 3504–3507.

[5] W. Ryu, "Dynamic Cluster Management of Hadoop Distributed Filesystem", Proc. Conference on Korea Information and Communication Engineering, KIICE, Oct. 2016, Vol. 20, No. 2, pp. 435–437.

Curves Similarity Based on Higher Order Derivatives

Florence Nicol†, Stephane Puechmorel‡

Ecole Nationale de l'Aviation Civile
Email: †nicol@recherche.enac.fr, ‡stephane.puechmore@enac.fr

***Abstract*—In many applications, data originate from the observation of a phenomenon depending on time. Trajectories of mobiles fall within this category and receive an increasing attention as many connected objects have the ability to broadcast their positions. When the raw location is the value of interest, several statistical procedures exist to deal with analysis of trajectories. Depending on whether the geometrical shape or the time to position relation is relevant, one will use a parametrization invariant distance or a simple L^2 metric to assess the similarity between any two trajectories. However, it is sometimes advisable to use higher order information like velocity or acceleration, while retaining some kind of geometrical invariance. The purpose of the present work is to introduce a framework especially adapted to such a situation.**

keywords*—*bundle metric, curve manifold, shape space.

I. Introduction

In many applications, the data of interest are measured values through time of a system in evolution. It is often the result of the observation of a physical phenomenon, obeying an underlying dynamics that may be unknown. As an extension, images can be modeled pretty much the same way, using two coordinates instead of a single time axis. Most algorithms designed to deal with such data rely on a sampled representation that is amenable to multivariate statistics.

Another approach was taken in the functional statistics framework, where the basic objects are mappings from a time interval to a given state space. Unfortunately, very little is known about probabilities in infinite dimension spaces, and one has to revert to finite dimensional representations during the implementation phase.

Several works were dedicated to the extension of classical multivariate algorithms to sample paths of Hilbert processes. As a starting point, data is first expanded on a truncated Hilbert basis [1], then, the vectors of expansion coefficients enter a standard finite dimensional analysis. A clever choice of the representation space and basis allows to take into account the prior knowledge about the studied process. Unfortunately, the dimension of the samples produced that way may be high, and varies with the geometric features of the sample paths. In particular, the presence of high curvature values will increase the number of expansion coefficients needed to keep a good approximation of the original function. In [2], an expectation maximization (EM) functional clustering algorithm is presented with an adaptive basis in each group, yielding an efficient numerical method to deal with this issue.

Another class of methods relies on a non-parametric approach [3][4]. A recent work [5] pertaining to this approach presents a hierarchical clustering principle, with application to electric power consumption.

Finally, some algorithms use a shape manifold [6] representation in order to derive a metric between sample paths. This last class of methods has distinguished benefits, like the ability to focus only on the shape of the curves and forget about a specific parametrization. The major drawback is a high computational cost, that may preclude its use on large data sets. While basically designed for using the first derivatives, it is possible to consider higher order information, although the notion of parametrization invariance becomes less intuitive.

The purpose of the present work is to introduce a framework in which the higher order derivatives are explicitly taken into account, but with a well controlled notion of invariance. It was motivated by an application in civil aviation, that is the assessment of runway adherence using only radar tracks of landing and taxiing aircraft. In this context, a full parametrization invariance is not advisable, as it will remove an important part of the relevant information. On the other side, a raw Sobolev distance between curves will be fooled by the diversity of aircraft and will induce false alarms.

In section (II), a general approach to the question of curve similarity is addressed. The main idea is to split between the observation and the geometrical object on which it lies, yielding a metric that gather in a controlled way the contribution of the underlying shape and the extra information borne by the measured data. Starting with a model of curves based on differential geometry, the data can be thought as a section of a vector bundle with base space the curve. Using a riemanian metric on it will be the key to obtain a measure of similarity between any two samples, in the spirit of the works dedicated to distances between shapes [6].

In section (III), the application of the general framework to the case of landing aircraft tracks will be discussed. Finally, a conclusion will be drawn, with a view towards future work on application on real and simulated data prior to an operational use.

II. Distance between bundles

A. *Problem statement*

The purpose of this section is to introduce a suitable state space for representing data that has both geometrical and cinematic features. It was motivated by the application that will be described later, where tracks of landing and taxiing aircraft must be clustered into homogeneous groups distinguished by

Figure 1. Runway clearing trajectories

the adherence of the runway. An example of a nominal (lower) and an abnormal (upper) track is given in Figure 1. The shape of the upper track is clearly different from the nominal one, and will not belong to the same cluster if one use a algorithm based for example on curvature. However, the divergence from the nominal curve may be due to low adherence condition or to a late turn. Only the first case must trigger a corrective action, that for the present situation is quite constraining: the runway has to be closed for the duration needed to perform an on-site adherence measurement. Using tangential acceleration will add a very discriminating feature since for the same shape, a high value means a high braking force, thus rejecting the hypothesis of low adherence. However, comparing raw velocity and acceleration induces two new issues:

- The aircraft type and airline procedures are varying, so that a shape comparison must be performed to minimize this effect;
- The time span of the trajectories is not the same. A registration procedure is needed, and it is a quite difficult problem to solve.

To summarize, neither parametrization invariant nor time dependent distances are fully satisfying. It is thus advisable to split the similarity computation into a purely geometrical part and a remainder that is not explained by shape variations.

All curves will be assumed to be smooth, that is indefinitely differentiable. This is not a real constraint in practical applications.

B. *Curves as manifolds*

In almost all applications, a curve is understood as a mapping γ from a real interval $[a, b]$ to a state space, generally $\mathbb{R}^p$. Furthermore, only curves with nowhere vanishing first derivative will be considered to avoid possible singularities. In practice, this condition is never an issue. This is the standard framework in which functional data statistics takes place, and is well suited to problems where the information is contained in the mapping. As an example, if one wants to analyze the delays occurring in road or air traffic, the time to position mapping is the most relevant data. However, it is quite common to encounter cases where the shape of the image $\gamma([a, b])$ holds the discriminating features. It obviously the case in image recognition algorithms, but also in spectrometric data [3], in biometric measurements (electroencephalogram, electrocardiogram) and generally speaking in all areas where the information will not change if the parametrization of the curves is changed. In the sequel, such a situation will be referred to as geometric data analysis (GDA).

The easiest approach to GDA is to let all curves be parametrized by arclength, which is defined as:

$$s : t \in [a, b] \to \int_a^t \|\gamma'(t)\| dt$$

The arclength has domain $[0, l(\gamma)]$ with $l(\gamma)$ the length of the curve. It comes at once that:

$$\frac{ds}{dt} = \|\gamma'(t)\|$$

so that taking the derivative with respect to s of a function of t can be done easily using the formula:

$$D_s = \frac{1}{\|\gamma'(t)\|} D_t$$

The arclength is related only to the shape of the image of γ. In fact, let $u \in [c, d]$ such that $t = \phi(u)$ with ϕ a strictly increasing smooth diffeomorphism from $[c, d]$ to $[a, b]$, it comes:

$$s(u) = \int_c^u \|D_u\gamma(t(u))\| du = \int_c^u \|\gamma'(t(u))\| \frac{dt}{du} du = \int_a^t \|\gamma'(t)\| dt \quad (1)$$

Many important features of the curve are naturally expressed with arclength: $D_s\gamma(s)$ yields the unit tangent vector $T_\gamma(s)$ while $\|D_{ss}\gamma(s)\|$ is the curvature at s.

For curve similarity computations, the drawback of the arclength is that its domain depends on the length of the curve and varies with the curves. A scaled version η with domain $[0, 1]$ is more convenient:

$$\eta = s/l(\gamma)$$

An obvious benefit of using η as a reference parametrization is that it solves the so-called registration problem, that consists of finding a common domain for all the functional samples [7]. It worth notice that in a sampled context, it is equivalent to have evenly spaced landmarks on the image of γ, as in [8].

It is worth noticing that the geometry of smooth curves with values in $\mathbb{R}^p$ is entirely defined by the so-called Frenet frame $(u_1, \dots u_p)$ and its associated curvatures $(\kappa_1, \dots, \kappa_{p-1})$. For the sake of completeness, the procedure for finding them is given by

$$u_1(t) = \gamma'(t)/\|\gamma'(t)\| \quad (2)$$

$$\tilde{u}_i(t) = \gamma^{(i)}(t) - \sum_{j=1}^{i-1} \langle \gamma^{(i)}(t), u_j(t) \rangle u_j(t), i = 2 \dots p \quad (3)$$

$$u_i(t) = \tilde{u}_i(t)/\|\tilde{u}_i\|, i = 2 \dots p \quad (4)$$

$$\kappa_i(t) = \frac{\langle u_i'(t), u_{i+1}(t) \rangle}{\|\gamma'(t)\|}, i = 1 \dots p - 1 \quad (5)$$

It is clear from the construction that changing the curve parametrization will keep the Frenet frame and the curvatures invariant: all information related to velocity, tangential acceleration and so on will be lost. In many applications, this is a major issue.

From a mathematical standpoint, one possible geometric model for a curve is a one dimensional riemanian manifold. It will be assumed in the sequel that the reader is familiar with the basic concepts of differential geometry that may be found in any textbook on the subject [9]. For shape analysis and recognition, one deals almost always with closed curves, that comply with the usual notion of manifold. However, when dealing with paths with distinct endpoints, the right model is a manifold with boundary. In the sequel, all curves will be represented that way.

Any real interval $[a, b]$ has the structure of a trivial one dimensional manifold with boundary $\{a, b\}$. Tangent vectors are couples (t, u) where t is the basepoint in $[a, b]$ and u is a one dimensional vector, that can be represented as a real number. One can think of a tangent vector (t, u) as the velocity at t of a point moving along the interval $[a, b]$. Boundary conditions impose $u(a) > 0, u(b) < 0$. A vector field defined on it is just a smooth mapping $u: t \in [a, b] \mapsto \mathbb{R}$ such that all derivatives admit a limit to the right (resp. to the left) at a (resp. b). These limits will define the field at the boundary, and are not required to comply with the conditions satisfied by tangent vectors.

A curve $\gamma: [a, b] \to \mathbb{R}^p$ with nowhere vanishing derivative is an immersion from the manifold $]a, b[$ to $\mathbb{R}^p$ that can be extended to $[a, b]$. As such, it inherits a metric from the local embedding in $\mathbb{R}^p$ by letting, for any $t \in]a, b[$ and real numbers u, v, interpreted as tangent vectors:

$$g_t(u, v) = \|\gamma'(t)\|^2 uv$$

The Levi-Civita connection on $]a, b[$ is given by:

$$\nabla_{\partial_t} u = \partial_t u + \frac{1}{\|\gamma'(t)\|^2} \langle \gamma'(t), \gamma''(t) \rangle u$$

The first term corresponds to the intrinsic variation with respect to the parameter t, while the second is the part of the tangential acceleration coming from the geometry of the immersion. When the immersion parameter is chosen to be the arclength, the second term in the right hand vanishes as $D_s\gamma$ is the unit tangent vector at s and $D_{ss}\gamma$ is orthogonal to it. The Levi-Civita connection reduces thus to derivative with respect to arclength. The same applies for the scaled arclength η.

While curvature is a very important information for curves, it is a characteristic of the immersion and not an intrinsic feature of the trivial manifold $[a, b]$. It can be recovered from the immersed normal bundle $\mathcal{N}$, whose elements are couples (t, v) with $t \in]a, b[$ and $v \perp \gamma'(t)$. It is a vector bundle with base manifold $[a, b]$ and typical fiber $\mathbb{R}^{p-1}$, and its sections can be easily recovered using the Frenet frame $u_1(t), \ldots, u_p(t)$ introduced earlier, as any vector normal to $\gamma'(t)$ lies in span$(u_2(t), \ldots, u_p(t)$. A section of $\mathcal{N}$ is then a smooth mapping $s: [a, b] \to R^{p-1}$, with $s(t)$ the coordinates on the frame $(u_2(t), \ldots, u_p(t))$.

The immersed normal bundle is the prototype of objects bearing vector information along a curve, and fulfilling the requirement of partial geometrical invariance mentioned earlier. For a single curve $\gamma: [a, b] \to R^p$, one can attach a vector $v(\theta)$ for each $\theta \in [a, b]$ that is interpreted as a sample at position $\gamma(\theta)$. Going back to the case of landing tracks, one can think of this vector information as the couple velocity/acceleration $v(\theta) = (u(\gamma(\theta)), D_t u(\gamma(\theta))$. It is important to note that the shape parameter θ is not related to time t, that is used to compute velocity and acceleration: at a given θ, $u(\theta), D_t(\theta)$ are the respective velocity and acceleration sampled at position $\gamma(\theta)$ on the trajectory. Different aircraft following the same curve but with different braking profiles will have different samples $v(\theta)$. Within the immersed bundle, they will be described by different sections. However, the geometric object underlying the sections, that is the base immersion γ will remain the same. When we let it vary, it appears that data can be compared at two well defined levels: the first one is the geometry and arises from the difference between the base immersions and the second is related to the sections themselves.

In a general setting, a immersed vector bundle will be defined as a vector bundle with base manifold $[a, b]$, typical fiber $\mathbb{R}^n$ and whose sections are of the form $s(t) = v(\gamma(t)), t \in [a, b]$, with $\gamma: [a, b] \to \mathbb{R}^p$ an immersion. As above, the geometry is encoded in γ, while the non-geometric information is described by the section.

The ability to deal with similarity between such objects relies on a notion of distance between them, that will be now introduced.

C. Distance between bundle sections

In order to simplify the derivations, all curves will be assumed to be immersions from $[0, 1]$ to $\mathbb{R}^p$, using the η parameter. The derivation of a distance between immersed bundles sections will closely follow the principle underlying the construction of geometric distances between curves, as presented in [10]. Let $\mathcal{E}_0, \mathcal{E}_1$ be immersed vector bundles on respective immersions γ_0, γ_1 with values in $\mathbb{R}^p$ and with typical fibers $\mathbb{R}^n$. Let s_0, s_1 be sections respectively of $\mathcal{E}_0, \mathcal{E}_1$, that will represent the vector samples along the respective curves γ_0, γ_1. An immersed path between s_0 and s_1 is a smooth mapping $\phi: [0, 1] \times [0, 1] \to \mathbb{R}^p \times \mathbb{R}^n$ such that:

- For all $s \in [0, 1]$, the mapping $t \in [0, 1] \mapsto \phi(s, t)$ is a smooth section the trivial bundle $\mathbb{R}^p \times R^n \mapsto^\pi \mathbb{R}^p$;
- For all $s \in [0, 1]$, $\pi \circ \phi(s, \bullet)$ is a smooth immersion in $\mathbb{R}^p$;
- For all $t \in [0, 1]$, $\phi(0, t) = s_0(t), \phi(1, t) = s_1(t)$.

For a given $s \in [0, 1]$, the mapping $t \in [0, 1] \to \pi \circ \phi(s, t)$ defines an immersion from $[0, 1] \to \mathbb{R}^p$ that interpolates between γ_1, γ_2 in the sense of [10][6]. This immersion defines in turn an immersed bundle, with typical fiber $\mathbb{R}^n$. It will be referred to as $\mathcal{E}_s$ in the sequel. Finally, if a metric g_s is available on each of the member of the family $\mathcal{E}_t$, it is possible to compute for a given ϕ a path length:

$$l(\phi) = \int_0^1 \int_0^1 g_s \left(\frac{\partial \phi}{\partial s}, \frac{\partial \phi}{\partial s} \right)^{1/2} dsdt \tag{6}$$

Having this measure at hand, the distance between s_0 and s_1 is defined the infimum of the values $l(\phi)$ over all the admissible paths ϕ.

For clustering applications, it may be convenient to use the energy of a path ϕ that is defined to be:

$$E(\phi) = \int_0^1 \int_0^1 g_s \left(\frac{\partial \phi}{\partial s}, \frac{\partial \phi}{\partial s} \right) dsdt$$

Paths minimizing the energy are the same as those minimizing the length. Since it saves a square root in the computation, the minimization is easier. However, if a distance is really needed at the end, it is enough to compute $l(\phi)$ on the minimizing path obtained. The way the interpolating bundles $\mathcal{E}_s$ can be constructed will be deferred to a future work; however, normal bundles (or closely related ones) are quite natural in applications. It was the choice made for the classification of landing aircraft tracks.

A second question is the choice of the metrics g_s. While out of the scope of the present paper, a requirement is that the family be smooth and natural in the sense of [11]. For the application, an ad-hoc metric will be derived in the next section.

III. A WORKED EXAMPLE: SKID DETECTION

A. *Problem statement*

The problem of early detection of runway bad adherence has a great importance in airport operational management. When the runway or the taxiways are in bad condition, the only reliable procedure used nowadays is a direct measurement using an especially designed vehicle. Unfortunately, the runway has to be closed for the duration of the operation, which has a high cost both from the economic and traffic management point of view. Attempts where made to infer adherence from clustering of landing trajectories obtained by the surface surveillance means (radars), but due to the diversity of aircraft and airline procedures, a registration must be applied to curves, which is quite awkward to design. Since both the geometry of the landing trajectories and the deceleration law are important to make the right decision, the above theoretical framework seems to be ideally suited. As the phenomenon of interest stems from contact mechanics, it is worth starting with the underlying physics to derive a suited bundle metric.

B. *From contact mechanics to curve similarity*

Landing aircraft may experience slip during deceleration phase when the runway is in degraded conditions. It may result from icing, snow, bad runway surface state but also from pilot's actions, namely a too strong braking action or sharp turn. In this last case, it is not related to runway condition and must not trigger a maintenance action from the airport services.

Slip can be detected on-board by comparing wheel rotation rate with aircraft velocity and computing the so-called wheel slip factor:

$$\lambda = \frac{\omega_w - \omega_a}{\max(\omega_w, \omega_a)} \tag{7}$$

where ω_w is the wheel angular velocity and $\omega_a = V_a/R_w$ is the expected angular velocity that can be computed as the ratio of the aircraft velocity to the wheel radius. Please note that on the real vehicle, several wheels are used, and the λ coefficient has to be understood as a mean value. Furthermore, due to tire elasticity, λ is not zero even if there is no actual slip: this is due to the fact that when a traction or a braking force is applied, the rubber will stretch, resulting in the tire outer part actually traveling more or less than expected from rigid body dynamics. This information is not yet downlinked in real time to ground centers and thus cannot be used in the intended application. From the ground standpoint, λ cannot be observed without on-board information, but some aspects of the landing or taxiing aircraft behavior may still be inferred. It is assumed in the sequel that Coulomb's law for friction [12] is applicable, so that the contact force F_c depends only on aircraft weight and tire/runway conditions:

$$F_c \leq \mu g M \tag{8}$$

with M the aircraft mass, g the gravity of the Earth and μ the adhesion coefficient. Without slip, μ is equal to the static friction coefficient μ_s and F_c can be increased until it reaches the upper bound in (8). At that point, slip occurs and μ drops to the value of the dynamic friction coefficient μ_d. F_c remains constant until it falls below $\mu_d g M$. In real world experiments, this simple behavior is no longer valid and one has to express μ as a function of λ, which can be found in [13]. Within this frame, the expression of the contact force is $F_c = \mu(\lambda) g M$, which is valid for both non-slip and slip case. Furthermore, in the case of aircraft, aerodynamics forces are exerted, with a net result of a braking force F_a that adds to the actual brakes action, but does not contribute to the friction analysis. Putting things together, the equation of motion along the aircraft trajectory γ can be expressed as:

$$\ddot{\gamma}(t) = \frac{F_a(t)}{M} + \mu(\lambda(t)) g \vec{u} \tag{9}$$

where $\vec{u}$ is a unit vector in the direction of the contact force F_c. Without making additional assumptions, it is not possible to use (9) for slip detection. However, if actions taken are assumed to be optimal, then F_a and $\vec{u}$ will be collinear so as to maximize the net braking effect. The expression of the aircraft dynamics becomes:

$$\ddot{\gamma}(t) = (K(t) + \mu(\lambda(t) g)\, \vec{u} \tag{10}$$

where the coefficient $K(t)$ accounts for the aerodynamic braking force intensity. As aircraft must loose speed fast, μ will be close to the maximum at least during the landing and the beginning of taxi. The same applies for K, as it will not impair adherence. It can then be deduced that aircraft will try to keep the ratio between longitudinal and normal acceleration as high as possible. An observable measurement of slip condition will then be given by:

$$\theta = \arctan\left(\frac{\kappa\|D_t\gamma\|^3}{\langle D_{tt}\gamma, D_t\gamma\rangle}\right) \tag{11}$$

where γ is the aircraft trajectory and κ its curvature. It can further reduced to:

$$\theta = \arctan\left(\frac{\det\left(D_t\gamma, D_{tt}\gamma\right)}{\langle D_{tt}\gamma, D_t\gamma\rangle}\right) \tag{12}$$

using the well known property $\kappa = \det\left(D_t\gamma, D_{tt}\gamma\right)/\|D_t\gamma\|^3$.

In good runway conditions, the longitudinal acceleration will be high and nearly constant, at least in the first part of the landing trajectory. As a consequence, one can expect θ to be relatively small and be proportional to $\det\left(D_t\gamma, D_{tt}\gamma\right)$. Reciprocally, under slip conditions, a trade off has to be made between path following and deceleration: the angle θ will thus increase towards the limiting value $\pm\pi/2$.

From the above discussion, it appears that θ makes sense as a weighting factor for curve comparisons.

C. An adapted metric

In the sequel, the symbol D_t will stand for the partial derivative with respect to variable t. Higher order derivatives with respect to variables $t_1 \ldots t_N$ will be written similarly as $D_{t_1t_2\ldots t_N}$. Please note that the same variable may occur several times.

A smooth planar curve $\gamma\colon [0,1] \to \mathbb{R}^2$ will be an immersion when the derivative $D_s\gamma$ is everywhere non vanishing in $]0,1[$. The set of such curves will be denoted by $\mathbf{Imm}([0,1],\mathbb{R}^2)$. Taking $\gamma \in \mathbf{Imm}([0,1],\mathbb{R}^2)$, its length is:

$$l(\gamma) = \int_0^1 \|D_t\gamma(t)\|dt \tag{13}$$

It is invariant under parametrization change $\gamma \to \gamma \circ \phi$ with $\phi\colon [0,1] \to [0,1]$ a smooth diffeomorphism. Given a path $\Phi\colon [-\epsilon,\epsilon] \to \mathbf{Imm}([0,1],\mathbb{R}^2)$ that can be seen as a smooth mapping $\Phi\colon [-\epsilon,\epsilon]\times[0,1] \to \mathbb{R}^2$, the variation of $l(\Phi(0,\bullet))$ can be computed :

$$D_s|_{s=0} l(\Phi(s,\bullet)) = \langle D_s\Phi(0,1), T(1)\rangle - \langle D_s\Phi(0,0), T(0)\rangle \tag{14}$$

$$+\int_0^1 \langle D_s\Phi(0,t), \kappa(t)\|D_t\Phi(0,t)\|^2 N(t)\rangle dt \tag{15}$$

with $T(t), N(t)$ the respective unit tangent and normal vectors to the curve $t \mapsto \Phi(0,t)$ and $\kappa(t)$ its unsigned curvature. The extension to more general immersions is quite straightforward [10]. In the same reference, the variation formula (14) is used to derive a riemanian metric on the quotient space $\mathbf{Imm}(\mathbb{S}^1,\mathbb{R}^2)/\mathbf{Diff}([0,1],\mathbb{R}^2)$.

In the present work, a similar approach will be taken. However, due to the fact that the slip condition must come into play as a weighting factor, it is not possible to keep invariance under change of parametrization. Furthermore, curves with vanishing second derivative must be excluded since the slip angle θ 11 is not defined at points where $D_t t\gamma(t) = 0$. The last condition boils down to the requirement that the curve $t \in [0,1] \mapsto (\gamma, D_t\gamma)$ be an immersion. The space of such objects will be denoted by $\mathbf{Imm}([0,1],\mathbb{R}^4)$.

As an arc tangent appears in the definition of θ, it is more convenient to use instead $sin(\theta)$ that has a simpler expression but otherwise similar behavior:

$$\sin(\theta(t)) = \frac{\kappa(t)\|D_t\gamma(t)\|^2}{\|D_{tt}\gamma(t)\|} = \frac{\det\left(D_t\gamma(t), D_{tt}\gamma(s)\right)}{\|D_t\gamma(t)\|\|D_{tt}\gamma\|} \tag{16}$$

Definition 1. Let γ be a smooth curve. An admissible variation of γ is a smooth mapping $\Phi\colon]-\epsilon,\epsilon[\to \mathbb{R}^2, \epsilon > 0$, such that $\Phi(0,\bullet) = \gamma(\bullet)$ and $\forall s \in]-\epsilon,\epsilon[, \Phi(s,0) = \gamma(0), \Phi(s,1) = \gamma(1)$.

An admissible variation defines a tangent vector at γ: it is the smooth vector field $t \in [0,1] \mapsto D_s\Phi(0,t)$.

The expression (16) has a nice variational interpretation as indicated in the next lemma.

Lemma 1. *Let $\gamma\colon [0,1] \to \mathbb{R}^2$ be a smooth path and Φ an admissible variation of it. Let ϕ be a smooth path such that $\phi(0) = \gamma(1)$, $\phi(1) = \gamma(0)$. Then:*

$$D_s A(0) = \int_0^1 \det\left(D_s\Phi(0,t), D_t(0,t)\right) dt \tag{17}$$

where $A(s)$ is the net area enclosed by the loop $\Phi(s,\bullet), \phi$ for $s \in]-\epsilon,\epsilon[$.

Using lemma 1, the integral :

$$\int_0^1 \frac{|\det\left(D_t\gamma(t), D_{tt}\gamma(s)\right)|}{\|D_t\gamma(t)\|\|D_{tt}\gamma\|}\|D_t\gamma(t)\|dt \tag{18}$$

may be interpreted as the total infinitesimal area swept by the curve γ when moved in the direction $D_{tt}\gamma$. This quantity is global indication of the slipping experienced along the path γ.

Turning back to bundles, if $\gamma\colon [0,1] \to \mathbb{R}^2$ is the immersion describing the geometry of the problem (with the η parametrization) and $v(\eta), v'(\eta)$ the respective velocity and acceleration at position $\gamma(\eta)$, the above metric can be adapted to yield a bundle metric. Without going into derivation detail, it can be expressed as:

$$g((u(\eta),u'(\eta)),(v(\eta),v'(\eta))) = \langle u(\eta)_N, v(\eta)_N\rangle\left(1+\kappa^2(\eta)\right) + \det\left(D_\eta\gamma(t), D_{\eta\eta}\gamma(s)\right) \tag{19}$$

Looking at the expression (19) reveals a sum of a geometric distance between immersions in the sense of Mumford-Michor and a proper vector variation. This bundle metric is injected in the procedure for computing distances between immersed bundles sections (6) to yield the desired similarity measure that discriminates skid conditions.

IV. Conclusion and Future Work

While quite developed from the theoretical standpoint, the work is still ongoing to assess performance in operational environment on real data. Unfortunately, there is no access to data correlated to adherence condition, as this information can only be obtained from direct measurements and is not communicated by airports authorities. The option taken was to develop a realistic taxi and landing simulator, that has been recently completed and will be released in open source. With the help of this tool, slipping and non-slipping trajectories can be simulated and the performance of the classification procedure assessed. On available landing data, and using an upper bound estimate of the distance based on a linear homotopy as an admissible path, promising results have been obtained. However, they cannot be matched against adherence conditions due to the aforementioned data availability issue. It is nevertheless expected, based on this experiment, that even the simplest linear homotopy procedure will outperform all the state-of-the-art algorithms investigated so far.

References

[1] J. Ramsay and B. Silverman, *Functional Data Analysis*, ser. Springer Series in Statistics. Springer, 2005.

[2] C. Bouveyron and J. Jacques, "Model-based clustering of time series in group-specific functional subspaces," *Advances in Data Analysis and Classification*, vol. 5, no. 4, pp. 281–300, 2011.

[3] F. Ferraty and P. Vieu, *Nonparametric Functional Data Analysis: Theory and Practice*, ser. Springer Series in Statistics. Springer New York, 2006.

[4] A. Delaigle and P. Hall, "Defining probability density for a distribution of random functions," *The Annals of Statistics*, vol. 38, no. 2, pp. 1171–1193, 2010.

[5] M. Boullé, R. Guigourès, and F. Rossi, *Advances in Knowledge Discovery and Management: Volume 4*. Cham: Springer International Publishing, 2014, ch. Nonparametric Hierarchical Clustering of Functional Data, pp. 15–35.

[6] D. Mumford, *Colloquium De Giorgi 2009*. Pisa: Scuola Normale Superiore, 2012, ch. The geometry and curvature of shape spaces, pp. 43–53.

[7] L. Sangalli, P. Secchi, S. Vantini, and V. Vitelli, "Functional clustering and alignment methods with applications," *Communications in Applied and Industrial Mathematics*, vol. 1, no. 1, pp. 205–224, 2010.

[8] I. Dryden and K. Mardia, *Statistical Shape Analysis*, ser. Wiley Series in Probability & Statistics. Wiley, 1998.

[9] F. Flaherty and M. do Carmo, *Riemannian Geometry*, ser. Mathematics: Theory & Applications. Birkhäuser Boston, 2013.

[10] P. W. Michor and D. Mumford, "Vanishing geodesic distance on spaces of submanifolds and diffeomorphisms," *Documenta Mathematica*, vol. 10, pp. 217–245, 2005.

[11] O. Kowalski and M. Sekizawa, "Natural transformations of riemanian metrics on manifolds to metrics on tangent bundles," *Bull. Tokyo Gagukei University*, vol. 40, no. 4, pp. 1–29, 1988.

[12] V. L. Popov, *Contact Mechanics and Friction: Physical Principles and Applications*. Berlin, Heidelberg: Springer Berlin Heidelberg, 2010, ch. Coulomb's Law of Friction, pp. 133–154.

[13] R. Rajamani, *Vehicle Dynamics and Control*, ser. Mechanical Engineering Series. Springer US, 2011.

Automated Generation of SQL Queries that Feature Specified SQL Constructs

Venkat N Gudivada*, Kamyar Arbabifard*, and Dhana Rao†
*Department of Computer Science, East Carolina University, USA
†Department of Biology, East Carolina University, USA
email: gudivadav15@ecu.edu, arbabifardk15@students.ecu.edu, and raodh16@ecu.edu

Abstract - SQL is an ISO standard language for querying relational databases. SQL queries are deceptively simple to write, but writing semantically correct queries requires a good understanding of the data model and SQL constructs. Often, this is a challenging task for beginners. Automatic generation of SQL queries that feature specified SQL constructs is useful for both informal self-testing and formal assessment. In this work-in-progress paper, we describe the automated question generation problem in a broader context, provide an overview of the current approaches, and discuss our approach to automatic generation of SQL queries. Our approach is based on the notion of *grammar graph*. We illustrate the approach using an arithmetic expression grammar and generalize this approach to SQL query generation.

Keywords—Context-Free Grammar; SQL Query Generation; Grammar Graph; Question Generation.

I. Context and Introduction

Recently, there has been tremendous interest in improving student learning in classrooms through innovative and inclusive pedagogy. Research in cognitive psychology, neuroscience, and biology provides insight into how humans learn [1]. Contrary to the conventional study habits such as cramming, re-reading, and single-minded repetition, techniques such as interleaving the practice of one skill or topic with another, and self-testing enable more complex and durable learning outcomes [2]. There is research-based evidence for seven key aspects of learning including effect of prior knowledge, organizing knowledge to effect learning, factors that motivate students, process by which students develop mastery, self-testing, kinds of practices and feedback that enhance learning, and the processes by which students become self-directed learners [3]. Several strategies exist to bring learning research into classroom environments across diverse disciplines [4] [5] [6]. In this paper, our focus is on enhancing learning through self-testing.

The National Academy of Engineering of The National Academies has identified advancing personalized learning as one of the fourteen Grand Challenges for Engineering in the 21st century [7]. Personalized learning has multiple dimensions. Providing a wide assortment of teaching and learning materials to suit the different learning styles of students is one aspect. Allowing students to progress through a course to meet their just-in-time learning goals is another aspect. More specifically, each student may potentially choose a different order for learning the course topics. The only constraints that limit the topic order are the prerequisite dependencies. A third aspect of personalization involves providing contextualized scaffolding and immediate feedback to students on assessment activities. The last aspect involves providing students authentic questions for self-assessment and preparation for exams.

Structured Query Language (SQL) is an ANSI and ISO standard declarative query language for querying and manipulating relational databases. Though writing SQL queries appears to be easy at a superficial level, students tend to make several types of errors [8]. The goal of this paper is to provide a question generation tool that automatically generates virtually unlimited SQL queries to support personalized learning in a database systems course. The tool will generate SQL queries that will contain the SQL constructs specified by the user. Given the complexity of the SQL language, we begin our investigation of automated question generation on a simpler problem: generation of arithmetic expressions. Once we understand the generation process and formalize an algorithm, we apply the algorithm to the generation of SQL queries.

In Section II, we provide motivation for automated question generation problem in a broader context and discuss related work. An automated approach to arithmetic expression generation is described in Section III. Extending this work to SQL query generation is outlined in Section IV. Section V provides conclusions.

II. Motivation and Related Work

The advent of Massive Open Online Courses (MOOCs), renewed interest in anytime and anywhere learning, the potential of personalization in revolutionizing learning, benefits of contextualized scaffolding, and automated and immediate feedback on learning assessments are the primary drivers for automated question generation. This is an area of interest to researchers across multiple disciplines. Approaches to automated question generation are as diverse as the disciplines themselves. Furthermore, the goal of question generation is not necessarily for learning assessment.

We categorize current approaches to question generation into three broad categories: template-based,

Natural Language Processing (NLP) based, and hybrid. Template-based approaches use knowledge structures such as ontologies and manually crafted templates. NLP-based approaches analyze natural language text for extracting semantic information and use that information for question generation. As the name implies, hybrid approaches draw upon templates and NLP techniques.

A. Template-based Approaches

Khalek and Khurshid present an approach to generating syntactically and semantically correct SQL queries [9]. The context for their investigation is testing of relational database engines. They translate the problem of generating SQL queries into a Satisfiability (SAT) problem. More specifically, they translate SQL query constraints into Alloy models, which generate SQL queries. They also generate data to populate databases and test database engines using the generated SQL queries.

Binnig et al. propose an approach to *query-aware* database for testing a Database Management System (DBMS) [10]. The purpose of this research is to ensure the availability of appropriate data in the database to enable matching the data returned by a query to the expected result. If the database does not contain the appropriate data, the query will execute but does not return any results.

An integrated Exploratorium for database courses is developed as a platform to investigate the technical problems and the pedagogical benefits of using diverse interactive learning tools in [11]. It provides personalized access to three types of interactive learning tools: annotated examples, self-assessment questions, and SQL lab. Over 400 self-assessment SQL questions are generated from 50 templates.

Do et al. propose an approach to SQL query generation using manually crafted templates and SQL ontology [12]. A major limitation of this approach is that the generated queries are limited to the pre-defined templates. Another approach to testing database applications using automatically generated test cases is discussed in [13].

Siddiqi et al. describe the development and evaluation of IndusMarker, a short-answer grading system for an object-oriented programming course [14]. IndusMarker targets factual answers and uses *structure matching* for determining correctness of students' responses. Lastly, Li and Sambasivam developed a *template-based* approach to automated question generation for intelligent tutoring applications [15, 16]. Template-based approaches are also used to generate both questions and expected answers to evaluate retrieval algorithms for unstructured data [17].

B. NLP-based Approaches

Automatic generation of factual *WH*-questions from texts with potential educational value is investigated in [18]. WH-questions are those that contain an interrogative pro-form. For example, words that begin wh-questions are who, what, when, where, why, and how. An automated system is developed for automated question generation, which uses natural language processing techniques, manually encoded transformation rules, and a trained statistical question ranker.

To assist the task of automatically assigning texts for students to read, vocabulary assessment must be performed first. A system for vocabulary assessment is discussed in [19]. It generates six types of vocabulary questions using WordNet data. Evaluation of the system performance indicates that the vocabulary skill measured using the generated questions correlates well with the same measured on independently developed human written questions. An extension of this system for the Portuguese context is discussed in [20]. Another approach to language learning and assessment is discussed in [21]. This system semi-automatically generates questions for testing grammar knowledge using manually-designed patterns and natural language processing techniques.

Three workshops were held on question generation [22]. The third workshop on Question Generation included a question generation shared task and evaluation challenge, which featured question generation from sentences and question generation from paragraphs [23]. A special issue of Dialog & Discourse journal featured NLP-based question generation topics [24].

C. Hybrid Approaches

Ontologies are knowledge structures which depict entities in a domain and relationships among the entities. Automated inference and reasoning were the two primary and original drivers for ontologies. Al-Yahya developed a system for multiple choice question (MCQ) generation using ontologies [25]. The system is called *OntoQue* and has been evaluated on two domain ontologies. The evaluation findings indicated a limited success of the approach and revealed a number of shortcomings from the perspective of educational significance of MCQs. This study also suggests a holistic approach, which incorporates learning objectives and content, lexical knowledge, and scenarios into a single cohesive framework.

III. Generation of Arithmetic Expressions

Our approach to question generation is based on Context-Free Grammars (CFG). Conceptually, a CFG is specified by a set of rules or productions. The use of CFG to describe grammars of natural languages traces back to Panini (6th - 4th century BCE), a Sanskrit grammarian. The mathematical formalism of CFGs was developed by Noam Chomsky in mid 1950s. CFGs became a standard formalism for describing the grammars of computer programming languages in late 1950s. A *parser* is a computer program which determines, given a string and a CGF, whether the string can be generated from the CFG. In other words, the parser determines whether or not the string is valid element in the language defined by the CFG.

TABLE I. A CONTEXT-FREE GRAMMAR (CFG) FOR ARITHMETIC EXPRESSIONS

<expr>	::= <term> [<expr1>]*
<expr1>	::= (+ | -) <term>
<term>	::= <factor> [<expr2>]*
<factor>	::= <base> [<expr3>]*
<base>	::= (<expr>) | <number>
<expr2>	::= (* | /) <factor>
<expr3>	::= ∧ <exponent>
<exponent>	::= (<expr>) | <number>
<number>	::= <digit> [<digit>]*
<digit>	::= 0 | 1 | 2 | 3 | 4 | 5 | 6 | 7 | 8 | 9

Efficient parsers exist to determine whether a program written a programming language such as Java conforms to Java CFG.

Though the CFG for a programming language is finite, one can generate an infinite number of programs in the language. However, these programs are manually constructed by programmers. Writing useful programs is an intellectual task and requires knowledge and skill. The problem we address in this paper is the automatic generation of strings from a given CFG, which contain user specified *keywords* or *constructs*. The latter are *literals* in the CFG. This problem is challenging because strings with certain combinations of keywords may not exist in the language defined by the CFG. The first step is to determine whether a string that contains the user specified keywords exists. If such a string exists, we then generate it. We demonstrate our approach on a simple grammar first and then generalize the approach to SQL query generation.

The CFG we use for generating arithmetic expressions is shown in Table I. Using CFG, we generate arithmetic expressions of arbitrary complexity. Operands in the expressions are integers and operators include addition (+), subtraction (-), multiplication (*), division (/), and exponentiation (∧).

We propose a graph-based representation for efficiently generating arithmetic expressions from CFG grammars. We refer to this as the *grammar graph* and is shown in Figure 1. This is similar to Deterministic Finite State Automata (DFSA) but the semantics are different. The grammar graph consists of a set of vertices and edges. The color coding, line types, and other markers capture critical information to aid the generation of arithmetic expressions. Each vertex in the graph corresponds to a *terminal* or *non-terminal* in the grammar. In Figure 1, there is only one terminal designated by the vertex labeled <digit>. Note the color of the vertex.

The graph node labeled <expr> is the start vertex for expression generation. The directed edge from <expr> to <term> indicates a *substitution* — the nonterminal <expr> is replaced by another nonterminal <term>. Next, consider the *red-dashed* directed edge from <term> to <expr1>. This denotes an *optional edge* and does not involve replacing <term> with <expr1>.

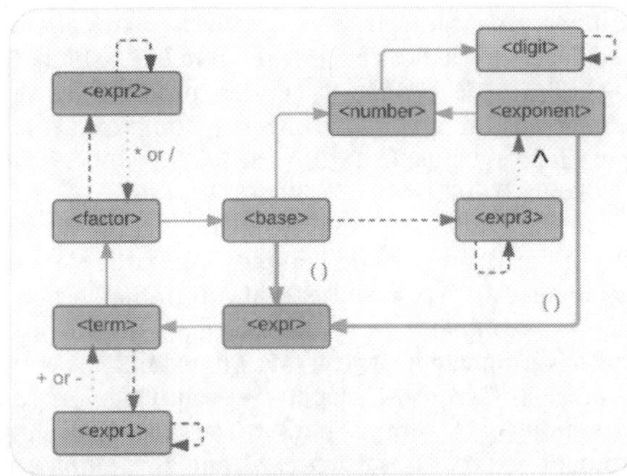

Figure 1. Graph representation of a Context-Free Grammar

The optional edge semantic is that whatever is generated through the optional edge gets appended to the <term>. In other words, instead of replacement something gets appended to the <term>.

The loop on the vertex labeled <expr1> denotes that zero or more copies of <expr1> are appended to <expr1>. Next, consider the *red-dotted* directional edge from <expr1> to <term>. Notice the edge label: plus (+) or minus (-). The semantic is that each copy of <expr1> is replaced by prefixing <term> with plus (+) or minus (-). For example, <expr1> can be replaced by either + <term> or - <term>. Lastly, consider the *thick-lined* directed edge from <base> to <expr> and notice the edge label: ( ). The semantic of this notation is that <base> is replaced by <expr> enclosed in parenthesis. That is, <base> is replaced by (<expr>).

Consider generating an arithmetic expression of the form: 32 + 65 − 173. As noted earlier, the generation process always starts at the vertex named <expr>. Next, since there is an edge from <expr> to <term>, we replace <expr> by <term>. Traversal of the edge from <term> to <expr1> is optional. If this path is chosen, we append to <term> rather than replacing it. We choose this optional edge and visit <expr1>. The loop indicates zero or more repetitions and each repetition generates one <expr1>. Let us generate two copies - <expr1> <expr1>. Next, consider the edge from <expr1> to <term>. Each copy of <expr1> will be replaced by a plus (+) or a minus (-) followed by the <term>. Assume that we chose plus in the first case and minus in the second case. Now we have the string <term> + <term> - <term>. Next, using the edge from <term> to <factor>, each copy of <term> is replaced by <factor> yielding <factor> + <factor> - <factor>. Similarly, we traverse from <factor> to <base> yielding <base> + <base> - <base>. Repeating this one more time using the edge from <base> to <number>, we get <number>

+ <number> - <number>. Using the <number> - <digit> directed edge and looping on the <digit>, each <number> in <number> + <number> - <number> can be replaced by a desired integer number, which yields 32 + 65 - 173. Using a similar procedure, we can generate any number of arbitrarily complex arithmetic expressions such as 9∧((8*9)∧5*(8*((5*(7∧(09/95)/9))+(9-(4∧(((6∧9)+2)+((81/877)∧5)∧9)))+8)∧3+8))/8.

In the grammar graph, we distinguish between two types of paths: simple and complex. All paths start at the special vertex <expr> and end at a terminal vertex (e.g., <digit>). A *simple path* is one that does not involve any loops or optional edge traversals. For example, <expr> → <term> → <factor> → <base> → <number> → <digit> is a simple path. Simple path traversals yield simplest arithmetic expressions such as 4 and 6. *Complex paths* are generated from simple paths by adding optional traversals, single- and multi-vertex loops. For instance, adding a single vertex loop, we can generate expressions such as 15 and 5674. An example of a multi-vertex loop is <expr> → <term> → <factor> → <base> → <expr>.

In our expression generation algorithm, a user can specify the complexity of the generated arithmetic expression. An user may use the terms *simple*, *moderate*, and *complex* to denote expression complexity. The algorithm quantifies the level of complexity using the length and the number of operators in the expression generated.

Our goal is to generate expressions of arbitrary complexity, which feature specified arithmetic operators from the set {add, subtract, multiply, divide, exp}. Given the size of the grammar, this task is not complex. As the size and complexity of the grammar increases, generating a query that features given operators is non-trivial. We address these issues in the context of generating SQL queries that contain specified SQL constructs.

IV. Generating SQL Queries

ISO/IEC 9075:2011 is the standard for the SQL database query language. The SQL language elements include operators, clauses, predicates, expressions, statements, and queries. Operators include the traditional mathematical ones such as ≤ and >, as well as database-specific ones such as Between, In, Exists, Is Not Distinct From, and Avg. Clauses are components of statements and queries. Predicates are conditions that evaluate to three-valued logic (true, false, unknown). Expressions, when evaluated, produce either scalar values or tables. Statements enable specifying a wide range of actions on the database. Lastly, queries enable retrieving data from the database. Queries do not change database contents and operate in read-only mode. SQL queries comprise a principal component of the ISO/IEC standard. Table II shows the generic structure of SQL queries. Only the first two components are mandatory. However, the components must occur in the order indicated. For example, a SQL query may have Select, From, and Group By without the Where clause. Likewise, we can have Select, From, and Order By without the Group By and Having clauses.

Table II. General structure of SQL queries

Select	<column names and transformations on column values>
From	<table names> and <join conditions>
Where	<row restrictions>
Group By	<column names for grouping rows in the result set>
Having	<condition specifying which groups to keep>
Order By	<sorting specification for displaying results>

Drawing upon our experience in generating arithmetic expressions, we will first create a grammar graph using the SQL grammar. We subset the SQL grammar to include only rules that are associated with the Select statement. Next, using the grammar graph we will determine if it is feasible to generate a query which contains the user-specified SQL constructs. This requires determining a path in the graph which encompasses, starting at the vertex which corresponds to the start symbol of the grammar (e.g., <expr)> in Figure 1), vertices and edges corresponding to all the SQL constructs specified by the user. Furthermore, the string traced by this path either contains only terminals or non-terminals that can be replaced with terminals.

V. Conclusions and Future Work

In this work-in-progress paper, we have presented a novel approach to automatic generation of SQL queries that feature user-specified SQL constructs. Our approach uses the notion of *grammar graph* to determine whether or not such a query exists, and to generate the query. We have demonstrated the validity of the approach on arithmetic expression generation. As a logical next step, we will apply the approach to the actual generation of SQL queries.

References

[1] L. D. Fink, *Creating significant learning experiences: An integrated approach to designing college courses*, Second. San Francisco, CA: Jossey-Bass, 2013.

[2] P. C. Brown, H. L. Roediger, and M. A. McDaniel, *Make it stick: The science of successful learning.* Cambridge, MA: Belknap Press, 2014.

[3] S. A. Ambrose, M. W. Bridges, M. DiPietro, M. C. Lovett, and M. K. Norman, *How learning works: Seven research-based principles for smart teaching.* San Francisco, CA: Jossey-Bass, 2010.

[4] V. Gudivada, J. Nandigam, and D. Guru, "A learning-centered approach to designing computer science courses," *J. Comput. Small Coll.*, vol. 21, no. 4, pp. 96–103, Apr. 2006.

[5] J. M. Lang, *Small teaching: Everyday lessons from the science of learning*, First. San Francisco, CA: Jossey-Bass, 2016.

[6] M. Weimer, *Learner-centered teaching: Five key changes to practice*, Second. San Francisco, CA: Jossey-Bass, 2013.

[7] National Academy of Engineering. (2017). Grand challenges, [Online]. Available: http://www.engineeringchallenges.org/cms/challenges.aspx (visited on 02/08/2017).

[8] A. Ahadi, V. Behbood, A. Vihavainen, J. Prior, and R. Lister, "Students' syntactic mistakes in writing seven different types of sql queries and its application to predicting students' success," in *Proceedings of the 47th ACM Technical Symposium on Computing Science Education*, ser. SIGCSE '16, Memphis, Tennessee, USA: ACM, 2016, pp. 401–406.

[9] A. S. Khalek and S. Khurshid, "Automated sql query generation for systematic testing of database engines," in *Proceedings of the IEEE/ACM international conference on Automated software engineering*, ser. ASE '10, New York, NY: ACM, 2010, pp. 329–332.

[10] C. Binnig, D. Kossmann, E. Lo, and M. T. Özsu, "Qagen: Generating query-aware test databases," in *Proceedings of the 2007 ACM SIGMOD international conference on Management of data*, ser. SIGMOD '07, New York, NY: ACM, 2007, pp. 341–352.

[11] P. Brusilovsky, S. Sosnovsky, M. V. Yudelson, D. H. Lee, V. Zadorozhny, and X. Zhou, "Learning sql programming with interactive tools: From integration to personalization," *Trans. Comput. Educ.*, vol. 9, no. 4, 19:1–19:15, Jan. 2010.

[12] Q. Do, R. Agrawal, D. Rao, and V. Gudivada, "Automatic generation of sql queries," in *Proceedings of the 121st ASEE Annual Conference & Exposition*, ASEE, Jun. 2014, pp. 1–11.

[13] D. Chays, "Test data generation for relational database applications," AAI3115007, PhD thesis, Brooklyn, NY, 2004.

[14] R. Siddiqi, C. J. Harrison, and R. Siddiqi, "Improving teaching and learning through automated short-answer marking," *IEEE Transactions on Learning Technologies*, vol. 3, pp. 237–249, 2010.

[15] T. Li and S. Sambasivam, "Question difficulty assessment in intelligent tutor systems for computer architecture," in *Proc ISECON*, EDSIG, 2003, pp. 1–8.

[16] T. Li and S. Sambasivam, "Automatically generating questions in multiple variables for intelligent tutoring," in *Society for Information Technology & Teacher Education International Conference (SITE)*, 2005, pp. 471–2005.

[17] V. Gudivada, "*TESSA* - an image testbed for evaluating 2-D spatial similarity algorithms," *ACM SIGIR Forum*, vol. 28, no. 2, pp. 17–36, Fall 1994.

[18] M. Heilman, "Automatic factual question generation from text," PhD thesis, Carnegie Mellon University, Pittsburgh, PA, 2011.

[19] J. C. Brown, G. A. Frishkoff, and M. Eskenazi, "Automatic question generation for vocabulary assessment," in *HLT '05: Proceedings of the conference on Human Language Technology and Empirical Methods in Natural Language Processing*, Morristown, NJ: Association for Computational Linguistics, 2005, pp. 819–826.

[20] R. Correia, "Automatic question generation for REAP.PT tutoring system," Master's thesis, 2010. [Online]. Available: http://www.inesc-id.pt/pt/indicadores/Ficheiros/5599.pdf (visited on 01/15/2017).

[21] C.-Y. Chen, H.-C. Liou, J. S. Chang, and J. S. Chang, "FAST – an automatic generation system for grammar tests," in *Proceedings of the COLING/ACL on Interactive presentation sessions*, 2006, pp. 1–4.

[22] P. Piwek and K. Boyer. (2010). The third workshop on question generation, [Online]. Available: http://oro.open.ac.uk/22343/1/QG2010-Proceedings.pdf (visited on 01/15/2017).

[23] V. Rus, P. Piwek, S. Stoyanchev, B. Wyse, M. Lintean, and C. Moldovan, "Question generation shared task and evaluation challenge: Status report," in *Proceedings of the 13th European Workshop on Natural Language Generation*, ser. ENLG '11, Stroudsburg, PA: Association for Computational Linguistics, 2011, pp. 318–320.

[24] P. Piwek and K. Boyer, "Special issue on question generation," *Dialog & Discourse*, vol. 3, pp. 1–322, 2012, http://elanguage.net/journals/dad/issue/view/347.

[25] M. Al-Yahya, "Ontology-based multiple choice question generation," *The Scientific World Journal*, no. 10.1155/2014/274949, pp. 1–9, 2014.

Data Visualization of A Cyber-Physical Systems Development Toolchain:
An Integration Case Study

Didem Gürdür*, Jad El-khoury
Department of Machine Design,
KTH Royal Institute of Technology,
Stockholm, Sweden
e-mail: {dgurdur, jad}@kth.se

Tiberiu Seceleanu, Morgan Johansson, Stefan Hansen
ABB AB,
Sweden
e-mail: {tiberiu.seceleanu, morgan.e.johansson, stefan.hansen}@se.abb.com

Abstract—**Development of Cyber-Physical Systems (CPS) requires various engineering disciplines, artifacts, and areas of expertise to collaborate. There are powerful software tools, which are used during CPS development, but it is often challenging to integrate these tools with each other. This paper proposes a data visualization approach to understanding current interoperability status and the integration needs in CPS development toolchains, and make decisions on potential integration scenarios accordingly. To this end, a case study is introduced based on a toolchain for the development of an embedded application at ABB Corporate Research. The node-link diagram (NLD) data visualization technique was used to understand integration needs and priorities. The study showed that the NLD visualization has the potential to inform toolchain architects about the interoperability situation and help them to make decisions accordingly, especially for small toolchains. Moreover, the integration solution is implemented and the result has been compared with the non-integration study.**

Keywords-toolchain interoperability; tool integration; interoperability visualization; toolchain visualization; data visualization; node-link diagram.

I. Introduction

Cyber-Physical Systems (CPS) rely on the tight interaction of real-time computing and physical systems [21]. CPS development involves the integration of computation and physical processes [1]. Moreover, this development process requires software tool support for the tasks associated with different engineering disciplines throughout the different phases of the Product LifeCycle (PLC) (see Figure 1). These tools are used to complete different PLC stages and they produce artifacts and data. Furthermore, there is a necessity to support intricate relationships between different stakeholder viewpoints at the people, model and tool levels [2].

The interoperability of these software tools is required to improve productivity and efficiency in a consistent manner for CPS development. Yet, the integration of these tools is especially challenging due to their heterogeneous nature. Even though the tool integration research field is progressing, there still are no well-defined methods to guide the toolchain architect to understand the current interoperability status of toolchains [3]. And yet, without understanding the current interoperability situation of the development toolchains, it is difficult to identifying the priorities, dependencies, and correct decisions necessary to improve the development process.

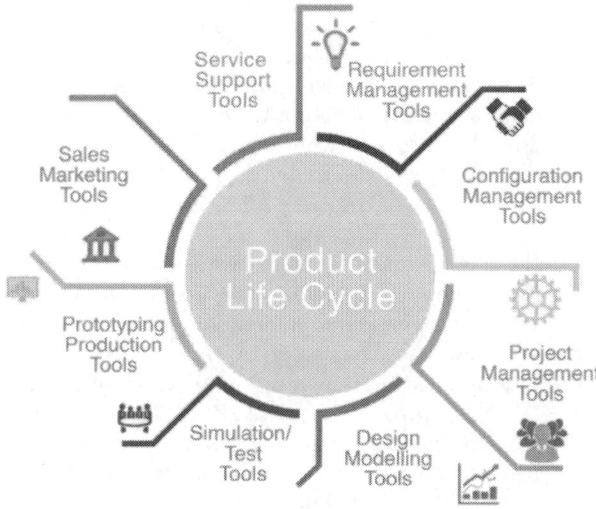

Figure 1. Product life cycle and various software tool categories [24].

Recent advances in computing and data storage technologies have made the existence of vast volumes of data possible, offering a powerful opportunity to discover new insights from the data. However, finding the valuable information in these vast data sets is not easy. Bendre and Thool [4] mention that data analytics and decision support tools in the manufacturing industry would handle, integrate, and analyze collected data and provide appropriate solutions "to improve manufacturing processes, control over production, market-oriented business avenues, and efficient customer service at lower costs, to increase profit and help manufacturers to stay in healthy competition". Visualization and visual analytics offer the opportunity to help understand interoperability with the added ability to promptly gain insight into the current interoperability of the toolchain. Visualization allows the extraction of patterns concerning relevant issues, such as workflow and tool usage, whilst visual analytics allows iterative work with these patterns [5]. In this way, the complexity and heterogeneity can be handled by analyzing the data visualizations of the development toolchains, allowing toolchain architects to focus on important aspects of integration. This study illustrates the application of visualization and visual analytics to help toolchain architects understand interoperability and support the decision making process in CPS development toolchains.

The study specifically looks at the use of the node-link diagram (NLD) [15] visualization technique. The proposed NLD visualization illustrates the toolchain *before* any integration is introduced in order to show the needs and thus supports the toolchain architect in making decisions according to the collected data about tool usage. Furthermore, this paper summarizes the integration method used to overcome the identified interoperability needs and highlights the change in tool interactions *after* the integration was introduced to underline the success of the integrated toolchain.

This paper is organized in six sections: Section 2 explains the background. Section 3 presents the case study. Section 4 discusses the rationale for the choice of the NLD visualization technique and the application of the technique in the context of toolchain interoperability, as well as summarizing the integration method and presenting the user activity data after integration. Section 5 summarizes the future direction of the study. Finally, the paper concludes with a summary of the study in Section 6.

II. Background

Interoperability is the ability of two or more systems, components or tools to exchange information and to use that information effectively [25]. Ford et al. [6] disclose at least 30 different definitions of interoperability from the last 30 years. Interoperability is a multidimensional concept, consisting of several perspectives and approaches from different domains. Although the definitions may differ, they all emphasize the importance of understanding interoperability. Our case study used in this paper is about the CPS development toolchains, focusing on the interactions between software tools to understand interoperability.

Assessing interoperability with well-chosen measures is essential for identifying priorities in product development and production. Many researchers have studied interoperability assessment models and proposed different approaches in literature [7-11]. In our earlier study [5], we examined interoperability assessment models and extrapolated that the literature mainly:

- Uses either complex metrics, separate levels, or combinations of these with little guidance on how such metrics can be used.
- Concentrates on selective aspects of interoperability.
- Focuses on structure and content, providing little guidance on how to deal with interoperability improvements.

Given these findings, we concluded/argued that a more flexible, data-oriented method to increase the understanding of interoperability is needed. Data visualization techniques were in the end chosen for the following reasons:

- Data visualization of toolchains provides an overview of the real situation of interoperability, where data can be filtered to ensure analytics for different stakeholders. Thus, the holistic, dynamic and bridged analysis could be possible to provide a better interoperability understanding for the stakeholders
- Data could be collected for different aspects of interoperability to extend the visualizations to cover more than one selective aspect, and to facilitate anaylsis of the interactions between different aspects. This is an important opportunity when addressing the overall interoperability status.
- Data analytics aims to guide the user towards better interoperability by allowing the toolchain architecture to see the big picture. Furthermore, this approach could be combined with some metrics such as cost, performance, and sustainability of the toolchain to guide the toolchain architect to take decisions according to these metrics.

Visualizations and visual technologies have also been pointed out by well-known initiatives that aim to contribute to better-integrated engineering environments, such as the Industrial Internet Consortium, the Advanced Manufacturing Partnership, Industrie 4.0, and La Nouvelle France Industrielle. These initiatives consider visual computing as a promising technology to be used to improve development environments. For instance, Industrie 4.0 mentions visual computing as a valuable support for acquiring, analyzing, and synthesizing data [12], while the Advanced Manufacturing Partnership organized workshops with the visualization, informatics, and digital manufacturing work groups to define fundamental research opportunities for these technologies with respect to smart manufacturing [13].

This study summarizes the work done in [22] where the Open Services for Lifecycle Collaboration (OSLC) [23] framework has been used to integrate software tools used in this case study. OSLC is an OASIS standard consisting of members from both industry and academia with a goal to standardize how tools should interact and share data. The OSLC standard is organized in work groups that each addresses a specific domain of tools such as requirements management, test management, change management or configuration management. Moreover, deriving all domains from the OSLC core specification ensures compatibility between domains. The earlier work [22] presents the details of how integration solution is developed by defining a version control domain based on the OSLC core specification, and describes how to represent versioned artifacts and perform version control operations. The study in [24] presents different visualization techniques and exercises their applicability before implementing any integration solutions. In this paper, we concentrate on the most successful data visualization approach from [24] and repeated the same development work by using the integrated toolchain and compare the non-integration and integration scenarios through data visualizations.

III. Case Study

The case study is about the development of a prototype application targeting the Cooling System for Transmission Plant (CSTP) (Figure 2) at ABB. The application is a closed loop control system where a number of sensor elements and actuators are connected by various interfaces. The system performs relevant actions depending on the input signals, the internal system state, the configurable logic, and possibly on operator commands. The system is required to perform a variety of computation-intensive operations, with very high real-time requirements, on data coming in concurrent streams.

This paper does not focus on the application of CSTP but rather on the creation and execution of a toolchain to support its development. Therefore, we collected data about the toolchain activities. During the development of the CSTP four different tools used such as Team Foundation Server 2005, Team Foundation Server 2015, HiDraw and Internet Explorer. Firstly, we installed user activity tracking software on one of the developers' computer. The tracking application worked on a dedicated computer for a period of time and saved information about tool usage. Secondly, we cleaned and filtered the data collected by the tracking application to remove unrelated tool accesses and to be able to understand tool interactions easier. As a third step, we used this data to develop data visualization of the toolchain. The aim was to visualize user activity during the development of CSTP to find out how much time was spent on each tool, and to see any patterns that might support a toolchain architect in making any decisions on integration scenarios. One important factor was the switching between tools, which can be explained as changing between tools. The data visualization was used to improve the understanding about the current interoperability situation. As a next step, integration need is identified and tools are integrated using the OSLC standard. The same developer was tracked again for the same amount of time on the same project in order to compare the toolchain performance before and after integration.

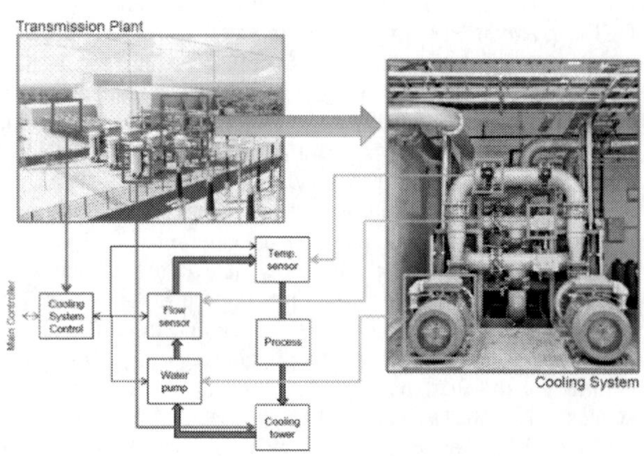

Figure 2. Cooling System for Transmission Plant [24].

During the development of the CSTP application, four main software tools are used. These tools are:

- Microsoft Visual Studio | Team Foundation Server 2005 (TFS 2005): used for storage of requirements, development artifacts and supporting documents, in addition to performing version control.
- Microsoft Visual Studio | Team Foundation Server 2015 (TFS 2015): used for storage of requirements, development artifacts and supporting documents, in addition to performing version control.
- HiDraw (HD): a proprietary graphical design tool, used to model the structure and functionality of the control application from which code can be generated, deployed and monitored. The generated code is then stored in TFS.
- Internet Explorer (IE): used as a support tool to access the TFS web interface to view and edit work items. The main reason for its usage, as explained by developers, is that ease of use of the IE, as compared to the TFS, especially for localizing work items.

The case study was designed to collect data about one developer's tool usage activity for a period of one month. A developer's activity was recorded by tracking the application to create data visualizations. This data is deliberately defined in a compact format in order to collect minimum information about the tool usage. In this way, we aimed to make the data collection, cleaning, and filtering process as simple as possible. The data only includes tool name, start time (defined as the time the developer activated a particular software tool) and end time (when the developer completed using the tool and switched to another tool). During the cleaning process, we merged the start and end time by introducing a new attribute called duration. We also filtered the data by combining some rows where the developer stopped using one tool but then start to use it again without switching to another tool. Table I is generated to summarize the total usage of each tool and the switching percentages between them (Table I).

TABLE I. FINAL DATA ABOUT THE TOOL USAGE AND INTERACTIONS DURING THE DEVELOPMENT OF CSTP.

	Total Usage	**HD**	**IE**	**TFS 2015**	**TFS 2005**
HD	53%	0%	48%	47%	5%
IE	33%	65%	0%	34%	1%
TFS 2015	13%	72%	28%	0%	0%
TFS 2005	1%	57%	43%	0%	0%

The same process was repeated after the integration of tools by tracking the same developer's activity for a similar amount of time. This second phase of the study observed the effect of integration on the developer's activity. The next section offers a discussion of the data visualization approach and comments on the understanding of toolchain interoperability needs, along with a brief summary of the integration details.

IV. DISCUSSION

In preparation for the collection and visualization of data, we organized meetings where different stakeholders of the toolchain discussed what factors are important to them in understanding interoperability better. These meetings concluded by identifying two main needs for understanding interoperability better:

- In any visual representation, each tool needs to be easily distinguished from the others. Each tool should be represented as a first-class element in the diagram. Different colors for each tool representation are used for this purpose.
- The most important information to be represented is the time spent using the tool by the developer For this reason, the size of tool representation should be proportional to this property. Interactive tooltips are also added to the graphical representations to provide more information about each tool.
- The interactions between tools are the main focus of current interoperability assessment methods. There is hence a need to reveal the interaction patterns in the studied case, which will then be a basis to prioritize mostly interaction tools for increasing interoperability. For this purpose, the interactions are added to the visualizations as an arc or link shape. The opacity of lines represents the interaction frequency between tools. In addition, the size of the shapes is proportional to the interaction rate.

To visualize the development toolchain we chose to use an NLD visualization technique. The two reasons behind this choice are:

Readability: NLDs are the most familiar representation of graphs in general.

Understanding: NLDs are intuitive, compact, and good at showing the overall structure of information. They are especially effective for small graphs.

An NLD is a tree-type data visualization that captures entities as nodes and relationships. The layout has the potential to use the entire two-dimensional space, offering a number of ways to represent interactions. This large variety of possible layouts allows different aspects of the data to be focused on, especially useful for large graphs. Battista et al. [14] presented an extensive collection of possible layout algorithms for drawing a graph of data using the NLD. This bibliographic survey attempts to encompass both theoretical and application-oriented papers from disparate areas. We refer the interested reader to this study for a detailed assessment of these algorithms.

Figure 3 shows the NLD visualization of the data we collected for the case study. Five data variables are used in this visualization - nodes, node labels, links, a qualitative attribute and a quantitative attribute. The mapping between data variables and visual variables in NLDs is as follows:

- The nodes are shown as circles to represent different tools;
- Each node has a label which is the name of the tool;
- There are links between nodes that are represented by line segments that show the interactions of tools.

A qualitative attribute is shown by the color of each circle and it is used to distinguish different tools. Lastly, the quantitative attribute is indicated by the size of the circle, which represents the usage frequency of the tool. In other words, the size of the circle is proportional to the time the user spent using in this tool. A link between two circles represents the switching behavior between the corresponding tools performed by the developer, where the opacity of the links is proportional to the switching frequency. A darker link color encodes higher interactions between tools. Thus, Figure 3 shows that the tool named HD is the most used tool during the development process, since the corresponding circle is the largest. Moreover, most of the tool switches occur either between TFS 2015 and HD or between IE and HD.

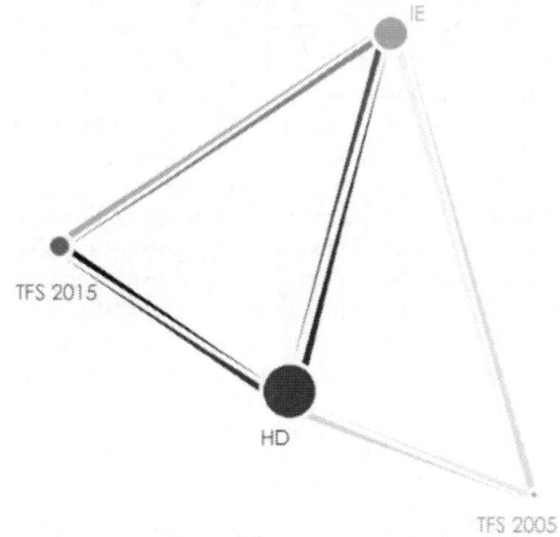

Figure 3. Node-link diagram of the development toolchain before integration [24].

The toolchain architect can easily distinguish the tools using the labels next to each circle. Since the visualization is interactive there is a possibility to include more information. There are tooltips, which inform the architect about the links and nodes. For instance, a toolchain architect can get more information about the time each tool was used, by hovering over the circles, or they can learn about the switching behavior by hovering over the links between tools.

NLDs help to observe global patterns of interactions in a toolchain. They make it easier to spot unexpected connections and understand the switching behavior between tools. Moreover, visual features such as color and size reveal the heterogeneity and time spent using each tool in the development process. One can make decisions about the toolchain interoperability according to the visualization and the graphic can be used to explain the need for interoperability in CPS development environments. Once the data was collected, and the visual diagrams were prepared, a meeting with the stakeholders was organized again. The toolchain architects found the visualization easy to read, and they were directly able to point out which parts of the toochain can best benefit from better interoperability.

The resulting NLD visualization of the CSTP shows the toolchain architect how much unnecessary time has been spent on IE to find information about the task. This visualization further used to show other stakeholders the necessity of integration, and supports communication about the problem. After having meetings and discussing the NLD visualization, it was decided that HD needs to be integrated with TFS 2005 and TFS 2015.

As a next step, ABB developed an integration solution based on the OSLC standard. In OSLC, data is represented as a Resource accessible and identified by a uniform resource identifier (URI). Other tools can look up, reference and interact with the resource by accessing the URI via RESTful services. OSLC resources are exposed by services through creation factories and query capabilities. An OSLC service is accessible via a service provider. Moreover, OSLC tool adapters are specialized tool extensions, which allow sharing data, signals or even parts of a user interface [22]. The integration solution requires building two tool adapters for the HD design tool and the TFS2015 version control tool. These adapters allow tools to integrate using an OSLC-compliant web service. The HD tool does not contain any version control specific implementation and can be integrated with any tool providing version control in the same OSLC manner. Moreover, through its OSLC adapter, TFS2015 can also offer version control functionality to any other tool which implements a client to the OSLC service.

This mentioned integration implementation "was applied on a set of project files and compared to existing direct tool-to-tool integration. The functionality of the OSLC tool adapter for TFS2015 and HD extension matched all existent functionality, demonstrating the integration of a design tool with a version control repository using the OSLC domain. The proposed approach also removes all TFS2015-specific code and functionality from the HD tool, eliminating the need to manage and update HD installation in case of changes to the version control system" [22]. The integration also addresses traceability between versioned items and items from an external requirements management tool. Introducing traceability is enabled by the fact that versioned items are exposed as OSLC resources, which can, in turn, be referenced by any other OSLC resource. The HD's OSLC extension allows selecting an OSLC requirement during the check-in operation, and attaching the newly created versioned item as the implementation of this requirement.

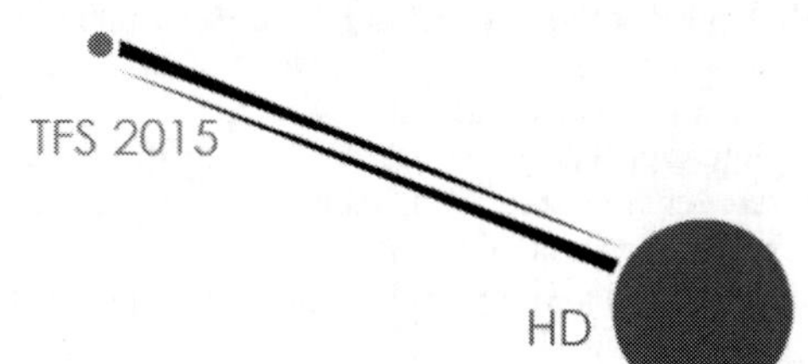

Figure 4. Node-link diagram of the development toolchain after integration.

Once the integration solution was implemented and deployed, we have used tracking software again to understand the effect of integration on the development toolchain. The same tracking application is used for this purpose with the same data collection format, for the same task. Moreover, the same developer has been tracked to minimize the effect of different user behavior. The results showed that the developer used HD 94% of the time and changed to TFS2015 only 6% of the time. Table II summarized the usage data after integration where developer only uses these two tools. Figure 4 shows the new NLD data visualization for the integrated toolchain. This new data shows that the developer does not need to switch between tools as much as the non-integrated scenario. One obvious reason behind this is the usefulness of the integration solution. Now, the developer uses version control through the HD adapter without a need to use IE to search for the information about the requirements. This also illustrated that the productivity of the developer increased since, after integration, the developer needed less time to complete the same task.

TABLE II. DATA ABOUT THE TOOL USAGE AND INTERACTIONS DURING THE DEVELOPMENT OF CSTP AFTER INTEGRATION.

	Total Usage	HD	IE	TFS 2015	TFS 2005
HD	94%	0%	0%	100%	0%
IE	0%	0%	0%	0%	0%
TFS 2015	6%	100%	0%	0%	0%
TFS 2005	0%	0%	0%	0%	0%

The case study included only one developer and this is one of the limitations that retain us to generalize the finding of the study. However, it still inholds valuable information about the importance of the understanding of current interoperability situation in development toolchains. This case study also illustrates how important the data is for improving the understanding of complex CPS development toolchains. Even with small data, the toolchain architect could have a better understanding and take decisions according to real data. Moreover, the study exemplified how this visualization can be used to develop common understanding about the interoperability state with other stakeholders.

V. FUTURE WORK

Although NLDs are a very successful way to show the overall picture, they do have some disadvantages. For instance, different layouts could create ambiguity when the node number increases [16]. Ghoniem et al. [17] showed that density has a strong impact on readability in these diagrams.

One way to approach this problem and increase the readability of NLDs is to use algorithms to obtain clustered graph layouts that optimize certain aesthetic criteria. For this reason, we suggest using a balloon layout [14, 15, 18, 19] for larger toolchain. Authors in [24] present different data visualization techniques including balloon layout to visualize the development toolchain. In future, repeating a similar case study for a larger toolchain and including more developers' activity would be beneficial to be able to further generalize the results.

VI. CONCLUSION

In this paper, we explained the interoperability challenge in CPS development environments, and presented data visualization as a promising approach for developing a better understanding of interoperability of CPS development toolchains. The studied development toolchain and the tools are described, in addition to the data collection and visualization process. The study showed that the NLD visualization has the potential to inform toolchain architects about the interoperability situation and help them to make decisions accordingly, especially for small toolchains. In the case study, this understanding lead to the integration of the two predominantly used tools, an HD design tool and a TFS2015 version control tool. This integration positively affected the performance of a developer and helped them to stay focused on one tool. The developer's tool usage data shows that integration eliminated the need for IE and increased the abilities of the HD tool. Last but not least, the study underlines the importance of data in the development environment and motivates the CPS industry to collect and use data in the decision-making process for better interoperability.

ACKNOWLEDGMENT

The research leading to these results has received funding from the ARTEMIS JU under grant agreement no 621429 for "EMC2 - Embedded multi-core systems for mixed-criticality applications in dynamic and changeable real-time environments", and from Vinnova under DIARIENR 2014-01225. The authors would like to acknowledge Vicki Derbyshire who performed language editing and proofreading.

REFERENCES

[1] E. A. Lee, "Cyber-physical systems-are computing foundations adequate". In Position Paper for NSF Workshop On Cyber-Physical Systems: Research Motivation, Techniques and Roadmap (Vol. 2), October 2006.

[2] M. Törngren, A. Qamar, M. Biehl, F. Loiret, and J. El-Khoury, "Integrating viewpoints in the development of mechatronic products," Mechatronics, pp.745-762, 2014.

[3] D. Gürdür, F. Asplund, J. El-khoury, F. Loiret, and M. Törngren, "Visual analytics towards tool interoperabilty: A position paper," In Proceedings of the 11th Joint Conference on Computer Vision, Imaging and Computer Graphics Theory and Applications, 2016a, pp. 139-145, ISBN 978-989-758-175-5.

[4] M. R. Bendre, and V. R. Thool, "Analytics, challenges and applications in big data environment: a survey," Journal of Management Analytics, pp.1-34, 2016.

[5] D. Gürdür, F. Asplund, J. El-khoury, "Measuring Toolchain Interoperability in Cyber-physical Systems," In Proceedings of the 11th International Conference on System of Systems Engineering, 2016b.

[6] T. C. Ford, J. M. Colombi, S.R. Graham, and D.R. Jacques, "Survey on Interoperability Measurement," Air Force Institute of Technology, 2007.

[7] G. E. Lavean, "Interoperability in defense communications," IEEE Transactions on Communications , 1980, pp.1445-1455.

[8] D. Mensh, R. Kite, and P. Darby. "A methodology for quantifying interoperability," Naval Engineering Journal, 1989.

[9] C. Amanowicz, and C. P. Gajewski. "Military communications and information systems interoperability," Military Communications Conference, 1996.

[10] T. Clark, and R. Jones, "Organisational interoperability maturity model for C2," In Proceedings of the 1999 Command and Control Research and Technology Symposium, June 1999.

[11] J. A. Hamilton Jr, J. D. Rosen, and P. A. Summers, "An interoperability road map for C4ISR legacy systems," Space and Naval Warefare Systems Center, 2002.

[12] J. Posada, C. Toro, I. Barandiaran, D. Oyarzun, D. Stricker, R. de Amicis, E. B. Pinto, P. Eisert, J. Döllner, and I. Vallarino, "Visual computing as a key enabling technology for industrie 4.0 and industrial internet," IEEE computer graphics and applications, 35(2), 2015, pp. 26-40.

[13] Smart Manufacturing Leadership Coalition. *SMLC-NSF Workshop* [Online]. Available from: https://smartmanufacturingcoalition.org/smlc-nsf-workshop

[14] D. G. Battista, P. Eades, I. G. Tollis, and R. Tamassia, Graph drawing: Algorithms for the visualization of graphs, 1999.

[15] I. Herman, G. Melançon, and M. S. Marshall, "Graph visualization and navigation in information visualization: A survey," Visualization and Computer Graphics, IEEE Transactions, 2000, pp. 24-43.

[16] R. Keller, C. M. Eckert, and P. J. Clarkson, "Matrices or node-link diagrams: Which visual representation is better for visualising connectivity models?," Information Visualization, 2006, pp. 62-76.

[17] M. Ghoniem, J. D. Fekete, and P. Castagliola, "On the readability of graphs using node-link and matrix-based representations: A controlled experiment and statistical analysis." Information Visualization, 2005, pp. 114-135.

[18] M. Dickerson, D. Eppstein, M. T. Goodrich, and J. Y. Meng, "Confluent drawings: Visualizing non-planar diagrams in a planar way," In Graph Drawing, September 2003, pp. 1-12

[19] D. Holten, "Hierarchical edge bundles: Visualization of adjacency relations in hierarchical data," IEEE Transactions on Visualization and Computer Graphics, 2006, pp. 741-748.

[20] M. Baur, and U. Brandes, "Multi-circular layout of micro/macro graphs," In Graph Drawing, September 2007, pp. 255-267.

[21] S. Emgell, "Cyber-physical systems of systems—definition and core research and innovation areas," Working Paper of the Support Action CPSoS, 2014.

[22] L. Lednicki, G. Sapienza, M, E. Johansson, T. Seceleanu, T. and D. Hallmans, "Integrating version control in a standardized service-oriented tool chain," In IEEE 40th Annual Computer Software and Applications Conference, June 2016, pp. 323-328.

[23] OSLC community, *Open Services for Lifecycle Collaboration*, [Online]. Available from: http: //open-services.net/

[24] D. Gürdür, J. El-khoury, T. Seceleanu, and L. Lednicki, "Making Interoperability Visible: Data Visualization of Cyber-Physical Systems Development Tool Chains," Journal of Industrial Information Integration, 2016, doi: 10.1016/j.jii.2016.09.002.

[25] M. Javanbakht, R. Rezaie, F. Shams, and M. Seyyedi, "A new method for decision making and planning in enterprises," In 3rd International Conference on Information and Communication Technologies: From Theory to Applications, April 2008, pp. 1-5.

Processing Information about Junior Specialists for Small IT-projects Teams Using Linked Data

Nafissa Yussupova
Computer Science and Robotics Department
Ufa State Aviation Technical University
Ufa, Russian Federation
e-mail: yussupova@ugatu.ac.ru

Dmitry Rizvanov
Computer Science and Robotics Department
Ufa State Aviation Technical University
Ufa, Russian Federation
e-mail: ridmi@mail.ru

Olga Smetanina
Computer Science and Robotics Department
Ufa State Aviation Technical University
Ufa, Russian Federation
e-mail: smoljushka@mail.ru

Artur Galyamov
Computer Science and Robotics Department
Ufa State Aviation Technical University
Ufa, Russian Federation
e-mail: galyamov.artur@profport.org

Konstantin Mironov
Computer Science and Robotics Department
Ufa State Aviation Technical University
Ufa, Russian Federation
e-mail: mironovconst@gmail.com

***Abstract*—In this paper, we develop an approach and Web-ontology model for globally distributed structured data processing related to junior professionals. This information is represented using linked data. The proposed approach is based on Representational State Transfer and Semantic Web technologies. The proposed approach and model were applied in a Web-application for extracting and searching information about competences of junior specialists to build teams for small IT-projects.**

Keywords- Linked data; OWL; RDFa; globally distributed data processing; web-ontologies; competences.

I. Introduction

According to some investigations [17], more than 50% of the industrial projects in the sphere of Information Technologies (IT-projects) are not successful. According to marketing research and experience of project managers [17], inadequate organizational structure of the project teams is one of the main reasons for the project's failure. Competence model can help to increase the validity of decisions taken by project managers in this situation. This paper is focused on elaboration of ontological competence model and its further use in the Web-application.

II. Related Work

The area of interest is explored in a number of scientific works [1-16]. Semantic search, semantic Web, Web-ontologies, descriptive logic are studied in [18-21]. Numerous researches are dedicated to knowledge representation models and architecture of global distributed information systems [11][13][15-16].

Here, we develop a competence model for knowledge representation. A competence model is a set of skills (or competences) [4], which are required to execute tasks of the project. In this case, the competence model will be assumed in the context of management and recruitment projects.

Competences can be classified as follows [5]:

- Corporate competences, which do not depend on the specific position and are common for all employees of the entire enterprise;
- Managerial competences, which are specific to managers who carry out strategic vision, business administration and other high-level tasks;
- Professional competences, specific to concrete units.

The authors of [5] added levels for each competence to the competence model. "Level" in this model means the assessment of competence, with specific descriptions. A clear competence model is constructed in [4], however the classification of competences is very diffuse (social competences, socio-psychological competences, conceptual competences, etc.). In [6], no clear distinction between competence and skill is made. The skills are separated into knowledge and abilities. All skills may depend on strengths and weaknesses (soft). Basically, this model was constructed for students of technical colleges, but it can be adapted to other areas. It is based on the ontological approach.

Competences in the model from [7, p.4] are divided into characteristics, motives, skills, knowledge and self-esteem. If they are directly used in the taxonomy of competences, they complicate the model too much and will not lead to desired results [7]. However, some of them may be useful as additional characteristics of competences, in the form of relations in the domain of competences. i.e., "negotiation with the customer" is a skill, and "overcoming stressful situations" is a feature.

In [9], IT-supported strategic competence management is considered as a part of a human resource management system. For the competence estimation, a scale from 0 (not assessed) to 9 (excellent) is used. The values are evaluated by using the period of time, when a person has used the competence.

More approaches to the solution of this classification problem, taken from the experience of HR managers [6, pp. 762], may be viewed as follows: skills, knowledge, ability, attitude. These competences are divided into 4 levels.

To assess the competences of students directly, the competences are classified as connected to computer science, business, or behavior [6]. In accordance with this classification, the score ranges from 0 to 1. Each competence is assessed by the level of knowledge (beginner, intermediate and advanced) and experience (basic, intermediate, advanced). The competence is determined by three attributes: the name (a unique identifier for use in HR-XML profile), the scale, and the traceable calibration to assess the strength. In [10], components of competence are knowledge, know-how and behavior. Knowledge is what gets people through the education system. Know-how can be obtained from personal experience and practice. Behavior is a personal characteristic, allowing knowledge to become a know-how. According to the HR-XML [10, p.762], it is necessary to admit a competence model comparison study (validity) and ensure the privacy of the information provided. The ability to compare two people in terms of possession of a competence can be achieved by describing the selection of competences from the dictionary, giving the relationship of similarity of competences and competence assessment.

III. Contribution Overview

Within the framework of this research a new approach is proposed, which we call "Globally Distributed Processing of Weakly Structured Data" (GDPWSD). The proposed model is slightly different from the existing approaches in three aspects: it uses Internationalized Resource Identifier (IRI) instead of Uniform Resource Identifier (URI), a three-tier architecture instead of the client-server, and mediators in the form of Web ontologies to unify the process of extracting heterogeneous data sources.

A novel technique is used for ontology creation. This technique is similar to the stages of database design (conceptual, data and physical description models). Its use allows the following:

• visualizing the relationship between the concepts of the domain in the form of a conceptual model;

• formalizing relations from the conceptual model in the form of a logical model;

• constructing an ontological model on the basis of the logical model.

IV. Globally Distributed Processing Information About Junior Specialists

The proposed hybrid approach is based on the Representational State Transfer (REST) approach and mediator-wrapper approach [11, p. 30; 12, p. 94], which uses Semantic Web technologies, including linked data formats.

The main concepts of the approach are the following:

- information processing is based on a three-level architecture (client, Web server, and a knowledge base / database server);
- the server does not store the view state. It applies a uniform interface to access the resources based on the use of IRI;
- three levels of abstraction are used:
    - o application layer, where the search is made (managed by users);
    - o intermediate level (the use of mediators), which implements data collection and aggregation; Web ontology, which brings together various descriptions, is developed at this level (managed by ontologists).
    - o data sources level, using linked data (managed by site administrators).
- The project and junior specialists are associated via role and competence;
- It is taken into account that some competences are equal (synonyms) and some can be part of others (meronyms).

The features of the proposed approach allow:

- flexible and scalable data processing;
- unified access to heterogeneous data sources by implementing semantic integration via Web Ontology;
- increasing the number of relevant search results.

V. Ontology Model Description

The ontology model is aimed at describing the necessary information [1-2]. It is possible to visualize the relationship between key concepts and roles using UML (OMG ODM standard). Description logic SHOIN (D) allows to define logical axioms. Web Ontology Language with description logics (OWL DL) is used to create Web-ontology and then utilize it in Web-applications. The basic classes of the research domain and their relationships are represented in Figure 1. It is assumed that competence and competency are synonyms.

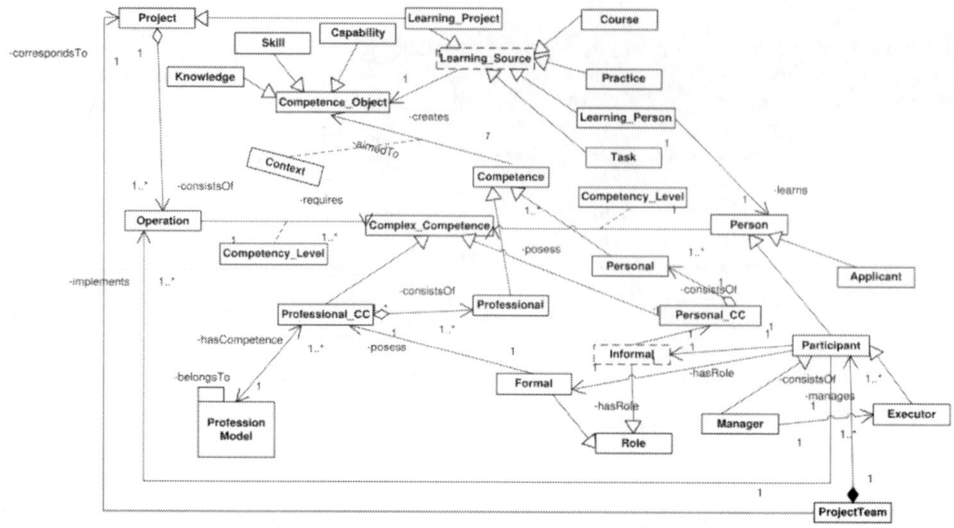

Figure 1. Representation of the Ontological Model Using UML Class Diagrams

Here, the concept of the project corresponds to *Project*, which consists of a series of operations *Operation*:

$$Project \equiv \forall \ consistsOf.Operation$$

The concept that corresponds to the notion of project team is *ProjectTeam*. In this model, it is a composition of roles in the project team:

$$ProjectTeam \equiv \forall \ consistsOf.Participant$$

In turn, the role *Role* can be formal and informal. Informal types of roles are taken from the socio-psychological models. Competence may be professional or personal. Hence, the formal role is associated with professional competence and the informal role is associated with personality:

$$Formal \subseteq \exists \ posess.Personal$$

$$Informal \subseteq \exists \ posess.Professional$$

The relation between the performer (Executor) and the Project is *Complex_Competence*, which is associated with the operation of the project *Operation*. Every complex competence consists of one or several single competences.

Each professional complex competence *Professional* is tied to a profession with the role *belongsTo*; it may be convenient to group competences, since sometimes one may need to immediately specify the profession a person should have to perform this role. For a hierarchy of occupations, the Standard Occupational Classification (SOC) was used, taking into account the specifics of the Russian employment market.

Each of the concepts belongs to its ontology. Their relationship is shown in Fig. 2.

Applying developed Web-application for searching about 100 various competences for 5 IT-projects showed increasing number of appropriate applicants for these projects by 10%.

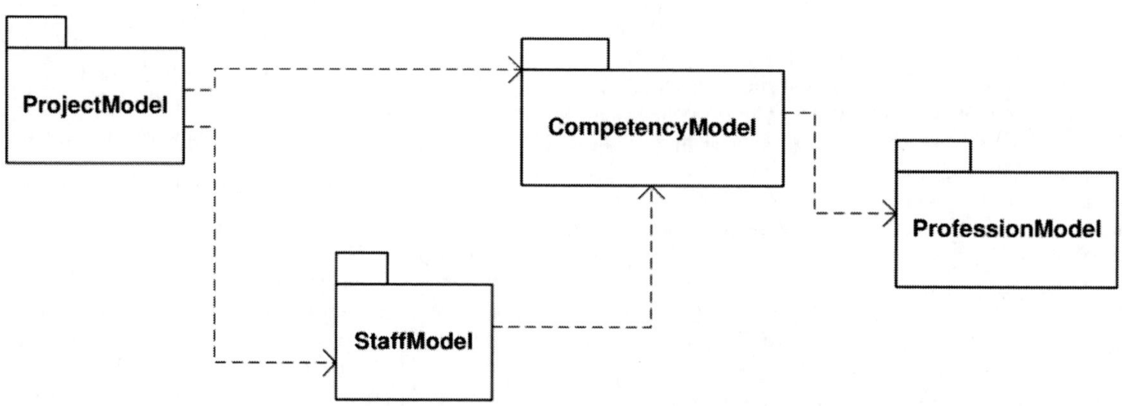

Figure 2. The Relationship of Ontology as a UML Package Diagrams

VI. WEB-APPLICATION

The Web-application based on our Web-ontology model, was implemented within the project ProfPort.org [14]. Information is extracted from the blogs and from the portfolios of the applicants and represented with RDFa, hCard microformat standard and simple HTML5/CSS3 sometimes. The Web-app is implemented with RubyOnRails framework as an application server, using document-oriented database MongoDB and RDF-store BigData. The deployment diagram and corresponding component diagram are presented in Fig. 3 and 4, respectively.

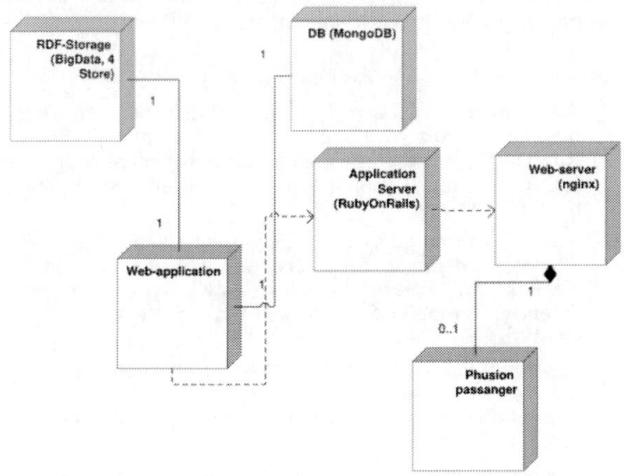

Figure 3. Deployment Diagram of the Web-App

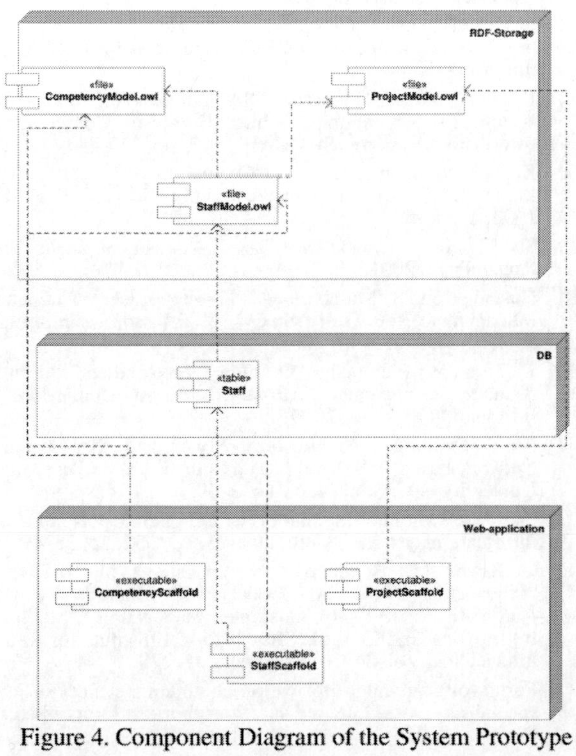

Figure 4. Component Diagram of the System Prototype

VII. EFFECTIVENESS ANALYSIS

The main purpose of the effectiveness analysis is to find out how the search results will change upon using synonymy and inheritance relations or without them. The main criteria that allows evaluating the effectiveness are completeness and relevance of the search.

Presently, 617 employment-seekers are registered in the ProfPort system; 428 competencies and 4 professions from the field of information technologies are introduced. These values allow rough designation of the search space.

To evaluate the speed of query execution, we use a standard personal computer with the following configuration:

- Processor: Intel Core i7-3770 @ 3.40GHz
- Motherboard: ASUSTek P8Z77-V LK
- Memory: DDR 3 Kingston 2xDIMM 4096 MB 800 MHz
- OS: Windows 8.1 Professional 64 bit
- SSD: OCZ Vertex3 224 GB
- Local server: Endels 1.64 Freeware

The fragment of the algorithm associated with the SPARQL query is used for the longest time using ARC2.The results of the experiment are shown in Table. 1.

TABLE I. SPEED OF EXECUTION OF VARIOUS REQUESTS

Experiment No. / Phrase	Programming in PHP (Separate Phrase)	Programming (Specific Competence)	Programming (Search Phrase)
1	58.366 s.	1.0568 s.	12.2957 s.
2	58.2956 s.	1.0506 s.	12.2085 s.
3	58.3636 s.	1.0572 s.	12.3267 s.
4	58.6011 s.	1.0502 s.	12.2845 s.
5	58.3122 s.	1.0415 s.	12.2504 s.
6	58.1308 s.	1.0635 s.	12.3185 s.
7	58.224 s.	1.0549 s.	12.3308 s.
8	58.1068 s.	1.0357 s.	12.2582 s.
9	58.1809 s.	1.0489 s.	12.2565 s.
10	58.2108 s.	1.0633 s.	12.3031 s.

Now, let us look at how the completeness is changed by using synonymy and inheritance relations. Coding is synonymous with the competence of Programming, which is the parent for several competencies, such as "Programming with PHP", "Programming in C#", "Programming with JAVA", and so on. Due to the use of ontology, these relationships can be taken into account in the search. Table 2 clearly shows the results of comparing the completeness of the results of the search for the keyword "Coding".

TABLE II. COMPARISON OF THE COMPLETENESS OF THE SEARCH

Inquiry	Number with synonymy and hierarchy	Number with synonymy only	Number with hierarchy only	Number without synonymy or hierarchy
Coding	10 competencies, 305 employment seekers	1 competency, 53 employment seekers	0 competencies, 0 employment seekers	0 competencies, 0 employment seekers

Based on the results shown in this table, it can be concluded that using an ontological approach for creating an information model that supports synonymy and inheritance relations, it has been possible to achieve a significant increase in the completeness of search results.

Let us now consider how the secondary search affects the relevance of the search results. For example, find employment seekers by searching the words PHP and git. By this query, quite a lot of results were found, about 10 competencies and 63 carriers of this competence. Let us assume the person conducting the search would want to clarify the results. To do this, it would be only necessary to enter those who are found in PHP. Accurate results are then obtained, with 6 competencies and 26 employment seekers, which more closely match search requests. After that, if there is a desire to find from the identified employment seekers only the ones with the competence of "Application of the basic PHPUnit testing techniques," our search would result in one specific competency left from the initial 6, and 6 employment seekers who own it. The search results and their quantitative estimates are summarized in Table 3.

TABLE III. THE IMPACT OF SECONDARY SEARCH ON THE RELEVANCE OF SEARCH RESULTS

Inquiry	"PHP Git"	"PHP"	Specific Competence
Results	10 competencies, 63 employment seekers	6 competencies, 26 employment seekers	1 competency, 6 employment seekers

The data given in Table 3 allows drawing the following conclusion: the use of detailed search for the results obtained has made it possible to increase relevance due to a gradual narrowing of the search area.

VIII. CONCLUSIONS

In this paper, an approach for processing information about junior specialists is proposed. It allows extraction and gathering of necessary information taking into account "synonyms" and "meronyms".

A Web-ontology model is created using the concepts of the proposed approach. It allows storing all necessary information about junior specialists and their competences.

A Web-application is developed using RubyOnRails framework. The created ontology is used for information representation. It allows a search for necessary specialists and building teams for projects.

Testing the developed Web-app showed an increased number of relevant junior specialists for IT-projects.

REFERENCES

[1] A.F. Galyamov, "Ontology knowledge base for decision making support to IT-project implementation," Proc. All-Russian winter school-seminar of postgraduates and young scientists «Actual problems of science and technique», Ufa, USATU, 2008, pp. 117-128.

[2] A.F. Galyamov, A.G. Abaytullin, and D.V. Popov, "Ontological model for decision support in IT consulting," Vestnik St. Petersburg University. Series "Information Science, Computer Science and Management, vol. 1, 2010, pp. 49-55.

[3] K. Zimin and M. Sukhanov, "Market research and prospects for the IT outsourcing," http://www.iemag.ru/researches/detail.php?ID=20002 (accessed Dec, 2011).

[4] E. Grebenyuk, "To assist HR-specialist: competence model," http://www.c-culture.ru/magazines/culture/2006-3-55 (accessed Dec, 2011).

[5] N. Volodina, "Competence model – it's easy," http://www.rhr.ru/index/rule/employees_certification/15320.html (accessed Dec, 2011).

[6] J. Dorn and M. Pichlmair, "A Competence Management system for Universities," Proc. European Conference on Information Systems, St. Gallen, 2007, pp. 759-770.

[7] K. Tucker and M. Cofsky, "Critical Keys to Competence-Based Pay," Compensation & Benefits Review, Nov.-Dec. 1993, pp. 46-52.

[8] Sh. Fletcher, "Competence-Based Assessment Techniques," Kogan Page, 2001.

[9] Hustad and Munkvold, "IT-Supported Competence Management: A Case Study at Ericsson," Information Systems Management, 2005.

[10] J. Dorn, M. Pichlmair, "Ontology development for human resource management," Proc. European Conference on Information Systems, 2009.

[11] R. T. Fielding, "Architectural Styles and the Design of Network-based Software Architectures," Dissertation. University of California, Irvine, 2000.

[12] Gio Wiederhold, "Mediators in the architecture of future information systems," Computer, 25(3), 1992, pp. 38–49.

[13] G. Kovacs, D. Bogdanova, N. Yussupova, and M. Boyko, "Informatics Tools, AI Models and Methods Used for Automatic Analysis of Customer Satisfaction," Studies In Informatics And Control (SIC). National Institute for R&D in Informatics, Vol. 24 (3), 2015, pp. 261–270.

[14] Portal for searching information about competences of junior specialists. Available at: http://profport.org/ (accessed: 12 December 2016)

[15] N. I. Yussupova, D. A. Rizvanov, K. R. Enikeeva, and O. N. Smetanina, "Knowledge representation models for decision making in complex systems management in uncertainty and resource restrictions," Proc. Information decision making technologies, Ufa, USATU, Vol. 2, 2016, pp. 24-27.

[16] N.I. Yussupova, D.R. Bogdanova, and M.V. Boyko, Processing structured information using artificial intelligence methods, Innovatsionnoe mashinostroenie, 2016.

[17] The Standish Group Report Chaos - Project Smart https://www.projectsmart.co.uk/white-papers/chaos-report.pdf

[18] L.R. Chernyahovskaya, V.N. Kruzhkov, and F.A. Dikova, "Ontological approach to development of decision support system," http://www.aselibrary.ru/datadocs/doc_917re.pdf.

[19] F. Baader, D. Calvanese et al. The Description Logic Handbook. Theory, implementation, and applications, Cambridge University Press, 2003, 340 p.

[20] V.A. Vittikh, "Ontological models of situations in the process of a collegial decision making," Proc. Problems of control and modeling in complex systems, Samara, 2009, pp. 405-410.

[21] T.A. Gavrilova, "Ontological engineering [in Russian]," http:// www.kmtec.ru/publications/library/authors/ontolog_engeneering.shtml.

Reproducible Evaluation of Semantic Storage Options

Jedrzej Rybicki* and Benedikt von St. Vieth†
Juelich Supercomputing Center (JSC)
Email: *j.rybicki@fz-juelich.de, †b.von.st.vieth@fz-juelich.de

***Abstract*—Distributed infrastructures are continuously challenged with the task of storing and managing different types of data. To this end, suitability and performance evaluations of different available technologies have to be conducted. We motivate our work with the concrete challenge of storing semantic annotations in an efficient way. We treat this problem from the resource provider perspective. The paper includes work in progress of evaluating possible storage engines for semantic annotations. The main focus, however, is on creating a framework to conduct such evaluations in a transparent and reproducible way. Our approach is based on Docker tools, and, therefore, the tests can be run on different platforms, and can be repeated if new version of the evaluated technologies become available.**

Keywords–Deploying Linked data; Reproducibility; Distributed infrastructures.

I. Introduction

Distributed research infrastructures like EUDAT (EUropean DATa [1]) provide generic services to manage research data in an efficient and cost-effective way. Since the research communities which use the services advance over time, they are constantly expressing new requirements with respect to kinds of data and possible usages that the infrastructure should be able to handle. To this end, resource and service providers are constantly evaluating possible approaches and new technologies. Such evaluation must adhere to scientific standards in terms of methodology, transparency, and reproducibility.

In our previous paper [2], we have shown how Docker [3] can be leveraged to provide on-demand instances of popular web services in context of a distributed research infrastructure. Although, such seamless provisioning of services can be used to conduct reproducible research, there are more aspects to it. In this paper, we will exercise a whole workflow from testing, through result processing, up to visualization of the outcomes. We will use Docker and `docker-compose` to conduct the steps in a transparent, sharable, and reproducible way. We will test our approach by evaluating storage options to handle semantic annotations.

Semantic annotations are a very powerful tool to work with data in distributed infrastructures. On the very high level, they allow to add comments to entities managed in the infrastructure. An example would be a keyword attached to a digital object, but more sophisticated examples are envisioned as well. We will explain the model in more detail later in this paper, but astute reader can imagine that efficient annotations handling should enable different types of queries. It should be possible to retrieve all annotations for a given object, but also reverse lookups (i.e., localizing all data objects with given keyword in our example) will be used. The uptake of this new service will only happen if sufficient performance of both kind of queries is offered.

There are many ways in which annotations can be stored. The EUDAT service plans to use the World Wide Web Consortium (W3C) Annotation Data Model [4]. Since it is based on JavaScript Object Notation for Linked Data (JSON-LD), an obvious approach would be to use document stores for the task. Since annotations are attached to data object, the whole data set forms a graph with nodes as managed entities and annotations as relations. Thus, graph databases could also serve as storage backends. Regardless of the technology used it should be possible to evaluate its performance and tune it to account for this particular use case. Such a tuning is usually done in an iterative way, where the results of each change are verified, it is critical to possess tools that can perform the benchmarking tests in a reproducible manner.

The rest of this paper is structured as follows. In Section II, we explain what semantic annotations are and discuss suitable storage options. Subsequently, a short introduction to Docker follows and technical details of our effort to make the evaluation reproducible are presented. Section IV comprises the preliminary results for selected storage options. We conclude the paper with an outlook.

II. Semantic Annotations

EUDAT is working on enabling semantic annotations of the objects stored in its distributed research infrastructure. The current approach is to use the W3C format for annotations. The W3C web annotation data format is pretty simple: Each annotation is a relation between a *body*, e.g., EUDAT data object, and *target*, e.g., metadata describing that object. Basic annotation model is shown in Figure 1.

It is important to notice that both target and body have unique identifiers. These are crucial from the user perspective. It can be expect that the users will be interested to view a list of all annotations for given body id, i.e., all metadata descriptions for a given data object. But also a reverse lookup producing all the data objects with specific tag (i.e., a retrieval by target id) embodies important functionality. These expected usage scenarios were used as corner stones for our benchmarks. In particular, we defined three metrics for the storage backend evaluation:

- creation times (creation of new, non-existing annotations),
- annotation retrieval by target id,
- annotation retrieval by body id.

There are many options to store semantic annotations. One obvious approach would be to stick to the JSON-LD rendering as proposed by W3C, use is also as internal storing format and find a storage backend which can support it. There are many NoSQL solutions on the market, which can store JSON documents, with MongoDB [5] being one of the most popular.

```
{
  "@context": "http://www.w3.org/ns/anno.jsonld",
  "id": "http://example.org/anno2",
  "type": "Annotation",
  "body": {
    "id": "http://example.org/analysis1.mp3",
    "format": "audio/mpeg",
    "language": "fr"
  },
  "target": {
    "id": "http://example.gov/patent1.pdf",
    "format": "application/pdf",
    "language": ["en", "ar"],
    "textDirection": "ltr",
    "processingLanguage": "en"
  }
}
```


Figure 1. Basic W3C Annotation Data Model

Another storage option is based on the observation that annotations and annotated objects form a graph (with annotations as edges). To account for this way of thinking, a graph database like neo4j [6] could serve as a storage backend. We decided not to include relation database systems in our evaluation. The reasons are twofold. As can be seen on the Figure 1, the model used for annotations is dynamic with optional fields (like format or language), such flexibility is hard to deal with when using relational database. Second reason was the fact that creation and explorations of data objects and annotations would involve a lot of joins in the case of relational model: One would have to jump from one annotation body (i.e., data object) to a target (e.g., keyword) and then again to body to identify objects similar to the starting node.

III. Experimental setup

To obtain meaningful evaluation results it is important to minimize the number of "moving parts" and reduce the testing environment to components which are absolutely necessary. In particular, we were not interested in the performance of the web interface that will be used to work with annotations or the performance penalty caused by its integration with other EUDAT services. Therefore, we have written a small program in Python, with methods for generating annotations with unique body and target identifiers, and for retrieval of the data. The methods use simple interfaces to access selected database stores: MongoDB and neo4j.

A. Docker

To enable easy reproducibility of the conducted tests, we have prepared a Docker-based environment. Docker is a lightweight virtualization solution which is using Linux Kernel features like *namespaces* and *cgroups* to isolate guest and host systems. Docker uses image templates to start containers (i.e., guest processes). Images are build in a hierarchical fashion by applying a "write-on-modify" principle. Thus, it is possible to trace back all the changes done in a given image during the installation and configuration of the software it comprises. Docker provides tools to easily exchange the images via a public Docker Hub [7], or private on-site repositories. Docker introduces notion of official images which are created and maintained by the providers of a given technology. There are official images for major Linux distributions but also for popular content management systems, or databases. Docker ecosystem embrace many tools, we will use `docker-compose` [8] which is an orchestration solution to start and manage more complex Docker-based deployments.

The main reason why we are using Docker is due to the virtualization it is possible to run our test programs on almost any platform (regardless of the operating system it uses). The images also contains the dependencies and libraries required, so again the configuration of the host system may be neglected. The possibility to review all the changes done in a particular Docker image enables transparency and understandability of the obtained results. Last but not least, by using Docker featured called volumes, it is possible to separate data from the programs, in our case: results and processing tools.

B. Solution details

Both technology providers (MongoDB and neo4j) offer official images for their databases which we used for our evaluation. We created a Docker image with our testing program and prepared a `docker-compose`-based testing environment. The source code and documentation is stored on GitHub [9], allowing for verification and repetition of the tests. In fact, we plan to reuse this framework to do some further testing of different EUDAT-inspired use cases in the future.

Given a system with a running Docker daemon and `docker-compose`, starting tests is a matter of merely issuing one command like:

```
docker-compose run tester --name exp1
```

The last parameter of the above command is not strictly required, it attaches a user-defined name to the particular experimental run which is convenient for the further analysis.

Also, Docker images for processing of the results and visualizing them are provided. The first step transforms the results from the evaluation by using following command:

```
docker run --volumes-from exp1 processor
```

Please note that we are using the name assigned to the experiment in the previous step (`exp1`), the `--volumes-from` parameter is used to attach storage volume with the data produced in the first step to the newly created Docker container.

Finally, the plots that we present in the following section are created with help of `gnuplot` [10] and other tools embodied in a Docker image which again uses volume with data from previous steps and can be run with a simple command:

```
docker run --volumes-from exp1 visualizer
```

To enable sequential processing of data, we internally agreed to store all the data (results, visualizations, etc.) in the same path defined as a Docker volume. Thanks to this contract, we can guarantee that data are not becoming part of the Docker images and thus will not hinder their reuse. Secondly, it is easily possible to extend the workflow by adding new steps or modify existing ones, for instance, if different types of visualization are required.

IV. Results

The tests are defined by three parameters:

1) *engine*: database engine (currently MongoDB and neo4j),

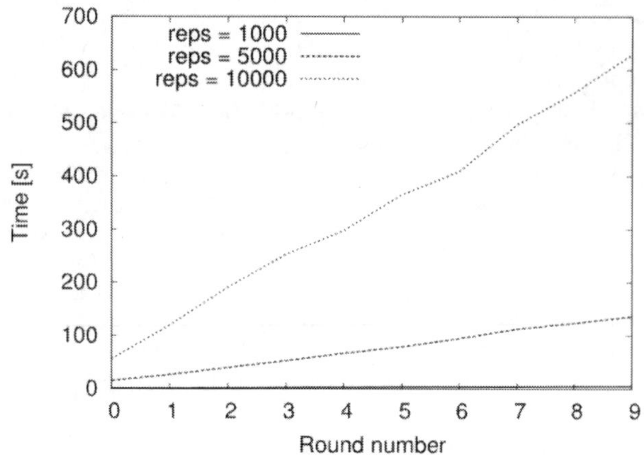

Figure 2. Retrieval scalability for MongoDB (*reps* records are added, and *reps* random records are retrieved in each round).

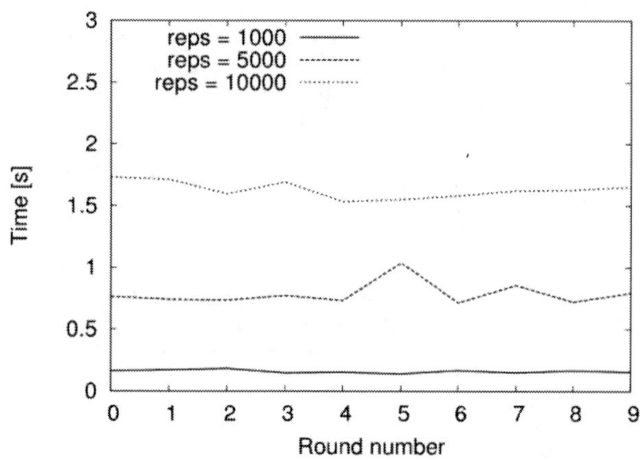

Figure 3. Retrieval scalability for neo4j (*reps* new records are added, and *reps* random records are retrieved in each round).

2) *rounds*: number of rounds,
3) *reps*: number of repetitions in each round.

The tests were divided into rounds and in each round all the above database operations were conducted in the given order. Firstly *reps* number of records were created, subsequently random (with repetition) *reps* annotations were retrieved by specifying existing *target.id*, finally *reps* random annotations were fetched by *body.id*. We measured time of each activity, that is complete time to create records, time to retrieve all *reps* record by target and body id. Three time measurements were made in each round. Please note, that no records were removed, i.e., for given $reps = 1000$, the database grown in each round by new 1000 record.

All the tests were run on the same virtual machine with 4 VCPUs, 4GB RAM, using Ubuntu 16.04.

In Figure 2 and Figure 3, we depicted the retrieval scalability of each database. For that we conducted three experiments with different values of *reps*, each had 10 rounds. Figure 2 shows that the performance of MongoDB is dramatically decreasing with the increasing number of records in store.

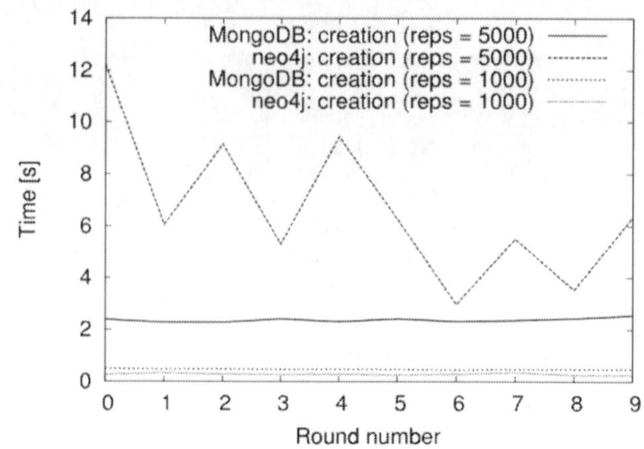

Figure 4. Comparison of creation scalability (*reps* new records are added in each round).

Also, the absolute values achieved by MongoDB are not very good, to retrieve 10 000 random annotations from a database with 90 000 documents, more than one minute is required.

The retrieval times for the same amount of data from the neo4j database of the same size are much smaller as can be seen in Figure 3 (please note that the y axis was scaled comparing to Figure 2). Also, the scalability of neo4j is much better, neo4j produces constant answer times regardless of the size of the database. For comparison with the MongoDB, to retrieve 10 000 random entities from a neo4j graph with 90 000 annotations, only $1.65s$ is required.

The situation is a little bit different for creation times. We depicted them in Figure 4. For smaller values of *reps* neo4j outperforms MongoDB but with $reps = 5000$ MongoDB is faster. We also conducted the tests for higher values of *reps* (not depicted for the sake of clarity) and MongoDB maintained its advantage in this regard. Neo4j also displays high variance in the creation times and the values decreased over time. This kind of behavior could be caused by the fact that neo4j is written in Java and Scala and the Java Virtual Machine can need some time to "warm up". Perhaps further investigations are required there, like warm-up phase before the actual tests to at least get rid of the high delay in the first round.

V. CONCLUSION AND FUTURE WORK

In this paper, we evaluate options for storing semantic annotations in a reproducible manner. We selected two technologies: MongoDB and neo4j. We believe that the presented approach is applicable also for other use cases. Our results support the hypothesis that annotations naturally form a graph and thus, can be efficiently stored in a graph database. Further investigations of the weak creation performance might be necessary.

It is clear that the presented work in progress is just a first step towards answering the question on how to efficiently manage annotation-like data. Both neo4j and MongoDB offer numerous possibilities to fine tune the performance to account for particular data and query types. Although, it was not the primary goal of this work we believe that by having a possibility to conduct performance evaluation in a repeatable way, such a tuning can be done much faster.

The challenge of constantly evaluating emerging technologies and dealing with the management of new kinds of data is common for distributed research infrastructures. Therefore, it is crucial to define evaluations in a reproducible manner. Our Docker-based toolkit has proven its potential as a basis for such reproducible computer-based experiments. In our future work, we will look into ways of extending this toolkit with a means of executing whole workflows rather that manually starting single steps as we currently do.

Acknowledgment

The work has been supported by EUDAT2020, funded by the European Union under the Horizon 2020 programme - DG CONNECT e-Infrastructures (Contract No. 654065).

References

[1] W. Gentzsch, D. Lecarpentier, and P. Wittenburg, "Big data in science and the EUDAT project," in *SRII Global Conference*, Apr. 2014, pp. 191–194.

[2] J. Rybicki and B. v. St. Vieth, "DARIAH Meta Hosting: Sharing software in a distributed infrastructure," in *MIPRO '15: 38th IEEE International Convention on Information and Communication Technology, Electronics and Microelectronics*, May 2015, pp. 217–222.

[3] (2016, Dec.) Docker. [Online]. Available: https://www.docker.com/

[4] (2016, Nov.) Web annotation data model. [Online]. Available: https://www.w3.org/TR/annotation-model/

[5] (2016, Dec.) MongoDB. [Online]. Available: https://www.mongodb.com/

[6] J. Webber, "A programmatic introduction to Neo4j," in *SPLASH '12: 3rd ACM Annual Conference on Systems, Programming, and Applications: Software for Humanity*, Oct. 2012, pp. 217–218.

[7] (2016, Dec.) Docker Hub. [Online]. Available: https://hub.docker.com/

[8] (2016, Dec.) Docker Compose. [Online]. Available: https://docs.docker.com/compose/

[9] (2016, Dec.) Annotations scalablity. [Online]. Available: https://github.com/httpPrincess/annotations-scalability

[10] (2016, Dec.) Gnuplot. [Online]. Available: http://gnuplot.sourceforge.net/

TLEX: A Temporal Analysis Tool for Time Series Data

Mohammed AL Zamil
Department of Computer Information Systems
Yarmouk University
Irbed, Jordan, 21163
Email: Mohammedz@yu.edu.jo

Bilal Abu AL Huda
Department of Management Information Systems
Yarmouk University
Irbed, Jordan, 21163
Email: abul-huda@yu.edu.jo

***Abstract*—Time is an essential dimension to many domain-specific problems, such as the medical and financial domains. This research introduces TLEX (Temporal Lexical Patterns), a framework to categorize temporal data that effectively induces semantic temporal patterns. TLEX is a rule-based classification framework dedicated to enhance the classification accuracy by focusing on eliminating outliers and minimizing classification errors. The contributions of this research are 1) formulating semantic temporal patterns as basic classification features, and 2) introducing an induction technique to discriminate semantic temporal patterns. To illustrate the design, the paper provides a detailed mathematical description that relies on set-theory to model the framework of TLEX. Furthermore, a detailed description of the proposed algorithms to facilitate implementing and reproducing the results has been described. Further, to evaluate the effectiveness of TLEX, extensive experiments have been performed on a weather temporal dataset. Accordingly, the F-measure and support values on weather dataset have been reported. Further, a sensitivity analysis to assess the capability of TLEX to work with temporal datasets has been provided. The findings indicate a significant improvement of Temporal-ROLEX over some existing techniques.**

Keywords- Temporal Data Mining; Classification of Temporal Data; Lexical Patterns.

I. INTRODUCTION

Time is an essential dimension to many domain-specific systems such as financial and medical data analysis. However, temporal data mining is concerned with such analysis in the case of ordered data records with temporal interdependencies. During the last decade, many interesting techniques of temporal data mining were proposed and shown to be useful in many applications areas. Since temporal data mining brings together techniques from different fields, such as statistics, machine learning and databases, the literature is scattered among many different sources.

Temporal data mining is commonly concerned with data mining of large sequential datasets that have been ordered chronologically with respect to some index. For example, time series constitute a popular class of sequential data, where records are indexed by time. Other examples of sequential data could be text, gene sequences, protein sequences, lists of moves in a chess game, etc. Here, although there is no notion of time as such, the ordering among the records is very important and is central to the data description and modeling.

Consider the temporal relation among three customers whose corresponding transaction sequences are as follows:

Cust. 1. $[\{X_1\ X_2\},\{X_3\ X_1\ X_4\},\{X_2\ X_5\}]$
Cust. 2. $[\{X_5\},\ \{X_1\ X_2\}]$
Cust. 3. $[\{X_1\},\{X_1\ X_2\ X_5\ X_6\}]$

where $\{X_i\}$ represents the items bought in a single transaction. For instance, customer 1 made 3 visits to the market. In her first visit, she bought 2 items $\{X_1\ X_2\}$. In her second and third visits, she bought 3 items $\{X_3\ X_1\ X_4\}$ and 2 items, $\{X_2\ X_5\}$ respectively. Temporal patterns are frequent sequences of actions that could be useful for analyzing data and predicting futures. In the above example, we can extract relations such as the sequence $[\{X_5\},\ \{X_1\ X_2\}]$ contained in $[\{X_1\ X_2\},\{X_3\ X_1\ X_4\},\{X_2\ X_5\}]$ but not in $[\{X_1\},\{X_1\ X_2\ X_5\ X_6\}]$.

This paper presents an efficient rule-based classification approach, called TLEX, for categorizing temporal data. The contributions of this research are: 1) formulating semantic temporal patterns as a basic classification features, and 2) introducing an induction technique to discriminate semantic temporal patterns.

TLEX framework relies on the formal definition of ROLEX-SP that has been introduced by M. AL Zamil and A. Can [1] to classify medical knowledge using a dedicated rule-based induction and learning techniques to come with efficient classification of domain knowledge. ROLEX-SP automates the induction and the learning processes by extracting textual patterns and building a specialized form of association rules. Such technique handles the problems of multiclass classification and feature imbalance problems.

To illustrate, consider the example of raining phenomena. A person might hear the thunder during and after its occurrence. Duration represents the persistence of an event over many time points. Also, rain and thunder might occur concurrently without a particular order. Finally, some events might intersect each other such as sun shining, raining and rising of the rainbow.

Section II discusses the related work. Section III provides background definitions of formalities that have been applied in this work. Section IV defines the temporal model as well as the form of the temporal pattern. Section V discusses the methodology for creating our proposed classifier. Section VI discusses the experiments and findings. Finally, Section VII concludes with a brief discussion of findings.

II. Related Work

Early works on mining temporal patterns rely on Apriori-style approaches such as the algorithm in [2], in which a breadth-first search strategy is applied to compute the support of item sets. As this strategy is not efficient on large datasets in terms of accuracy [3], recently efficient algorithms based on unsupervised elicitations of temporal relations have been proposed for the purpose of enhancing the performance of temporal classifiers. H-DFS [4] and KarmaLego [5] are based on an enumeration tree structure to classify temporal information. The implementation of enumerated decision trees supports the accuracy of classification results in an unsupervised manner.

Winarko and Roddick [6] have introduced ARMADA, which is an algorithm to discover interval time temporal rules. Recent work in this field asserts that time-stamps relationships such as the "during" relation could be more useful than solid time interval. Unlike ARMADA association rules, our work relies on discovering hybrid temporal rules that could be represented using during relation. In [7], TPrefixSpan has been introduced to apply prefix span technique using interval boundaries pruning patterns. Also, IEMiner [8] has implemented a prior based strategy with counters and pruning to improve the accuracy of IEClassifier; that is used to classify temporal sequential records.

Attempts have been made to construct temporal features in order to construct association rules such as those discussed in Bruno and Garza [9], Miao et al. [10], and Chiang et al. [11]. In Bruno and Garza [9], association rules have been developed to cope with outlier detection using functional quasi dependency. The technique does not model time-delay as a part of association rules. The technique in Bruno and Garza [9] handled time-delay explicitly which affects the overall performance as well as efficiency of the classification process, which is not crucial in outlier detection task.

Chiang et al. [11] have proposed a mathematical model to extract temporal patterns to track customer buying habits. Our proposed methodology focuses on time intervals as well as single point of time events. Similarly, our proposed technique benefits from the formal definition in Chiang et al. [11] in that we formulate the temporal patterns using similar mathematical aspects. Zhang et al. [12] have proposed a method to extract during temporal patterns DTP. DTP is a special case of interval temporal patterns. Kong et al. [13] have presented the notion of multi temporal patterns using predicates: before, during, equal and overlap.

Temporal datasets dimensions are characterized as huge ones. Techniques to reduce such dimensionality are important to produce scalable temporal mining systems. The proposed technique applied methods in Stacey and McGregor [14] and Wang and Megalooikonomou [15] to reduce the dimensionality of time series.

III. Background

Definition 1 (Temporal Sequence):

A temporal sequence is a chronologically ordered set of events of the form:

$$TSq = \{e_1(st,et), e_2(st,et),\ldots, e_n(st,et)\}$$

where (st,et) is a nonempty set in which sd is the start-time of an event and ed is the end-time of the same event, i.e., $st,et \in TIME$.

Definition 2 (Temporal Sequence Similarity):

Two temporal sequences are said to be similar, i.e. $Sim(TSq_1,TSq_2)$, if and only if all the following conditions hold:

1. $\forall(i)\{e_i(TSq_1) = e_i(TSq_2)\}$
2. $\forall(i)\{Len[e_i(TSq_1)] = Len[e_i(TSq_2)]$
3. $TSq1 \wedge TSq2$ are not empty

where $Len[(e_i(Sq)]$ refers to the event duration (i.e. $et - st$). This relation is useful to eliminate redundancy resulted from later categorization process.

Definition 3 (Temporal Sequence Dissimilarity):

Two temporal sequences are said to be dissimilar, i.e. $Dis(TSq_1,TSq_2)$, if $\neg Sim(TSq_1,TSq_2)$ holds.

Definition 5 (Support of Temporal Sequence):

The function $Supp(Tsq,D) \leftarrow \{Si \mid Si \in D \wedge Tsq \in Si\}$ is used to determine the support of a frequent pattern Tsq in a given dataset D, in which Si is a sequence fragment. Xingzhi et al. [16] illustrate the application of support model in data mining by theorem proving and case studies.

IV. Temporal Classification

The temporal classification problem is defined according to the learning description of ILP (Inductive Logic Programming) Lavrac and Dzeroski [17], as follows: given

1. A finite set TC of independent temporal classes of the form $\{Tc_1, Tc_2, ..., Tc_k\}$ where $k > 1$, meaning that there are many temporal classes and the classification results of a class do not affect the classification results of other classes.

2. A set $E = \{e_1, e_2, \ldots, e_n\}$ of events such that $\forall(j)\exists(Tsqi \subseteq TC \wedge |Tsqi| = v) : e_j \in Tsqi$ where $1 \le v \le k$ and $1 \le j \le N$, meaning that an event might belong to more than one temporal class; Si is a subset of the set of temporal classes.

3. A set of states $S = \{s_1, s_2, \ldots, s_m\}$ each of which represents a state of the current environment such as: raining and shining in the weather dataset.

4. A set of time-intervals $T = \{t_1, t_2, \ldots, t_n\}$, where $t_i = \{st_i, et_i\}$ represents the start and end time of a given event e_i.

5. A set P_{ci}^{+} of positive patterns consisting of ground logical facts of the form $p_{ci}^{+} \in E_{Tci}$ such that $(p_{ci}^{+} \in e \wedge e \in E_{Tci}) \Rightarrow e \in Tci$; a positive pattern under class Tci that occurs in the subset E_{Tci}, which represent a set of events that belong to class Tci.

6. A set P_i^{-} of negative facts; patterns that represent an event but does not refer to class Tci. In other words, they represent outliers or rare cases.

7. The function $g(a_\alpha) = \{e_1(a_\alpha, t_1), e_2(a_\alpha, t_2), \ldots, e_k(a_\alpha, t_k)\}$ includes all the interval times in which the state a_α occurs.

A classifier H_{ci} should be consistent with all positive and negative patterns. In other words, the classifier is a set of association rules to predict a temporal class or a set of temporal classes of a given set of events based on the presence or absence of some patterns in that set.

If a positive example p_{ci}^{+} occurs in document $g(a_\alpha)$ and none of the negative patterns occur in $g(a_\alpha)$, the classifier will assign event e under class Tci. Notice that negative patterns are prevented from undoing the effect of other categories' positive ones.

V. CLASSIFICATION METHODOLOGY

Let $e_j = \{s_i, t_j\}$ and $e_k = \{a_l, t_k\}$ be two events in the temporal dataset. Both e_j and e_k are called during events if e_j has executed during the execution of e_k. For any two given states a_i and a_k, a_i is called to be during a_k denoted as $a_i \Rightarrow^d a_k$. Our goal is to define a set of positive and negative predicates to predict during temporal patterns.

Instead of accuracy formula that has been applied in the previous version of ROLEX-SP, the function *support* that has been defined in [19, 20, 21] has been used to induce positive and negative patterns as well. Given $|g(a_\alpha)|$; the number of the time intervals included in all instances (records in the dataset) of a_α, the maximum number of time intervals among all sates $|g_0|$:

$$Support(a_\alpha) = \frac{|g(a_\alpha)|}{|g_0|} \quad (1)$$

It represents the relative frequency of time intervals for a given state with respect to the number of time intervals for a most frequent state. LSP Generator, Figure 1, implements our proposed methodology to induce classification rules.

LSP Generator

Goal: to extract positive and negative syntactic patterns from the set TS
Input: TS, C.
Output: P^{+}, P^{-}
Method: Apply the following instructions

Begin
$P^{+} = \{\}, P^{-} = \{\}$
For each $ci \in C$
For each $d \in TSc$
$P = parse(d, \text{Re}\, c(ci))$
For each $p \in P$
$Support(a_\alpha) = \frac{|g(a_\alpha)|}{|g_0|}$
if $Support(a_\alpha) \ge threshold$ *then*
$P_{ci}^{+} = P_{ci}^{+} \wedge p$
Elseif
$P_i^{-} = P_i^{-} \wedge p$
Next p
Next d
Next ci
return(P^{+}, P^{-})
End

Figure 1 The Relationship between Execution Time and The Number of Rules

The validation is responsible for evaluating the extracted rules and generating a classifier H_{ci}. Therefore, the classifier should contain the best rules to represent an event.

Definition 6 (Representative Set RS): given a set of rules sorted according to its support, RS is the set of rules of the form

$$c \leftarrow p_{ci}^{+} \in d, \quad \neg(p_{i1}^{-} \in d) \wedge \neg(p_{i2}^{-} \in d) \wedge \cdots \wedge \neg(p_{iM}^{-} \in d)$$

that have the highest support. Given a rule R and a set of events $E_{ci} \in C \times E$; a set of events that belong to a specific category, let $n_{covers}(R, ci)$ be the number of events covered by R under category ci , and $|E_{ci}|$ be the number of events in E_{ci} :

$$coverage(R, ci) = n_{covers}(R, ci) / |E_{ci}|$$

Accordingly, the validation phase, then, tries to optimize the problem such as: given $R = \{R_{c1}, R_{c2}, \cdots R_{ck}\}$ where $R_{ci} = \{R_1, R_2, \cdots, R_W\}$ and $w = |P_{ci}^{+}|$, the algorithm is responsible to produce the set $RS_{ci} = \{R_1, R_2, \cdots R_x\}, where\ x \leq w\ and\ RS_{ci} \subseteq R_{ci}$, of rules such that: $Coverage(RS_{ci})$ is the maximum.

Definition 7 (Redundant Rule): a rule Rj is a redundant rule if one of the following conditions holds:

1. $(\forall i)(\exists j): R_i = R_j \wedge i \neq j$
2. $(\forall i)(\exists j): Coverage(R_j) \subseteq Coverage(R_i) \wedge i \neq j$

Thus, getting rid of redundant rules, which are equal rules or rules that cover the same set of another rules, will enhance the overall performance of the classification task.

VI. Experiment and Results

During our experiment, the proposed technique has been applied on a weather dataset. The dataset has been collected from a weather station in Jordan in 2009. The empirical dataset holds 14 attributes: wind direction, average wind speed, maximum wind gust, average hourly temperature, percentage relative humidity, global hourly radiation, hourly sunshine duration, hourly precipitation duration, hourly precipitation amount, horizontal visibility, fog, snow, etc. The dataset has been processed to discriminate and convert the records into temporal ones consisting of event name, start time, end time, and state. The F-measure achieved during experiments is 81% at minimum support ranges up to 20% as shown in Figure 2

Figure 2 shows that the overall performance of our proposed technique is directly affected by the number of generated rules. Therefore, the higher the number of rules, the better the performance achieved by TLEX.

Figure 3 shows that additional running time is required while increasing the number of rules in our classifier. In fact, the results showed that the required time increased linearly as the number of rules in-creased.

Figure 4, on the other hand, shows that the time required by processing events is much greater than the one for events. However, a linear relation is clear between the running time and the number of events.

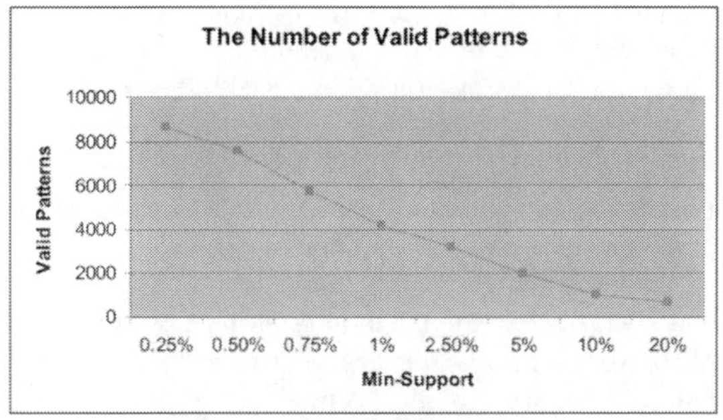

Figure 2 The Relationship between Number of valid Patterns and Minimum Support

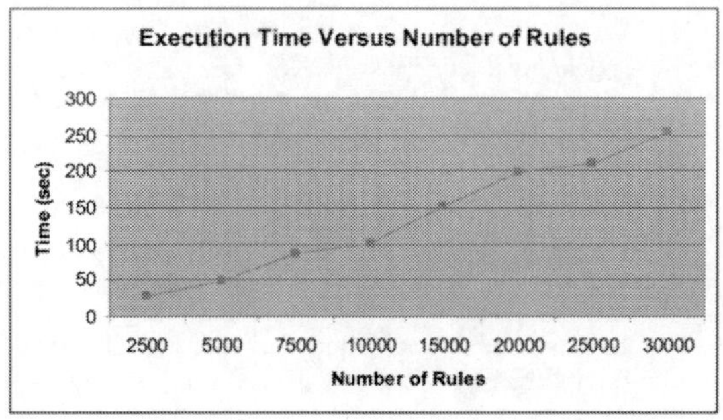

Figure 3 The Relationship between Execution Time and The Number of Rules

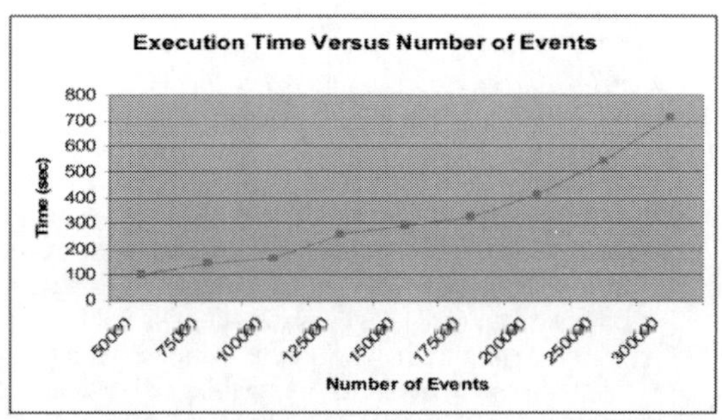

Figure 4 The Relationship between Execution Time and Number of Events

VII. Conclusion

In this paper, we presented a rule-based method for categorizing temporal records. The contributions of this research are 1) formulating semantic temporal patterns as a basic classification features, and 2) introducing an induction technique to discriminate semantic temporal patterns. We performed experiment on a weather dataset in order to evaluate the proposed method and compare our work with well known algorithms in the literature. Specifically, Temporal-ROLEX achieve significant enhancement using sequential temporal pattern. On the other hand, Temporal-ROLEX achieves average performance using hybrid temporal patterns.

Also, the improvement achieved by Temporal-ROLEX is statistically significant. The use of syntactic patterns, both positive and negative, contributes on increasing the accuracy of Temporal-ROLEX over the other method.

In addition, we also provided a sensitivity analysis to the performance of Temporal-ROLEX as a function to the number of rules and the number of records in the training set. The results indicated that Temporal-ROLEX was positively affected by the number of rules. On the other hand, our observations during experiments indicated that the number of records in the training set does not affect the overall performance of the learning process.

REFERENCES

[1] M. G. Al Zamil and A. B. Can. ROLEX-SP: Rules of lexical syntactic patterns for free text categorization. Knowledge-Based Systems, 24(1), 2011, pp. 58-65.

[2] R. Agrawal, T. Imieliński, and A. Swami. (1993, June). Mining association rules between sets of items in large databases. In Acm sigmod record (Vol. 22, No. 2, pp. 207-216). ACM.

[3] T. Page, A. L. Heathwaite, L. J. Thompson, L. Pope, and R. Willows. Eliciting fuzzy distributions from experts for ranking conceptual risk model components. Environmental Modelling & Software, 36, 2012, pp. 19-34.

[4] P. Papapetrou, G. Kollios, S. Sclaroff, and D. Gunopulos. Discovering frequent arrangements of temporal intervals. In Data Mining, Fifth IEEE International Conference on, November 2005, pp. 1-8. IEEE.

[5] R. Moskovitch and Y. Shahar. Medical temporal-knowledge discovery via temporal abstraction. In AMIA, 2009, pp. 452–456.

[6] E. Winarko and J. F. Roddick. ARMADA–An algorithm for discovering richer relative temporal association rules from interval-based data. Data & Knowledge Engineering, 63(1), 2007, pp. 76-90.

[7] S. Y. Wu and Y. L. Chen. Mining nonambiguous temporal patterns for interval-based events. IEEE transactions on knowledge and data engineering, 2007, 19(6).

[8] D. Patel, W. Hsu, and M. L. Lee. Mining relationships among interval-based events for classification. In Proceedings of the 2008 ACM SIGMOD international conference on Management of data, June 2008, pp. 393-404. ACM.

[9] G. Bruno and P. Garza. TOD: Temporal outlier detection by using quasi-functional temporal dependencies. Data & Knowledge Engineering, 69(6), 2010, pp. 619-639.

[10] Q. Miao, Q. Li, Q., and R. Dai. AMAZING: A sentiment mining and retrieval system. Expert Systems with Applications, 36(3), 2009, pp. 7192-7198.

[11] D. A. Chiang, Y. H. Wang, and S. P. Chen. Analysis on repeat-buying patterns. Knowledge-Based Systems, 23(8), 2010, pp. 757-768.

[12] L. Zhang, G. Chen, T. Brijs, and X. Zhang. Discovering during-temporal patterns (DTPs) in large temporal databases. Expert Systems with Applications, 34(2), 2008, pp. 1178-1189.

[13] X. Kong, Q. Wei, and G. Chen. An approach to discovering multi-temporal patterns and its application to financial databases. Information Sciences, 180(6), 2010, pp. 873-885.

[14] M. Stacey and C. McGregor. Temporal abstraction in intelligent clinical data analysis: A survey. Artificial intelligence in medicine, 39(1), 2007, pp. 1-24.

[15] Q. Wang and V. Megalooikonomou. A dimensionality reduction technique for efficient time series similarity analysis. Information systems, 33(1), 2008, pp. 115-132.

[16] M. G. Zamil and S. Samarah. Dynamic event classification for intrusion and false alarm detection in vehicular ad hoc networks. International Journal of Information and Communication Technology, 8(2-3), 2016, pp. 140-164.

[17] S. Dzeroski and N. Lavrac. Inductive logic programming: Techniques and applications. 1994.

[18] P. Rullo, V. L. Policicchio, C. Cumbo, and S. Iiritano. Olex: effective rule learning for text categorization. IEEE Transactions on Knowledge and Data Engineering, 21(8), 2009, pp. 1118-1132.

[19] M. G. Zamil and S. Samarah. Dynamic rough-based clustering for vehicular ad-hoc networks. International Journal of Information and Decision Sciences, 7(3), 2015, pp. 265-285.

[20] M. A. Zamil, S. Samarah, A. Saifan,, and I. A. Smadi. Dispersion–based prediction framework for estimating missing values in wireless sensor networks. International Journal of Sensor Networks, 12(3), 2012, pp. 149-159.

[21] S. Samarah, M. A. Zamil, A. Aleroud, M. Rawashdeh, M. Alhamid, and A. Alamri. An Efficient Activity Recognition Framework: Toward Privacy-Sensitive Health Data Sensing. IEEE Access. DOI: 10.1109/ACCESS.2017.2685531. 2017

Empirical Evaluation of Open Government Data Visualisations

Elena Ornig, Jolon Faichney, Bela Stantic
School of Information and Communication Technology
Griffith University
Gold Coast, Australia
email: elena.ornig@griffithuni.edu.au
email: {j.faichney,b.stantic}@griffith.edu.au

Abstract—**The Open Government Data (OGD) movement has seen governments around the world embrace the concept of opening their data. However, the large amounts of data released have not resulted in wide acceptance of the data by end-users. This is partly due to the emphasis on *machine-readability* rather than *human-usability*. Recently, some data portals have included visualization techniques to make the portals more usable. In this work, we report on user studies conducted to evaluate different OGD visualization techniques. The techniques were evaluated both quantitatively, through recorded tasks, and qualitatively, through a post study survey. We found that geographic map visualizations were reported by users to provide the highest level of qualitative satisfaction, which correlates with the quantitative results requiring the shortest time to complete the tasks. This study provides insights into empirical evaluation of visualization techniques to aid OGD providers in making decisions about the best way to present data in their portals.**

Keywords- ***data visualizations*; *open government data*; *empirical evaluation*;**

I. INTRODUCTION

The amount of OGD released for public use, reuse, and redistribution is rapidly growing. Currently, 18 million OGD datasets have been published around the world [1] and according to dataportal.org there are 520 registered government portals [2]. At the International Open Government Dataset Search there are 192 catalogs in 24 languages representing 43 countries [3]. These numbers represent a growing supply of OGD for users. However, the uptake by users has been limited. One possible cause, which we investigate in this paper, is the limited usability of open data.

The primary focus of the OGD movement has been on ensuring the release of the data so that it can be accessed. Additionally, the desired format of the data is one that is machine-readable, in formats such as Comma Separated Values (CSV) and eXtensible Markup Language (XML), preferably in the most raw and primal forms [20]. The motivation is based on transparency, so that the community has access to the data in its original form without modification. A downside to this motivation is that it is only usable by a small percentage of the community, those with technical computer skills, such as computer programmers and data analysts. The focus on *machine-readability* has limited the data's *human-usablility* [17].

One strategy to increase end-user uptake of OGD is to present the data using visualizations [18][19]. Graves and Hendler [4] conducted a detailed study on the use of visualisations for OGD. Their research focussed on end-users with some knowledge of data analysis such as researchers, journalists, and government data providers and consumers. They also identified a user profile of "Common Citizen" but did not include them in their study. They expressed an interest to investigate the remaining open question of how to empower "Common Citizens" and make it easier for them to consume OGD.

In our study, we are particularly interested in those who don't have skills in data analysis, but have an intention to use and benefit from open data.

Since there are many different groups of consumers and more than a hundred techniques of data visualisation [7], we singled out a group of consumers, defined by Graves et al [4] as common citizens to evaluate three different visualizations. We planned to find out what can make it easier for common citizens to use OGD data. To answer this question we conducted a field experiment in order to empirically evaluate human-usability of OGD visualisations by common citizens with the aim to inform designer and practitioners. In addition we evaluated what stops common citizens to use OGD with the aim to inform OGD community. To conduct field experiment we engaged common citizens in random locations, assigning them only if they had no knowledge in how to create, modify and manage data visualisations.

In Section II, we describe the relationship between data, visualization, and evaluation. In Section III, we explain the methodology used and how it was implemented. In Section IV, we report our results and finding. In Section V, we discuss the results significance and implications; our assumptions and limitations. Section VI describes our conclusions.

II. BACKGROUND

Visualization is an effective technique for communication of data, due to our natural ability to understand patterns [8].

When selecting a visualization technique there are a number of considerations: the underlying scientific principles of human perception and cognition; design guidelines; and the empirical evaluation of the technique.

One challenge with visualization as a science is that it currently does not have a unified general theory [10].

Demiralp [9] identified several causes for a lack of general theory. One issue is that visualization works at several domains in human perception and cognition. Additionally, visualization isn't necessarily limited to what we perceive, but may include an interactive element, which may have a significant impact on the success of the visualization. Demiralp [9] concludes that the question of how to measure and construct effective visualizations in general is an unsolved problem.

In terms of design principles, more work has been done and is somewhat well established. Shneiderman [5] introduced a type-by-task taxonomy to guide designers: overview first; zoom and filter; then details-on-demand [11], which has become the extended principles to guide designers of visualizations.

To judge a particular quality of a system or interface researchers and practitioners use evaluation, which is the last step in the process of the creation of visualizations [12], preferably empirically-driven [13]. Evaluation helps to understand the visualisation tool, visualisations themselves, and the complex process that this tool supports [13], as well as its potential and limitations [6]. This process represents the relationship between data, visualization, and evaluation.

III. METHODOLOGY

To evaluate the usability of open data visualization techniques we performed field experiments using the DataViva [21] open data web portal. DataViva is a web portal for Brazil's open data developed in partnership with the MIT Media Lab. Since starting this study, MIT Media Lab have also launched the Data USA [22] open data portal, which contains updated visualizations. We did not evaluate Data USA in this study.

The field experiment focused on three visualization techniques provided by DataViva: TreeMap, Map, and Stacked. Examples of these visualizations are shown in Figures 1-3.

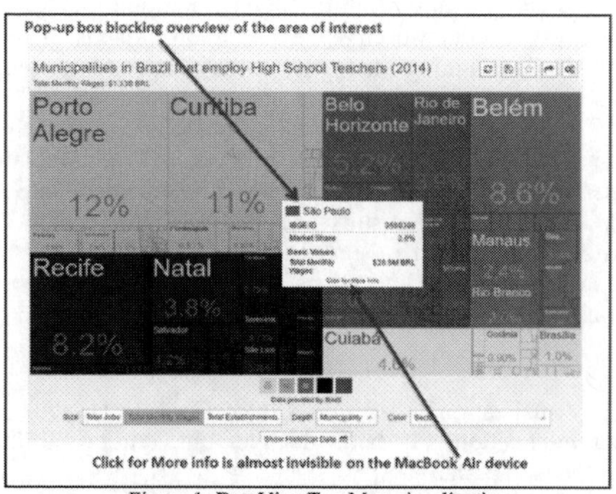

Figure 1. DataViva TreeMap visualization.

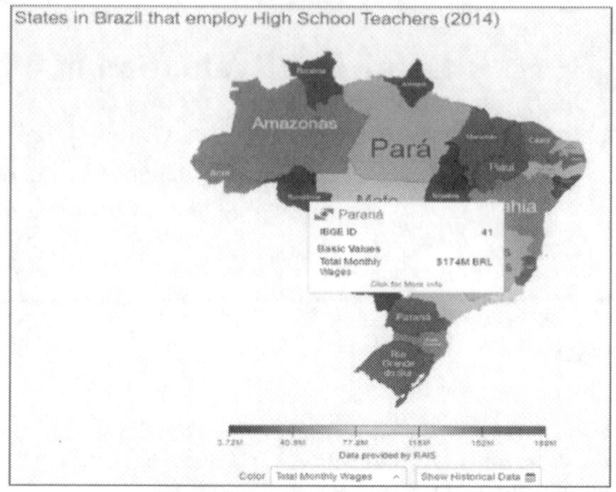

Figure 2. DataViva Map visualization.

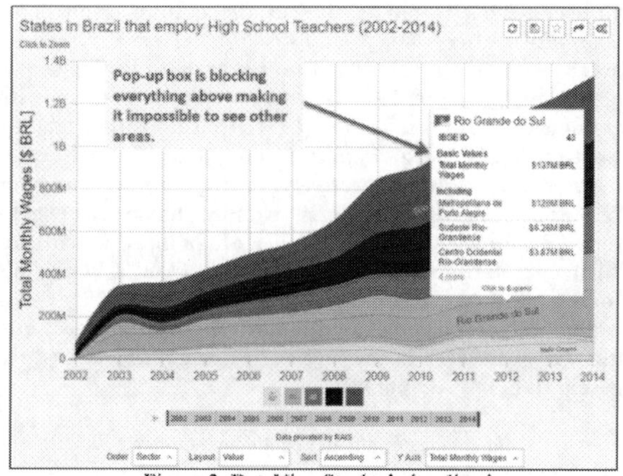

Figure 3. DataViva Stacked visualization.

We engaged our users at 7 different locations around Gold Coast city, Australia, in public places where Wi-Fi access was freely available. To conduct the experiment we used a MacBook Air laptop. DataViva was used to explore simple questions on the Brazilian economy. As a tool for video and audio data collection we used Software Debut.

Our goal was to test at least 10 participants as this is a suitable number according to Faulkner [16].

To balance the control between observer and the users and to balance the trade-offs between generalization, precision, and realism [14], the experiment was broken down into two stages: preliminary stage and controlled-testing stage.

The preliminary stage included presenting the participant with an information sheet about the study and conversational questioning to find out what stops common citizens from using OGD and concluded with the formal signing of the consent form.

The controlled-testing stage included 5 minutes of device and interface familiarization which was followed by performance tasks designed as a motivational scenario based on an envisaged real situation and setting. Tasks were designed to solve real problems with real data. The user's interaction was captured with screen recording software and audio that were later analyzed to calculate completion time. We used an unenforced *think aloud* protocol to support the identification of possible usability issues. Users were given 3 tasks to complete, each using a different visualization technique and a different task for that visualization. The tasks are shown in Table 1.

TABLE 1. VISUALIZATION TASKS COMPLETED BY PARTICIPANTS

Number	Technique	Description
Task 1	TreeMap	How many jobs are in Sao Paulo?
Task 2	Map	What is the nominal wage growth in Sao Paolo?
Task 3	Stacked	What is the total of monthly wages in Sao Paolo?

This was followed by preferential rating to quantify user's opinions for overall assessment of each single visualization interface. Finally, the participants were asked a single open question: Why do you prefer this particular visualization compared to others?

IV. RESULTS

Our experiment sample was based on 12 users. Their average age was 54 years. As shown in Figure 4, 33% had a university degree, 42% had a college education and 25% were educated at TAFE (a technical training institution).

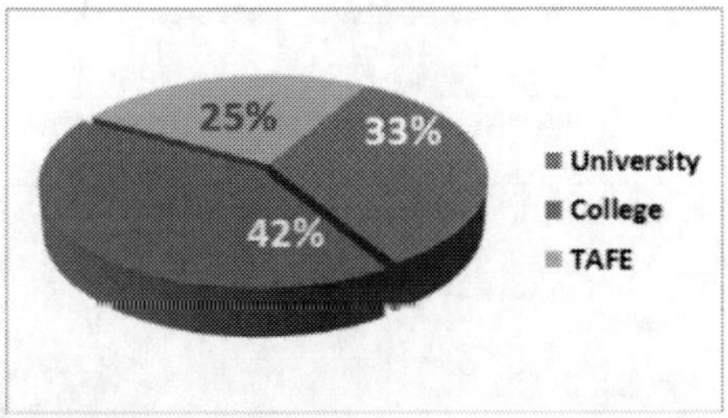

Figure 4. Distribution of participants' occupations.

The time spent per participant to complete the tasks took on average 11 minutes, excluding 5 minutes given to participants to familiarise with the DataViva interface and the time spent to answer an open-ended question.

At the preliminary stage we approached participants with the conversational questioning to find out what stops them from using OGD. 83.2% of participants answered that they had never heard of OGD; did not know OGD existed; or what it means. However, after their interaction with open data, 66.6% had expressed an interest to know more.

The average time to complete each task was calculated and the results are shown in Table 2. The Map visualization was the quickest, followed by Stacked, and then TreeMap.

TABLE 2. CONSISTANCY BETWEEN TIME PERFORMANCE & PREFERABLE CHOICE

Visualizations	Average time per participant	Preferable choice
Map	1 min	First
Stacked	1min 13sec	Second
TreeMap	1min 19sec	Last

Participants were asked to rank the visualizations in order of preference. The participants were asked the question: "What visualization they prefer or perceive as the easiest to use and why?" Figure 5 shows the results of the ranking.

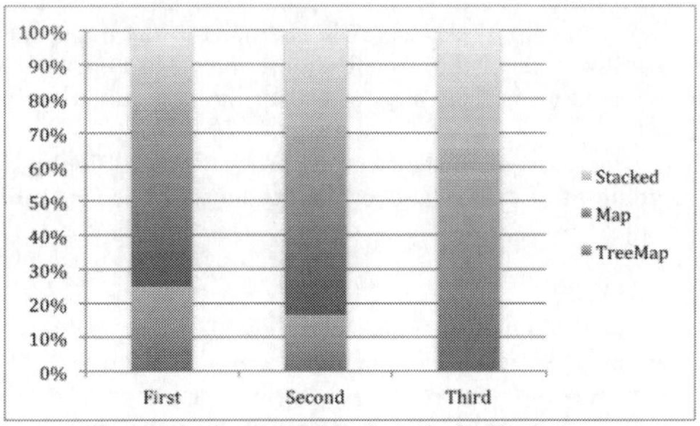

Figure 5. Preferential ranking for each visualization type.

The Map visualization had the most number of first choice rankings, it also had the most number of second choice rankings, and no participants placed it last. The ranking of TreeMap and Stacked were very similar with Stacked having one more ranking in second place and hence one less ranking last. As a result the order of preference for the participants was Map, Stacked, and TreeMap, which correlates with the time it took to complete each task as shown in Table 2.

Participants also provided reasons why they gave visualizations the particular ranking. The Map visualization was chosen because it was perceived as a familiar shape, that of a geographic map, and easy to use.

The Stacked visualisation had contradictory perception. Some perceived it as easy to understand and clear. Others found it confusing and reported that it "didn't make sense".

Participants that rated the TreeMap first found it easy to find information. Those that rated it second stated that it was "not clear". Those that rated it last said it was confusing, busy, and more difficult to find information.

V. DISCUSSION

The field experiments highlighted a number of issues with open data usability. Firstly, only 16.6% of participants had previously heard of open data. Secondly, TreeMap is a very common visualization tool used commonly in data journalism. However, we found that participants had the most trouble with it, both in terms of taking the longest time to complete the task, and also in response to the open question.

The most significant usability problem with all three visualisations was a feature known as the tooltip plugin or more commonly as pop-up box. With all three visualizations, the pop-up box was blocking the overview. Taking into consideration the extended principles for designers of data visualizations: overview first, zoom and filter; then details-on-demand [5] we demonstrated that this feature was blocking overview with details shown in Figures 1-3.

The problem with the feature is that it appears on a mouse rollover. As the user is navigating to interact with the visualization, the popup box occludes the area they want to interact with.

We have provided possible solutions to the popup box issue for each of the visualizations, shown in Figures 6-8. The solution is generally to display the popup box to the side.

Other issues that users reported were difficulty in reading titles or headings or the headings not being visible at all.

VI. CONCLUSIONS

The OGD movement is maturing with large quantities of data being released by governments around the world. The embracing of OGD hasn't necessarily translated into uptake by OGD consumers. We propose that this is because of the focus on machine-readability rather than human-usability. Recent efforts are focusing on providing interactive visualizations of OGD. In this paper, we evaluated one OGD portal to identify strengths and weaknesses between data visualization techniques, specifically for common citizens, which currently hasn't been investigated in the literature.

Even though our participants were unfamiliar with OGD, after a short introduction they were able to answer the problems on average in under 2 minutes, showing the advantage visualizations have over technical and raw data. This serves as a strong argument for OGD portals to provide visualizations to increase end-user uptake by common citizens.

Comparing three different types of visualizations, the clear preference was for Map visualization which presents the data on a geographical map. The basis for Map being the greatest preference both qualitatively and quantitatively is due to its familiarity to the users. Concrete concepts are quicker to grasp than abstract concepts. The TreeMap and Stacked visualizations present data more abstractly and require a greater conceptual leap for common citizens to grasp.

Therefore to encourage end-user uptake of OGD, visualizations should be selected that are concrete and familiar to end-users, such as Map visualizations, and to avoid more abstract visualizations. Note that visualizations such as TreeMap have been designed to address many usability and visualization factors, however, we have found that for common citizens, concreteness and familiarity are more important than other usability factors.

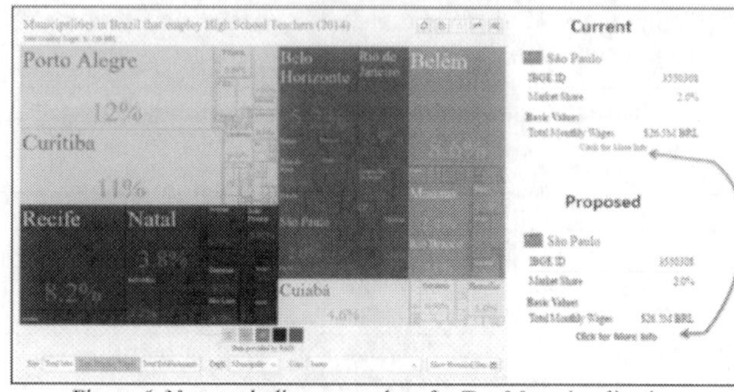

Figure 6. Non-occluding popup box for TreeMap visualization.

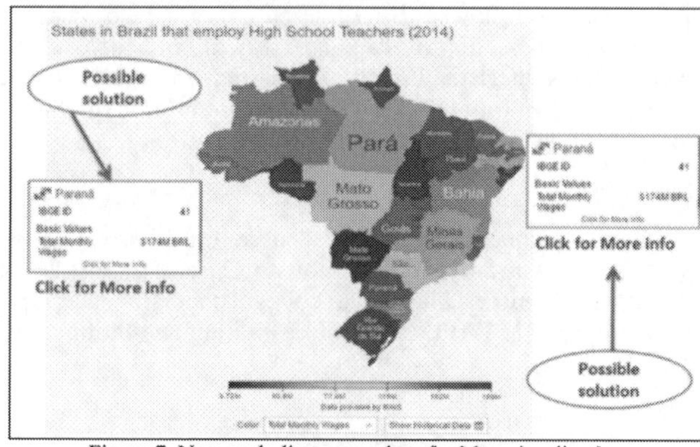

Figure 7. Non-occluding popup box for Map visualization.

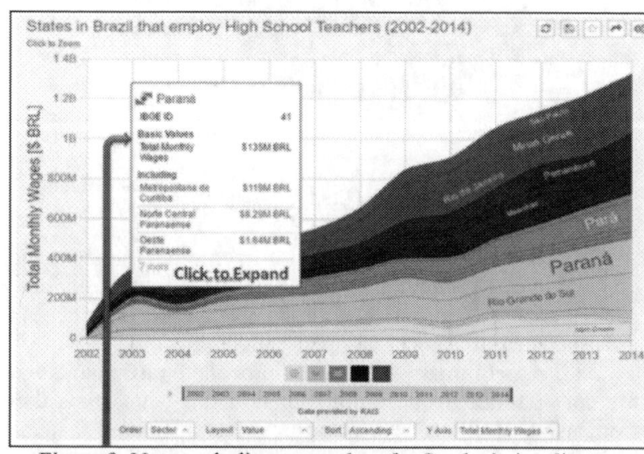

Figure 8. Non-occluding popup box for Stacked visualizaton.

Our study also identified smaller issues such as popups, where a simple and useful feature when poorly implemented can grossly impact the effectiveness of a visualization and reinforces the need not just for visualizations, but for end-user testing to verify the effectiveness of the visualizations.

Our study compared three visualization techniques. Future work will investigate broader visualization techniques and investigate newer data portals such as Data USA and a new version of DataViva. Additionally more comprehensive tasks can be evaluated that provide greater insights into the strengths and weaknesses of different techniques and enhance the benefits of each.

As Demiralp [9] has identified there is currently no general unified theory of designing and evaluating visualization techniques. We are interested in drawing together the science of perception, design principles, and empirical evaluation to enhance and improve the consumption of OGD.

ACKNOWLEDGMENT

We would like to acknowledge all participants who greatly contributed their time and effort to support this project.

REFERENCES

[1] data.world, "data.world launches to make the world's data easier to find, use, and share." 11 July, 2016, retrieved: March, 2017. [Online]. Available: https://globenewswire.com/news-release/2016/07/11/855045/0/en/data-world-Launches-to-Make-the-World-s-Data-Easier-to-Find-Use-and-Share.html

[2] Data Portals, "A Comprehensive List of Open Data Portals from Around the World", retrieved: March, 2017. [Online]. Available: http://dataportals.org/

[3] Tetherless World Constellation Linking Open Government Data (TWC LOPG), "IOGDS: International OGDset Search". retrieved: March, 2017. [Online]. Available: https://logd.tw.rpi.edu/demo/international_dataset_catalog_search

[4] A. Graves & J. Hendler, "A study on the use of visualizations for OGD". Information Polity, 19(1, 2), pp. 73-91, 2014.

[5] B. Shneiderman, "A Grander Goal: A Thousand-fold Increase in Human Capabilities". Educom Review, 32, 6, 4-10. HCIL-97-23, Nov-Dec 1997.

[6] C. Plaisant, "The challenge of information visualization evaluation." In Proceedings of the working conference on Advanced visual interfaces (pp. 109-116). ACM, May, 2004.

[7] R. Lengler & M. J. Eppler, "Towards a periodic table of visualization methods for management." In IASTED Proceedings of the Conference on Graphics and Visualization in Engineering (GVE 2007), Clearwater, Florida, USA, Jan, 2007.

[8] C. Ware, "Information visualization: Perception for design". Elsevier. Third edition, 2013.

[9] C. Demiralp, D. H. Laidlaw, J. J. Van Wijk, and C. Ware, "Theories of Visualization—Are There Any?" Brown University. Panel discussion. 2 Sep, 2016. retrieved: March, 2017. [Online]. Avaialable: http://hci.stanford.edu/~cagatay/projects/vismodel/TheoriesOfVisualization-Vis11.pdf

[10] B. Rogowitz, "Visualization Theory: Putting the Pieces Together," IEEE Visualization VizWeek, 29 Oct, 2010. retrieved: March, 2017. [Online]. Available: https://sites.google.com/site/bernicerogowitz/theory-of-visualization

[11] B. Shneiderman, "The eyes have it: a task by data type taxonomy for information visualizations," Visual Languages, 1996. Proceedings., IEEE Symposium on, Boulder, CO, 1996, pp. 336-343. DOI= 10.1109/VL.1996.545307.

[12] A. R. Teyseyre and M. R. Campo, "An Overview of 3D Software Visualization," in IEEE Transactions on Visualization and Computer Graphics, vol. 15, no. 1, pp. 87-105, Jan.-Feb. 2009. Doi: 10.1109/TVCG.2008.86

[13] H. Lam, E. Bertini, P. Isenberg, C. Plaisant and S. Carpendale, "Empirical Studies in Information Visualization: Seven Scenarios," in IEEE Transactions on Visualization and Computer Graphics, vol. 18, no. 9, pp. 1520-1536, Sept. DOI=2012.doi: 10.1109/TVCG.2011.279, 2012.

[14] Carpendale, S, "Evaluating information visualizations," (pp. 19-45). Berlin, Heidelberg: Springer Berlin Heidelberg. doi:10.1007/978-3-540-70956-5_2, 2008.

[15] C. Chen, "Top 10 Unsolved Information Visualization Problems." IEEE Comput. Graph. Appl. 25, 4, pp. 12-16. DOI=http://dx.doi.org/10.1109/MCG.2005.91, July, 2005.

[16] L. Faulkner, "Beyond the five-user assumption: Benefits of increased sample sizes in usability testing." Behavior Research Methods, Instruments and Computers, 35(3), 279-383. doi=10.3758/BF03195514, 2003.

[17] C. Martin, "Barriers to the OGD Agenda: Taking a Multi-Level Perspective," Policy & Internet, 6(3), 217-240, 2014.

[18] N. Shadbolt, et al., "Linked OGD: Lessons from data.gov.uk," IEEE Intelligent Systems, 27(3), 16-24, 2012.

[19] J. Hendler, J. Holm, C. Musialek, & G. Thomas, "US government linked open data: semantic.data.gov," IEEE Intelligent Systems, 27(3), 0025-31, 2012.

[20] Sunlight Foundation, "Ten principles for opening up government," 2010, retrieved: March, 2017. [Online]. Available: http://sunlightfoundation.com/policy/documents/ten-open-data- principles/

[21] DataViva. retrieved: March, 2017. [Online]. Available: http://dataviva.info.

[22] Data USA. retrieved: March, 2017. [Online]. Available: https://datausa.io/

Analyzing Browsing and Purchasing Across Multiple Websites Based on Latent Dirichlet Allocation

Nadine Schröder*, Andreas Falke*, Harald Hruschka*, Thomas Reutterer†
* Department of Marketing
University of Regensburg, Regensburg, Germany
Email: see http://www.uni-regensburg.de/wirtschaftswissenschaften/bwl-hruschka/lehrstuhl/index.html
† Institute for Service Marketing and Tourism
WU Vienna University of Economics and Business, Vienna, Austria
Email: thomas.reutterer@wu.ac.at

Abstract—**The increasing importance of online channels for retailers and service providers is paralleled by a rising interest in gaining insights into the customer journey to online purchases. Most attempts to shed light to this issue are restricted to data available for only few particular sites. Our research focuses on mining online shoppers' website visitation patterns across 472 individual websites. We propose a methodological framework to uncover latent interests which we assume to underlie observable online browsing behavior. Using one year of clickstream data for a random sample of comScore panelists, we show that there is heterogeneity among shoppers regarding online browsing habits, combinations of latent interests, and their conversion into online purchases. Our analysis finds that a relatively small fraction of online shoppers realizes 70% of online spending. In addition, we detect substantial segment-specific differences of shopping behavior with respect to 59 product categories.**

Keywords–Topic Models;Latent Dirichlet Allocation; Internet Usage and Purchasing Behaviour; Behavioral Segmentation

I. Introduction

Although online retail sales have grown at substantially high rates in recent years and the internet continues to play an increasingly important role in information acquisition throughout the purchase funnel prior to sales [11][4] sales conversions remain at very low rates [18][23]. Consequently, online retailers aim at engaging their visitors in staying longer on their websites and exploring more pages or, in other words, to create "stickiness", which has been shown to be associated with higher profitability [5][23]. However, most of the research focuses on the browsing and purchase behavior within a given retailer's website. In this research, we expand this view by investigating the browsing behavior of online shoppers across different websites and link this behavior with their purchases in several product categories.

We found nine studies analyzing browsing behavior of individual online shoppers across multiple web sites in the marketing and management science literatures [16][13][14][20][6][8][7][17][22]. Seven of these studies do not look at browsing at individual website, but aggregate websites to site types (e.g., travel, book, or music sites).

Let us summarize the novel aspects of our study against to the previous literature. We do not introduce fixed site types, but characterize individual sites as mixtures of latent interests which are based on site visits. Our approach differs from Trusov et al., who also use a topic model, but look at the number of times a consumer visits 29 fixed website types (e.g., services, social media, entertainment) [22]. In other words, these authors aggregate visits to the level of site types before analyzing them. As we avoid aggregation to fixed site types the latent interests, which we obtain, should be better in line with the perspective of consumers. We allow for correlations between all sites which most previous studies have excluded. We consider 59 product categories. The maximum number of categories in previous studies amounts to 29. In contrast to the majority of previous studies, we consider purchase as an additional dependent variable. We compare yearly purchase frequencies between 59 product categories in different segments of online shoppers. These segments are determined by clustering the importances of topics for each individual panelist. Note that only one previous study considers purchases differentiating between (three) different product categories. Finally, by analyzing a total number of 472 unique sites our research provides a much more comprehensive picture of website visitation behavior across multiple sites than the overwhelming majority of previous studies.

In Section II we present the methodological framework, which we adopt to derive latent interests embedded in online shoppers' website visitation patterns. We employ Latent Dirichlet Allocation (LDA), a commonly used technique in text mining to identify latent topics in large texts, which already has also seen promising applications in marketing. In Section III we explain how we obtain the analyzed data by selecting websites and online users participating in the comScore Web Behavior Panel for 2009. In Section IV we present the results of applying LDA to these data. We also segment online users based on their combinations of latent interests and study how different types of online browsing behavior get converted into purchases in a variety of product categories. In Section V we summarize results and outline possible extensions of our approach.

II. Latent Dirichlet Allocation

In text mining, topic models are often used quite successfully to extract mixtures of topics represented in documents [3][2]. In the following, we define a visit as a list containing all the sites accessed by an individual online shopper in a calendar week. Such a list contains multiple entries for any site, which a shopper accesses several times during a calendar week. We apply LDA, the most widespread topic model, to our data and interpret topics as latent interests. LDA implies the assumption that the sites visited by a shopper are generated by a mixture of latent interests. Let I, J and T denote the number of visits, sites and latent interests, respectively. Probabilities ϕ_{jt} and θ_{ti}

indicate the importance of site j for latent interest t and the importance of latent interest t for visit i, respectively. Please note that the Dirichlet distribution with hyperparameters α and β serves as prior for these probabilities.

Finally, the probability p_{ij} that visit i contains site j is related to the importance of this site for latent interests and the importance of latent interests for this visit in the following manner [9]:

$$p_{ij} = \sum_{t=1}^{T} \phi_{jt}\theta_{ti}. \tag{1}$$

We see several advantages of LDA in comparison to traditional cluster analytic methods. LDA simultaneously forms soft clusters of sites and visits. It explicitly takes the sparseness of the data into account (as a rule, most sites are not contained in a visit). LDA also considers multiple accesses of the same site during a visit. LDA does not rely on distance measures. It is based individual visits and does not loose information by aggregating across visits.

III. Data

We analyze clickstream data from the comScore Web Behavior Panel, which were collected from January 1, 2009 to December 31, 2009. Because our research emphasizes purchase behavior, we only include web sites at which at least one purchase is made in one of the 59 categories during the entire observation period. Furthermore, as mentioned before, we use the calender week as time frame. The resulting visits of panelists comprise a large variety of websites with highly skewed frequencies. Following common data preprocessing practice in text mining, each site whose number of visits is lower than the 5 percentile or greater than the 95 percentile is removed. Aggarwal and Zhai recommend to remove very frequent sites (words), as they are not discriminative between latent interests (topics) [1]. Many empirical studies in text mining adhere to this recommendation [10][24]. In fact, our procedure removes only three sites of the top-100 U.S. retail websites in 2009 [15].

Finally, panelists who never visited any of the remaining 472 web sites are removed. The final data set consists of 138,213 visits made by 7, 235 comScore panelists. Each visit is defined as a list of websites accessed by an individual panelist during a specific calender week. To give an example, a list (qvc.com, hsn.com, gap.com, childrensplace.com, qv.com) indicates that a panelist accesses these website (and qvc.com twice) in the respective week. On average panelists make 19.1 weekly visits. The average number of visits per site amounts to 1,035, the average number of sites per visit is 3.5.

IV. Major Results

A. *LDA Results*

We estimate LDA models using blocked Gibbs sampling. The first 1,000 iterations are discarded for burn-in and estimates are based on the next 1,000 iterations. α is estimated and β is set to a constant value of 0.1. To avoid local optima we let the number of latent interests vary between 2 and 110.

We evaluate model performance by the Bayesian information criterion (BIC), which penalizes model complexity [21]:

$$BIC = LL - 0.5\, n_p \log(I) \quad \text{with} \quad n_p = TJ. \tag{2}$$

According to Equation (2) the BIC is based on the log-likelihood LL, the number of visits I and the number of parameters n_p of the topic model. The number of parameters equals the number of latent interests T multiplied by the number of sites J. The model with the highest BIC is to be preferred. The log likelihood LL of a LDA model (n_{ij} indicates how often site j is contained in visit i) is computed as follows [19]:

$$LL = \sum_{i=1}^{I}\sum_{j=1}^{J} n_{ij} \log\left(\sum_{t=1}^{T} \phi_{jt}\theta_{ti}\right) \tag{3}$$

We obtain the best BIC value for 86 latent interests and conclude that 86 latent interests best describe the browsing behavior of our sample of households. Hence, our 472 websites are compressed into 86 latent interests and browsing patterns of online shoppers are generated by combinations of multiple latent interests.

TABLE I. Performance of LDA models

# interests	BIC	# interests	BIC	# interests	BIC
2	-2,315,613	10	-1,570,939	20	-1,276,315
30	-1,120,628	40	-1,033,775	50	-963,837
60	-923,595	70	-905,408	80	-876,826
81	-879,668	82	-878,211	83	-871,994
84	-870,503	85	-877,192	86	-865,820
87	-887,090	88	-871,641	89	-874,598
90	-873,709	100	-881,801	110	-889,039

BIC values rounded to nearest integer

Both the derived latent interests and the sites reflected by these interests differ in their contribution to characterize the observed visitation or browsing patterns. Table II represents the twelve most important latent interests. The importance of each interest t is measured by its expected frequency, which we obtain by summing θ_{ti} across all visits $i = 1, \cdots, I$. The interest with the highest expected frequency is considered to be the most important one. In addition, we indicate importance of a site j for each interest t by the estimated ϕ_{jt} value excluding small values $\phi_{jt} < 0.01$.

Table II illustrates the six most important latent interests. The most important interest # 1 is related to two sites, i.e., qvc.com and hsn.com. Based on the contents offered by these sites we label this topic "home shopping". On the other hand, interest # 2 is related to only one site satisfying the condition $\phi_{jk} < 0.01$, namely usps.com. Both interests # 3 and # 5 also refer to similar sites. Given the relatively broach combination of underlying sites, we label interest # 3 as "apparel". Whereas sites like gap.com and bananarepublic.com are rather classical online apparel stores with mainly adult customers, childrensplace.com and gymboree.com offer apparel for babies and kids. This is in contrast to the sites associated with interest # 5, which we label as "young adults apparel". These sites focus primarily on casual and lifestyle products. Sites belonging to interest # 4 are clearly serving amateurs' needs and we therefore label this interest "home improvement". Interest # 6 consists of two different kind of sites, i.e. toys and layette. However, as site toysrus.com dominates this interest we label this interest "toys". The remaining latent interests can be characterized in an analogous manner.

TABLE II. Six most important latent interests

1 = "homeshopping"		2 = '"postal service 1"	
qvc.com	.641	usps.com	.986
hsn.com	.350		
3 = "apparel"		**4 = "home improvement"**	
gap.com	.616	lowes.com	.538
childrensplace.com	.147	homedepot.com	.412
oldnavy.com	.129	acehardware.com	.036
gymboree.com	.047		
bananarepublic.com	.030		
piperlime.com	.016		
5 = "young adults apparel"		**6 = "toys"**	
aeropostale.com	.325	toysrus.com	.930
ae.com	.295	babyage.com	.014
abercrombie.com	.139	etoys.com	.011
urbanoutfitters.com	.084	diapers.com	.011
delias.com	.053		
abercrombiekids.com	.045		
alloy.com	.041		

gives sites j with ϕ_{jt} >= .010 for latent interest t

TABLE III. Segmentwise browsing behavior

	1	2	3	4	5	6	7
panel ists in %	11	13	15	16	17	17	12
visits in %	26	23	19	15	10	5	1
average # visits per panelist	45.6	34.2	25.3	17.9	11.5	5.9	2
average # sites per visit	5.7	3.5	2.8	2.5	2.1	1.9	1.6
Interest							
travel service			H	H			
department store 1	H		L		L	L	
apparel	H	H		H		L	L
travel	L		H		H		
entertainment tickets	L		H	H	H	H	L
home shopping	H			H		L	L
books	L						
apparel & news	H	L	L	L	L		
department store 2	H						L
travel service (discount)	L	H	H				

average importance less than lowest quartile (L), greater than highest quartile (H)

B. Segment-Specific Website Browsing Behavior

To gain a better understanding on how online shoppers combine these latent interests over time, we aim at generating segments of panelists and study their differences with respect to discriminating latent interests and implications for purchase behavior. We first group panelists based on the results of the selected LDA model using k-means clustering. For clustering the panelists we calculate the expected frequency f_{ht} of each interest t by summing θ_{ti} across all visits of each panelist h and logit-transform it as follows:

$$\log f_{ht} - \log(\max_{h'} f_{h't} - f_{ht} + 0.00001). \qquad (4)$$

We let the number of segments k vary between 2 and 60 and choose a seven segment solution, which reproduces 91.8% of the total sum of squares. Anyway, based on experience with data sets for similar numbers of respondents we did not expect to obtain more than ten segments.

Table III describes the seven resulting segments. In terms of number of panelists segments 5 and 6 are the two largest segments each containing 17%, while segment 1 is the smallest. By looking at the number of website visits we obtain quite different results. Segment 1 is largest in this regard and segment 7 the smallest, representing just one percent of overall website visitations.

It turns out that panelists' browsing behavior differs substantially across the derived segments (see table III). Members of segment 1 are active almost throughout the whole year, i.e., in 45.6 out of 53 examined calendar weeks. In contrast, panelists in segment 7 seem to browse quite irregularly with an average number of active weeks of just 2. Those households who are active throughout the year also combine more websites in their weekly visits; while segment 1 members visit, on average, 5.7 websites per week, the respective number for segments 6 and 7 are just below 2 websites with the potential of being purchase relevant.

Next we explore whether the derived segments also differ regarding the latent interests characterizing the segment members' online browsing patterns and if so, which specific interests are discriminating between segments the most. To this end, we test each of the 86 latent interests for significant differences in average visitation importances (measured as average expected frequencies) across the seven segments using a series of oneway analyses of variance. Ten latent interests turned out to differentiate significantly between the segments ($\alpha < 0.05$). For these ten significant latent interests, table III indicates for each segment whether the average importances are less than the lowest quartile (L) or greater than the highest quartile (H). As an example, consider the interest "travel service". It consists of the sites travelocity.com, orbitz.com and cheaptickets.com and is very important for segments 3 and 4. We find interests related to online shopping activities for product categories offered by department stores including apparel and fashion goods, which shape the browsing behavior of the highly active segment 1 representing around 11% of our panel household sample. On the other side, we find a substantial fraction of panel households, in particular those gathered in segments 3 or 5, which score relatively low on these dimensions but browse the interned particularly for travel and ticketing purposes.

C. Segment-Specific Purchasing Behavior

In addition, we examine how latent interests are translated into purchasing behavior. Table IV shows the percentage of panelists making at least one online purchase in 2009. Whereas most panelists in segment 1 purchase at least once, about the same fraction of online panelists in segment 6 never purchases online.

The conversion of weekly website visits into purchases is also much higher for segment 1 (with almost 12% of visits) when compared to other segments. In addition, online shoppers who purchase more frequently also tend to buy more products and spend more money. Again, panelists in segment 1 purchase more products and spend higher amounts online than all the other panelists do. About 25 percent (segment 1 and 2 members) realize about 70 percent of overall online sales.

To gain a more thorough understanding which product categories benefit the most from the conversion of site visits into purchases, we systematically compare differences in average numbers of purchases among 59 product categories in each of the seven discussed segments. To this end, we conduct $0.5 \times 59 \times 58 = 1711$ pairwise comparisons of category purchases, which implies a Bonferroni corrected significance level of $\alpha = 0.05/1830$ [12]. In six out of seven segments, we obtain significantly different category pairs. Note that for

TABLE IV. Segmentwise purchasing behavior

	1	2	3	4
purchasing panelists	81%	69%	56%	44%
visits with purchase	11.78%	7.61%	5.95%	4.80%
average # of products bought per purchase	4.35	3.13	3.09	2.18
average # of products bought per visit	0.256	0.106	0.063	0.029
total $ sales	530,768	264,745	184,431	100,715
$ sales per panelist	664.29	284.06	175.31	86.90
	5	6	7	
purchasing panelists	32%	18%	5%	
visits with purchase	4.3%	3.78%	3.00%	
average # of products bought per purchase	2.15	2.13	1.89	
average # of products bought per visit	0.017	0.008	0.002	
total $ sales	37,502	21,465	2,010	
$ sales per panelist	31.20	17.70	2.29	

segments with very low conversion rates (as given in table IV) the number of significant differences between product categories decreases considerably. On the two extremes, in segment 7 with very few purchase incidences no significant differences between product categories can be observed, while we find in segment 1 most significant differences.

TABLE V. Segmentwise comparisons of purchase frequencies between product categories

segment 1		segment 2	
Apparel	59	Apparel	58
Food & beverage	52	Food & beverage	55
Other services	47	Air travel	46
Health & beauty	45	Photo printing services	42
Air travel	45	Other services	39
Shoes	38	Shoes	35
Photo printing services	38	Event tickets	33
Unclassified	33	Hotel reservations	33
Event tickets	31	Books & magazines	32
Bed & bath	26	Mobile phones & plans	27
Car rental	25	Car rental	26
Arts, crafts & party supplies	24		
segment 3		**segment 5**	
Apparel	56	Apparel	53
Air travel	49	Food & beverage	49
Food & beverage	45	Air travel	47
Photo printing services	45	Hotel reservations	22
Event tickets	30		
Shoes	28		
Hotel reservations	27	**segment 6**	
Unclassified	27	Air travel	36
Car rental	22	Food & beverage	30
		Apparel	27
segment 4			
Apparel	55		
Food & beverage	49		
Air travel	49		
Photo printing services	45		
Hotel reservations	37		
Event tickets	34		
Shoes	24		
Books & magazines	23		

Contains categories with 20 or more significant comparisons. Reading example for apparel and segment 1: for segment 1 the yearly purchase frequency of apparel is significantly higher than the purchase frequencies of 58 other categories.

Table V represents, for each segment, a list of product categories ranked in descending order of their respective number of significant comparisons. Note that these lists can be interpreted as rankings of product categories with respect to their importances for online purchases made by the respective segment members. Interestingly, categories apparel and food & beverage are always among the top three positions in these segment-specific lists, which implies that these two categories dominate virtually all online shopper segments.

However, the "big picture" of a subset representing about a quarter of panel households (i.e., segment 1 and 2) being particularly active, purchase a lot, and — in addition — do so across a wide range of assortment is confirmed by this category specific view of online purchase activities. On contrary, segments 5 and 6 show only few product categories with purchase frequencies higher than those of other categories. But there are also some notable differences between the highly active segments 1 and 2 in terms of their purchase behavior. For example, health & beauty and books & magazines attain higher purchase frequencies only in segments 1 and 2, respectively. For segment 2 members, hotel reservations clearly play a much more important role as they do in the visits of segment 1. The contrary applies to categories arts, crafts & party supplies or bed & bath, which dominate more of the other categories in segment 1 as opposed to segment 2.

V. CONCLUSION AND FUTURE WORK

Weekly clickstream data of panelists across 472 websites can be adequately compressed into a mixture of 86 latent interests. Using k-means clustering of the panelists' importances devoted to these latent interests, we determine seven online shopper segments. These segments are characterized by remarkable differences both in terms of the way they combine various latent interests and in the intensity of their overall online activity. Moreover, these segments also show marked differences in their online purchasing behavior, both in individual product categories and at a more aggregate level. We find that around 25 percent of online shoppers (segments 1 and 2) realize 70 percent of online sales and apparel as well as food & beverage are in all of the examined online shopper segments among the dominating product categories. However, we also detect substantial segment-specific differences of shopping behavior across categories.

The approach presented in this paper also faces some limitations which offer opportunities for future research efforts. Here we pursue a two step approach, starting with a topic model, which provides discrete latent variables. In the second step we obtain clusters of panelists based on the importances of these latent variables for the visits of each panelist. To develop and apply a topic model, which integrates these two steps by also taking heterogeneity of panelist into account constitutes an interesting future research endeavor. Another possibility consists in allowing latent variables (interests) to evolve over time. For such an extension, dynamic effects must be included in a topic model. However, such an extension also requires more data spanning over several years.

REFERENCES

[1] C. C. Aggarwal and C. Zhai, A Survey of Text Clustering Algorithms: Springer, New York, 2012, pp.77-128, in Aggarwal, C. C., Zhai, C., Mining Text Data.

[2] D. M. Blei, "Probabilistic Topic Models," in Communications of the ACM, vol. 55 , 2012, pp. 77-84.

[3] D. M. Blei, A. Y. Ng, and M. I. Jordan, "Latent Dirichlet Allocation," Journal of Machine Learning Research, Vol. 3, 2003, pp. 993-1022.

[4] B. Bronnenberg, B. J. Kim, and C. F. Mela, "Zooming in on Choice: How Do Consumers Search for Cameras Online?," Marketing Science, vol. 35 , 2016, pp. 693-712.

[5] R. E. Bucklin and C. Sismeiro, "A Model of Web Site Browsing Behavior Estimated on Clickstream Data," Journal of Marketing Research, Vol. 40, 2003, pp. 249-67.

[6] P. J. Danaher, G. W. Mullarkey, and S. Essegaier, "Factors Affecting Web Site Visit Duration: A Cross-Domain Analysis," Journal of Marketing Research, vol. 42, 2006, pp. 182-194.

[7] P. J. Danaher and M. S. Smith, "Modeling Multivariate Distributions Using Copulas: Applications in Marketing," Marketing Science, vol. 30, 2011, pp. 4-21.

[8] A. Goldfarb, "State Dependence at Internet Portals," Journal of Economics & Management Strategy, vol. 15, 2006, pp. 317-352.

[9] T. L. Griffiths and M. Steyvers, Finding Scientific Topics, in: Proceedings of the National Academy of Sciences (Suppl. 1), Vol. 101, 2004, pp. 5228-5235.

[10] M. D. Hoffman, D. M. Blei, C. Wang, and J. Paisley, "Stochastic Variational Inference," Journal of Machine Learning Research, vol. 14, 2013, pp. 1303-1347.

[11] P. Huang, N. H. Lurie, and S. Mitra, "Searching for Experience on the Web: An Empirical Examination of Consumer Behavior for Search and Experience Goods," Journal of Marketing, vol. 73, 2009, pp. 55-69.

[12] J. D. Jobson, Applied Multivariate Data Analysis. Volume I: Regression and Experimental Design. Springer, New York, 1991.

[13] E. J. Johnson, S. Bellman, and G. L. Lohse, "Cognitive Lock-In and the Power Law of Practice," Journal of Marketing, vol. 67, 2003, pp. 62-75.

[14] E. J. Johnson, W. W. Moe, P. S. Fader, S. Bellman, and G. L. Lohse, "On the Depth and Dynamics of Online Search Behavior," Management Science, vol 50 , 2004, pp. 299-308.

[15] E. Leuenberger, Top 100 Retail Websites of 2009, 2009 (http://www.zencartoptimization.com/2009/01/12/top-100-retail-web sites-of-2009/ Accessed 14.12.16).

[16] S. Li, J. C. Liechty, and A. L.Montgomery, Modeling Category Viewership of Web Users with Multivariate Count Models. Working Paper, Carnegie Mellon University, Pittsburgh, PA, 2002.

[17] G. Mallapragada, S. R. Chandukala, and L. Qing, "Exploring the Effects of "What" (Product) and "Where" (Website) Characteristics on Online Shopping Behavior," Journal of Marketing, vol. 80, 2016, pp. 21-38.

[18] W. W. Moe and P. S. Fader, "Dynamic Conversion Behavior at E-Commerce Sites," Management Science, vol. 50 , 2004, pp. 326-335.

[19] D. Newman, A. Asuncion, P. Smyth, and M. Welling, "Distributed Algorithms for Topic Models," Journal of Machine Learning Research, vol. 10, 2009, pp. 1801-28.

[20] Y. H. Park and P. S. Fader, "Modeling Browsing Behavior at Multiple Websites," Marketing Science, vol. 23, 2004, pp. 280-303.

[21] G. Schwarz, "Estimating the Dimension of a Model," The Annals of Statistics, vol. 6, 1978, pp. 461-464.

[22] M. Trusov, L. Ma, and Z. Jamal , "Crumbs of the Cookie: User Pro ling in Customer-Base Analysis and Behavioral Targeting," Marketing Science, vol. 35, 2016, pp. 405-426.

[23] V. Venkatesh and R. Agarwal, "Turning Visitors into Customers: A Usability-Centric Perspective on Purchase Behavior in Electronic Channels," Management Science, vol. 52, 2006, pp. 367-382.

[24] D. Yogatama, C. Wang, B. R. Routledge, N. A. Smith, and E. P. Xing (2014), "Dynamic Language Models for Streaming Text," Transactions of the Association for Computational Linguistics, vol. 2 , 2014, pp. 181-192.

A Vision on Prescriptive Analytics

Maya Sappelli
TNO
Data Science, The Hague, The Netherlands
Email: maya.sappelli@tno.nl

Maaike H.T. de Boer
TNO and Radboud University
Data Science, The Hague and Nijmegen, The Netherlands
Email: maaike.deboer@tno.nl

Selmar K. Smit
TNO
Modelling, Simulation& Gaming, The Hague, The Netherlands
Email: selmar.smit@tno.nl

Freek Bomhof
TNO
Data Science, The Hague, The Netherlands
Email: freek.bomhof@tno.nl

***Abstract*—In this paper, we show our vision on prescriptive analytics. Prescriptive analytics is a field of study in which the actions are determined that are required in order to achieve a particular goal. This is different from predictive analytics, where we only determine what will happen if we continue current trend. Consequently, the amount of data that needs to be taken into account is much larger, making it a relevant big data problem. We zoom in on the requirements of prescriptive analytics problems: impact, complexity, objective, constraints and data. We explain some of the challenges, such as the availability of the data, the downside of simulations, the creation of bias in the data and trust of the user. We highlight a number of application areas in which prescriptive analytics could or would not work given our requirements. Based on these application areas, we conclude that domains with a large amount of data and in which the phenomena are restricted by laws of physics or math are very applicable for prescriptive analytics. Areas in which the human or human activities play a role, future research will be required to meet the requirements and tackle the challenges. Directions of future research will be in integrating model-driven and data-driven approaches, but also privacy, ethics and legislation. Whereas predictive analytics is often already accepted in society, prescriptive analytics is still in its infancy.**

Keywords*–*Prescriptive Analytics; Requirements; Applications

I. Introduction

Prescriptive analytics is one of the big data buzzwords from recent years. Being able to automatically prescribe actions in order to attain some goal would mean a huge step forward in decision support or automatic decision making for any field, especially growing fields like industry [1]. However, the problem of prescriptive analytics is its complexity [2], [3] Nevertheless, there are more and more indications that the increase in computer power allows for more complex calculations. Think only of the field of deep learning in which continuous progress is made on a wide variety of application areas. This suggest that it is time to investigate when and how we can and should apply prescriptive analytics.

In order to assess the feasibility of prescriptive analytics in any application area it is important to understand the complexity of the prescriptive analytics field. In this paper we aim to do so, by analyzing the characteristics of prescriptive problems and how it has been applied so far. We start off by explaining the difference between prescriptive analytics and its brothers descriptive and predictive analytics in Section II. We continue with the challenges and requirements in prescriptive analytics in Section III. In Section IV we use several application domains, such as oil and gas, law enforcement, healthcare and logistics, to explain in which situations prescriptive analytics might be fruitful and in which it will not. This paper ends with a direction of future prescriptive analytics research.

II. Descriptive, Predictive and Prescriptive Analytics

The number of organizations that base their results on data analysis is growing. In the simplest form, the data analysis of organization entails a form of **descriptive** analytics [4]. In this form of analytics, a (typically large) dataset is described quantitatively on its main features with the aim to reduce the amount of data into 'human consumable information'. An example is the extraction of simple statistics, such as average number of products that <u>has been</u> sold per day.

The next step of analytics is **predictive** analytics. In predictive analytics, typically a prediction is made about the future based on information from the past and current situations [5]. An example is the prediction of how many products <u>will be</u> sold in one month, or one year. These predictions are based on correlations and patterns in past data. A simple predictive model can be a linear regression model that assumes that the average number of sales per day decreases each month. More complex models can take into account other aspects that could influence the number of products that will be sold.

In **predictive** analytics, the underlying question is: 'What will happen?' The next step is **prescriptive** analytics: 'What <u>should I do</u> to make this happen?' [4]. This means that **prescriptive** analytics is focused on finding the action that should be taken to optimize some outcome, rather than focused on what will happen if I continue to do the same thing. In the sales example, an example of **prescriptive** analytics would be to prescribe the action or actions that should be undertaken to increase the average number of sales with a certain amount.

Just as descriptive and predictive analytics have tight bonds, **predictive** and **prescriptive** analytics are also strongly connected. One important reason is because **prescriptive** analytics also include predictions to estimate the effect of possible actions. However, note that these are very different kind of predictions. In prescriptive analytics, the prediction of the effect of a (sequence of) actions or interventions is central. This type of prediction deals with more complex situations such as interaction between actions or hypothetical effects for which no historical data is available. Predictive analytics only involves predictions in a single dimension based on the current and historical situations.

Imagine that a car seller wants to get some insight in his business. First, he starts with some **descriptive** analytics and calculates the number of sales and profit he made the past 5 years. He also defines some cohorts of interest, such as high end cars and low end cars and the profit he made on each of those cohorts. Then, he moves on to **predictive analytics** and calculates what his expected profit is for the next month, based on the current and past situation. He also calculates a more advance **prediction**, such as the expected number of sales if the supplier prices go up five percent. In the **prescriptive** analytics case, the car seller goes one step further. He wants to increase his total profit by five percent and wants to know what he should do; should he a) find a new supplier, b) stop selling low-end cars, or c) start an advertisement campaign. To answer this question he will most likely use some **predictions** but, since the seller has never done an advertisement campaign before, and has always used the same supplier he needs to rely on other sources of data to calculate the expected effect of strategies a) and c). Moreover, the optimal solution can also be a combination of actions a), b) and c). And, the actions can also interact. For example: an advertisement campaign may not have the same impact when the car seller stops selling low-end cars, because low-end cars might attract precisely those buyers that are attracted through the campaign, making the campaign irrelevant when the low-end cars are not available anymore.

Although a **predictive** analysis itself can also lead to a prescription, this is typically one that is straightforward: 'if the stock prices are expected to go up, I buy'. Although the question behind this **prediction** is an optimization problem (optimizing profit), the optimization itself is not part of **predictive** analytics. An example of a solution to such an optimization problem stems from optimal control theory. This is a mathematical theory dealing with finding a control law to achieve an optimality criterion [6]. On the other hand, a **prescriptive** analysis typically involves two aspects: 1) exploration of possible actions and 2) generation of the prescription. It leads to a complex prescription, such as the prescription of combinations or sequences of actions, which requires more complex predictions. Typically, the decision space for **prescriptive** analytics tends to be larger; multiple situations with many variables, options and constraints are taken into account.

Moreover, the interpretation of the prediction may not always lead to an unambiguous decision. Therefore, an important aspect of prescriptive analytics is the transparency of the method: the algorithm must be able to explain why a certain strategy is prescribed.

This also illustrates the close link between **prescriptive** analytics and **business** analytics. Business analytics has been defined as 'a process of transforming data into actions through analysis and insights in the context of organizational decision making and problem solving' [7]. Hence, **prescriptive** analytics is a method for automating this manual process that is specifically suited, as all automation methods, when the job is dull, dirty, dangerous, demanding or difficult.

III. Requirements and Challenges

For a problem space to be relevant for prescriptive analytics, there are a couple of requirements that need to be present. The relevance of each requirement is determined by the application domain, but is typically present for interesting applications of prescriptive analytics. An overview of the criteria is presented in Table I, based on [2].

First and foremost the decision space needs to be complex. Complexity can arise from the number of possible actions that need to be evaluated, number of context parameters that need to be taken into account and the influence of a decision on the search space itself. Moreover the **impact** of the decision should be significant. For simple decision spaces, it is most likely sufficient to predict the outcome of the alternative situation compared to the current situation and the analysis is complete. For example, in the stock market example, the impact of the decision will be very limited (except if you are a big player) and hardly influence the new situation.

The same is true if it is not the profit on a single stock that needs to be optimized, but a complete strategy or portfolio. Hence, it is not about optimizing a single action, but a sequence of actions that needs to be executed in a coordinated manner. For such a **complex** situation in which there are multiple variables and multiple interventions that need to be optimized, a prescriptive analytics approach is more suitable for the decision maker to oversee the impact of his decision.

Another important requirement is that the objective is definable, i.e. there is a **clear quantifiable objective**, such as long-term profit. Moreover, this objective often competes with other objectives, making the decision space more complex. For large pension funds for example, the decision to buy or sell will have so many implications that the decision will not only depend on an expected stock price. Another complication that increases the complexity of the decision space even more, are possible **constraints**, for example when limited resources are available.

Finally, the required **data** should be **available**, specifically data on previous actions, decisions and the consequent situation. As predictive analytics can map the current situation to some point in the past and assume that they will progress similarly, prescriptive analytics can map the current situation to a point in the past, and the possible interventions to previous interventions and assume that the response will be similar. Hence, prescriptive analytics requires not only time series as input, but also the actions performed previously.

This specific requirement of the availability of data and specifically the actions taken is often a big challenge. It is something that is often lacking, either because of (privacy) concerns and legislations or simply because the required data is not monitored. For example, it might be very useful for the car sales-manager in the previous example, to constantly monitor the actions and emotions of employees and customers to derive the best sales tactic. However, this is probably both not desired and hard to record. The data about these employees and customers should thus be collected in a non-intrusive manner, meaning that the individuals that are monitored should not get disturbed.

In the case of little data, simulation models can provide a solution, but this can lead to simulation or knowledge-driven prescriptions, and does not exploit the full capabilities

TABLE I. REQUIREMENTS AND DESCRIPTION FOR PRESCRIPTIVE ANALYTICS

Nr	Name	Description
1	Impact	Is the expected impact worth the effort?
2	Complexity	Is the problem sufficiently complex (i.e. more than one possible action and multiple alternatives).
3	Objective	Does the problem have a clear quantifiable objective that can be optimized?
4	Constraints	Are there boundaries on the decision space that make the problem more complex?
5	Data	Is there data on the possible actions, decisions and the consequent situation?

of prescriptive analytics, hence some hybrid solution is needed. Furthermore, in simulations physical systems are easier to model through the laws of nature compared to the behavior of people. This is because human behavior tends to be less rational or predictable, whereas physical laws tend to be strict. Moreover, a generic 'human simulation model' will not capture the diversity in drives, needs and motivations that are an integral part of an individuals actions.

Another challenge regarding the data is that when (implicitly) including previous decisions to the dataset, the decisions might get towards a certain decision. To illustrate this, we move to an example in policing. Imagine that prescriptive analytics is used to steer surveillance against drugs dealers. Increasing the police surveillance in a specific area of a city will increase the number of catches in that area (and not in other areas). This will cause a prescription algorithm to increase surveillance in that area (since the expected number of dealers caught is the highest there) and creates an infinite loop. This loop for the example of prescriptive policing is visualized in Figure 1.

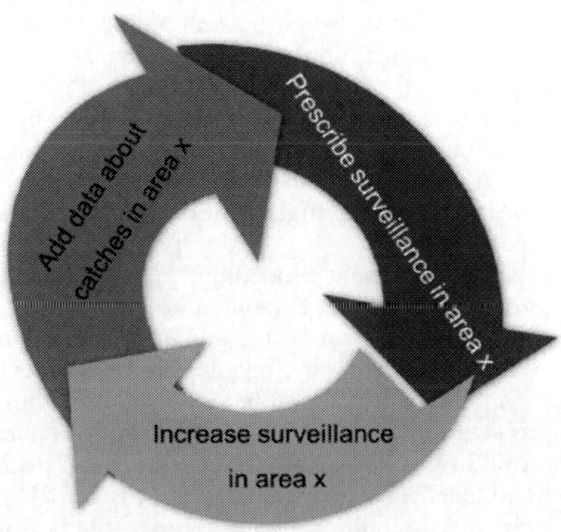

Figure 1. Loop in Surveillance

Besides challenges regarding the data, an important challenge is related to the user and trust. The system should produce decisions that are transparent, explainable and traceable in order for a user to trust and accept the decision of the system. On the other hand, the user should not overtrust the system in cases it provides a suboptimal solution. As explained before in the challenges regarding the data, the system has no creativity and can only produce results based on the data it has seen. The user is needed to validate whether the decision is right in the situation, because humans are able to use their creativity and adaptation capabilities in novel situations. Balancing between those extremes will be a major challenge in any practical application.

IV. APPLICATIONS

We will elaborate on four application areas to provide an example of how, and in what kind of application areas prescriptive analytics might be useful. We indicate to what extent they meet the mentioned requirements. Note that these areas are merely used as an example, and are not an extensive list of possibilities.

A. *Oil, Gas and Offshore*

Oil, gas and offshore are a group of domains in which prescriptive analytics can be very beneficial and in which it is already applied [8]. Costs are very high and any reduction, no matter how small, can lead to big profits. Due to the nature of the field, the (sensor) data has nice properties, such as that they are rich, readily available and relatively accurate. The most promising application of prescriptive analytics is, confusingly, predictive maintenance [9]. Three example applications within this domain are:

(a) Predictive maintenance. Any minute a plant or turbine is not working can cost thousands of euros, especially when this occurs unplanned. Hence, maintenance is of major importance to this area. It should not be performed too late; otherwise a breakdown will cost a massive amount of money. But also performing it early is not the solution, since replacement parts are also very costly. Predictive maintenance could come to rescue by suggesting (or prescribing) the ideal moment for maintenance given weather conditions, expected demand, and sensor data indicating the current state of each part. For offshore specifically, the algorithm should also take into account that a bulk replacement might be cheaper than just-in-time.

(b) Where to drill, lift or frack. Within the area of oil and gas, prescriptive analytics can also be used to determine where to drill (or where not to) and with which techniques. Even though at first sight it does not seem to be a very dynamic problem, in practice the dynamics of an (oil) field are very volatile. The technique used for drilling or lifting at one place, affects the performance on other places and is dependent on the type of well.

(c) Automatic drill support. Prescriptive analytics can support horizontal drilling and hydraulic fracturing operations by automatically interpreting real-time sound, video and other forms of data to automatically make real-time adjustment to the parameters of the machines.

For each of the application, the relation to each of the requirements is shown in Table II.

TABLE II. APPLICATIONS IN OIL, GAS AND OFFSHORE IN RELATION TO THE REQUIREMENTS OF PRESCRIPTIVE ANALYTICS (green is requirement met, orange is neutral and red is requirement not met)

	Impact	Complexity	Objective	Constraints	Data
a. Predictive maintenance					
b. Where to drill					
c. Drill support					

TABLE III. APPLICATIONS IN LAW ENFORCEMENT AND JUSTICE IN RELATION TO THE REQUIREMENTS OF PRESCRIPTIVE ANALYTICS (green is requirement met, orange is neutral and red is requirement not met)

	Impact	Complexity	Objective	Constraints	Data
a. Prescriptive Policing					
b. City Planning					
c. Sentencing					

B. Law Enforcement and Justice

Predictive Policing is one of the hot topics within law enforcements all over the world. A typical application is to predict where and when a certain type of crime will occur [10]. Currently, applications exist that use predictive analytics to predict who is most likely to be the victim or the perpetrator, or who is most likely to recidive. Although these applications provide some insight into the dynamics of crime, they are not necessarily of much use directly. Since the objective is to prevent crime from happening, it is more important to know what will be the effect of your intervention; this leads to Prescriptive Policing. This is a challenging field, not only because of the human behavior that is included, but more importantly because of the privacy, bias and other concerns, such as ethical profiling. Furthermore, it is to be expected that explainability of the outcomes is necessary to stand a chance in court. Examples of possible applications of prescriptive modeling in the law enforcement domain are:

(a) Prescriptive Policing. As mentioned above, Prescriptive Policing is applying prescriptive analytics in order to determine the best possible intervention to prevent crime from happening. Problems are all over the 'requirements spectrum'; constraints are unclear, data is not available or legislated by law, the impact is hard to monetarize. Even the objective is not clear: do you want to prevent crime, or catch criminals?

(b) City Planning & Legislation. From Environmental Criminology it is known that the environment, and specifically the buildings, parks and infrastructure can have a great impact on the actual and the perceived amount of crime [3]. As local government can, more or less, control them, predicting the effect of city planning and legislation could lead to safer cities. Again impact and constraint are unclear, however data is readily available.

(c) Sentencing. Law firms can use algorithms that offer predictions on certain cases and based on how similar cases fared in the same jurisdiction give a prediction how new cases could work out. The small Californian law firm Dummit, Buchholz & Trapp already uses such technology, developed by LexisNexis, to determine in 20 minutes whether a case is worth taking or not [11]. One might even imagine that judges are replaced by prescriptive algorithms that determine the appropriate sentence. This could lead to a more objective and consequent practice. Whether society would accept such developments is, however, highly uncertain.

Table III shows for each application which of the requirements are met.

C. Healthcare

The domain of healthcare is typically well-suited for the application of prescriptive analytics [12]. The impact of decisions in the healthcare-domain is large and the decision space, with patient types and possible treatments is complex. There are also clear trade-offs and constraints in healthcare that cannot be ignored. Especially with additional constraints coming from insurance companies, decision making and optimization is important for hospitals and other healthcare professionals. However, the reason why it has not yet been applied in healthcare often is that it usually requires the modeling of a human action. As explained earlier, this is more difficult than modeling physical systems because their range of choices and actions is much more diverse and less predictable. Examples of possible applications of prescriptive modeling in the healthcare domain are:

(a) Activity planning for the optimization of an individuals well-being. In this example a prescription can look like a sequence of actions that an individual would need to take in order to improve their well-being [13]. Actions can include adapting sleeping behavior, eating behavior, physical activity or a combination. Problems in this example is the effort and privacy issues involved with collecting data on an individuals sleep, eat and activity behavior. Moreover, the objective - increasing well-being - is ill-defined and highly subjective, making it harder to optimize.

(b) Hospital constraint modeling reduce cost and increase throughput. Another example is on the level of optimizing cost and throughput in a hospital. This problem is highly complex since many people are involved. Especially constraints on availability of employees can make the problem difficult. There are multiple objectives that play a role in this scenario. Not only cost and throughput are important, but patient satisfaction as well. The impact is large, since sending patients home too early is undesirable in the long run. It is likely that hospitals have a sufficient amount of data to work on these prescriptive scenarios. Sir Mortimer B. Davis Jewish General Hospital has been looking into enterprise optimization using prescriptive analytics [14].

(c) Personalized decision support for medical experts. A final example in the healthcare domain would be the prescription of a treatment plan, personalized for an individuals specific situation. The biggest problem in this scenario is the availability of required data and the privacy issues that are involved once aspects, such as sleep, food and activity are involved.

Table IV gives an overview of the relation between the requirements and each application.

TABLE IV. APPLICATIONS IN HEALTHCARE IN RELATION TO THE REQUIREMENTS OF PRESCRIPTIVE ANALYTICS
(green is requirement met, orange is neutral and red is requirement not met)

	Impact	Complexity	Objective	Constraints	Data
a. Activity planning					
b. Hospital constraint modeling					
c. Personalized decision support					

D. *Logistics*

The logistics domain seems an interesting domain for the application of prescriptive analytics. Although humans are often in the loop, they are typically not the core of the objective that needs to be optimized. This means that a less advanced human model is required, making the application of prescriptive analytics more realistic. Examples of possible applications of prescriptive modeling in the logistics domain are:

(a) Routing of ships and trucks for loading and unloading on docks [15]. A possible example of a routing problem is the case where multiple companies are cooperating. This makes the problem complex and interesting, since there are strong interactions between actions, i.e. if a single driver pauses, than this effects other trucks and ships as well. Moreover, there is a clear objective reducing time and optimizing throughput. Constraints are also clear, for example local speed limits. With the increase in use of GPS trackers, there is a continuous availability of streaming data. The optimization of the activities of all parties involved at a dock can have a large impact on total revenue and throughput.

(b) Dairy farm optimization. In the food industry, farms collect a lot of data about their farm and their animals [16], [17]. This ensures an optimal flow of milk and other animal products. Food industry in general has a large impact on society, however the impact of a single farm might be small. There is an interesting overlap between optimizing the health of animals and optimizing the health of people. Constructing animal models might be less complex than constructing human models, making this a particularly interesting example application. Moreover, optimization in dairy farms could also be focused on optimizing supply-demand flows. This makes the decision space, from cow to retailer elaborate and complex.

The relation of these two applications in the Logistics domain to the requirements of prescriptive analytics is shown in Table V.

TABLE V. APPLICATIONS IN LOGISTICS IN RELATION TO THE REQUIREMENTS OF PRESCRIPTIVE ANALYTICS
(green is requirement met, orange is neutral and red is requirement not met)

	Impact	Complexity	Objective	Constraints	Data
a. Routing on Docks					
b. Dairy farm optimization					

V. CONCLUSION AND FUTURE RESEARCH

It is immediately clear from the applications in the previous section that the low hanging fruit of prescriptive analytics is in those areas with lots of data and in which the phenomena can be described with physics or math. Logistics and oil, gas and offshore are just two examples, but automotive, chemistry and additive manufacturing can also benefit from prescriptive analytics.

The areas which are more challenging are areas in which we do not have the data available or in which we have a gigantic number of possible actions or a large degree of freedom. In these circumstances, models and knowledge can come to aid as these can fill in the gaps of missing data [18]. Human behavior is the most typical example here. Healthcare, Law Enforcement, Human Resource Management, Force Protection, Sustainability; each of them has the promise of major (societal) impact. In terms of algorithms, this means adapting or combining current predictive algorithms, self-learning algorithms and knowledge-driven algorithms to deal with the complexity of a prescriptive analytics problem.

Within a few years Google, Facebook, IBM and other companies will deliver prescriptive algorithms - 'as a service'. Any company can, and will, move towards a more data-driven approach in decision making. Prescriptive analytics is the Holy Grail in this area; whereas descriptive and predictive algorithms still make you do the thinking, prescriptive algorithms are the first that actually deliver actionable insights. However, although building such algorithms is easy, controlling them and keeping them clear from biases is not. These dynamics are complicated to grasp and require extensive knowledge from both self-learning algorithms and the application area.

Finally, privacy, ethics and legislation are important issues in some of those areas and should not be overlooked. We should not fear a Minority Report; predictions and prescriptions are no forecast, they are just math. We should be careful also to treat them as such. Humans are intrinsically lazy, and will readily comply, even if the prescription is coming from a machine. Hence, machines that are making prescriptions are not that different from autonomous systems, and should therefore be considered equal. If we do not want autonomous weapons, we should also not build prescriptive ones either.

ACKNOWLEDGMENT

We would like to thank the Early Research Program 'Making Sense Of Big Data' of TNO for their financial support.

REFERENCES

[1] A. Banerjee, T. Bandyopadhyay, and P. Acharya. Data analytics: Hyped up aspirations or true potential? [Online]. Available: http://www.vikalpa.com/pdf/articles/2013/04-Perspectives.pdf (2013)

[2] C. Centurion. Prescriptive analytics in healthcare. [Online]. Available: http://www.riverlogic.com/prescriptive-analytics-in-healthcare (2014)

[3] S. Smit, B. van der Vecht, and L. Lebesque, "Predictive mapping of anti-social behaviour," European Journal on Criminal Policy and Research, vol. 21, no. 4, 2015, pp. 509–521.

[4] D. Delen and H. Demirkan, "Data, information and analytics as services," 2013.

[5] M. A. Waller and S. E. Fawcett, "Data science, predictive analytics, and big data: a revolution that will transform supply chain design and management," Journal of Business Logistics, vol. 34, no. 2, 2013, pp. 77–84.

[6] D. E. Kirk, Optimal control theory: an introduction. Courier Corporation, 2012.

[7] M. J. Liberatore and W. Luo, "The analytics movement: Implications for operations research," Interfaces, vol. 40, no. 4, 2010, pp. 313–324.

[8] S. Gupta, L. Saputelli, M. Nikolaou et al., "Applying big data analytics to detect, diagnose, and prevent impending failures in electric submersible pumps," in SPE Annual Technical Conference and Exhibition. Society of Petroleum Engineers, 2016.

[9] R. K. Mobley, An introduction to predictive maintenance. Butterworth-Heinemann, 2002.

[10] S. Smit, A. de Vries, R. van Kleij, and H. van Vliet, "From predictive to prescriptive policing," TNO report, The Hague, 2016.

[11] S. Thammaboosadee, "Big data and big lawyer," TIMES-iCON2016, p. 193.

[12] W. Raghupathi and V. Raghupathi, "An overview of health analytics," J Health Med Informat, vol. 4, no. 132, 2013, p. 2.

[13] S. Koldijk, W. Kraaij, and M. A. Neerincx, "Deriving requirements for pervasive well-being technology from work stress and intervention theory: framework and case study," JMIR mHealth and uHealth, vol. 4, no. 3, 2016.

[14] P. Troy, A. Berg, J. Richards, G. Pellerin, and L. Rosenberg, "A prescriptive analytics project for maximizing healthcare value generation," 2015.

[15] A. G. Dominguez, "'smart ships": Mobile applications, cloud and bigdata on marine traffic for increased safety and optimized costs operations," in Artificial Intelligence, Modelling and Simulation (AIMS), 2014 2nd International Conference on. IEEE, 2014, pp. 303–308.

[16] G. Leopold. Dairy industry asks: Got big data? [Online]. Available: https://www.datanami.com/2014/10/31/dairy-industry-asks-got-big-data/

[17] R. Schrijver, P. Berentsen, R. A. Groeneveld, A. Corporaal, and T. de Koeijer, "Development of nature-oriented dairy farm systems with an optimization model: the case of 'farming for nature' in 'de langstraat', the netherlands," Agrarwirtschaft, vol. 55, no. 5/6, 2006, pp. 280–289.

[18] M. J. Mortenson, N. F. Doherty, and S. Robinson, "Operational research from taylorism to terabytes: A research agenda for the analytics age," European Journal of Operational Research, vol. 241, no. 3, 2015, pp. 583–595.

Statistical Analysis of Aircraft Trajectories: a Functional Data Analysis Approach

Florence Nicol

Université Fédérale de Toulouse
Ecole Nationale de l'Aviation Civile
Toulouse, FRANCE
Email: florence.nicol@enac.fr

***Abstract*—In Functional Data Analysis, the underlying structure of a raw observation is functional and data are assumed to be sample paths from a single stochastic process. When data considered are functional in nature thus infinite-dimensional, like curves or images, the multivariate statistical procedures have to be generalized to the infinite-dimensional case. By approximating random functions by a finite number of random score vectors, the Principal Component Analysis approach appears as a dimension reduction technique and offers a visual tool to assess the dominant modes of variation, pattern of interest, clusters in the data and outlier detection. A functional statistics approach is applied to univariate and multivariate aircraft trajectories.**

Keywords–curve clustering; principal component analysis; functional statistics; air traffic management.

I. INTRODUCTION

In many fields of applied research and engineering, it is natural to work with data samples composed of curves. In air transportation, aircraft trajectories are basically smooth mappings from a bounded time interval to a state space. The dimension of the state space may considerably increase if Quick Access Recorders (QARs) provide a full bunch of flight parameters. Most of the time, aircraft trajectories are observed on a fine grid of time arguments that span the time interval. The size and the dimension of the observed samples are usually important, especially if the flight data recorders are used. Data collected in air transportation thus present some characteristics of big data: complexity, variety and volume. These characteristics are inherent to air traffic and require using specific statistical tools that take into account the diverse and complex nature of data and efficient numerical algorithms.

In Air Traffic Management (ATM), analyzing aircraft trajectories is an important challenge. A huge amount of data is continuously recorded (flight data recorder, maintenance softwares, Radar tracks) and may be used for improving flight, as well as airport safety. For instance, trajectories coming from flight data recorders might help the airlines to identify, measure and monitor the risk of accidents or to take preventive maintenance actions. On airports, landing tracks observations may indicate bad runway or taxiway conditions. Therefore, it is of crucial importance to propose relevant statistical tools for visualizing and clustering such kind of data, but also for exploring variability in aircraft trajectories.

Aircraft trajectories, that are basically mappings defined on a time interval, exhibit high local variability both in amplitude and in dynamics. Because of the huge amount of data, visualizing and analyzing such a sample of entangled trajectories may become difficult. A way of exploring variability is then to identify a small number of dominant modes of variation by adapting a Principal Component Analysis (PCA) approach to the functional framework. Some of these components can help to visualizing how major traffic flows are organized. This approach can also address the aircraft trajectories clustering that is a central question in the design of procedures at take-off and landing. Moreover, identifying atypical trajectories may be of crucial importance in aviation safety. Resulting clusters and outliers may be eventually described relatively to other variables such as wind, temperature, route or aircraft type.

In this study, we will focus on Functional Principal Component Analysis (FPCA) which is a useful tool, providing common functional components explaining the structure of individual trajectories. First, in Section II and III, the state of the art and the general framework for functional data analysis are presented. Next, in Section IV, the PCA approach is generalized to the functional context. The registration problem is then considered when phase variation due to time lags and amplitude variation due to intensity differences are mixed. Finally, in Section V, FPCA is applied to aircraft trajectories that can be viewed as functional data.

II. PREVIOUS RELATED WORKS

Most of the time, aircraft trajectories are observed on a fine grid if time arguments that span the time interval. Data are first sampled then processed using multivariate statistics. While simple, this process will forget anything about the original functional dependency. Most of studies conducted on air traffic statistics make use of the sampled data only as is proposed in [1] and forget all about their functional nature, dropping some extremely valuable information in the process. One of the most salient shortcoming of the discrete samples methods is they do not take into account with the correlation in the data while functional data exhibit a high level of internal structure and intrinsic characteristics (geometry of trajectories). Moreover, as noted in [2], standard methods of multivariate statistics have became inadequate, being plagued by the "curse of dimensionality". In a standard multivariate approach, a PCA is performed on matrix data in which the number of variables may be much more important than the number of individuals. As a result, statistical methods developed for multivariate analysis of random vectors are inoperative and trying to crudely apply traditional statistical algorithms on this kind of data may induce some severe numerical instabilities.

The quite recent field of functional statistics [2] [3] provides a more adequate framework for dealing with such data that are assumed to be drawn from a continuous stochastic process taking its value in an Hilbert space. Data are no longer point values but the complete trajectories, all statistical procedure being performed on them. A major asset of working with functional data instead of points is the ease of adding a priori information by carefully selecting the Hilbert space. In air transportation, few studies using the functional framework have been carried out.

In [4], random forest for functional data are used for minimizing the risk of accidents and identifying explanatory factors in the context of aviation safety. This approach is not suitable to visualizing how major traffic flows are organized. In [5] [6], a new approach based on entropy minimization and Lie group modeling is presented, in which the geometry of trajectories are taken into account to cluster the traffic in groups of similar trajectories. Although this approach deals with the aircraft trajectories clustering, the objective is quite different. Indeed, this metod is intended to be a part of a future automated trajectory planner. Given a sample of planned trajectories, the classification algorithm creates clusters such that the mean line of each of them is similar to an airspace route. Geometrical constraints have then to be considered.

In [7], a FPCA was performed on a sample of unidimensional aircraft trajectories, especially trajectory altitudes. This approach generalizes the standard multivariate principal component analysis described in [1] to the functional context. In the following, this approach is extended to the multivariate FPCA (MFPCA), in which we want to study the simultaneous modes of variation of more than one function. Particularly, the simultaneous statistical analysis of the longitude and latitude coordinates may give some insights on the nowadays traffic and then allow to forecast the expected one.

III. Dealing with Random Functions

A. Problem statement

Functional Data analysis (FDA) deals with the study of infinite dimensional objects with a time or spatial structure to be processed, such as curves or images. This point of view differs from standard statistical approaches, the underlying structure of a raw observation being functional. Rather than on a sequence of individual points or finite-dimensional vectors as in a classical approach, we focus on problems raised by the analysis of a sample of functions. Functional data $x_1(t), \ldots, x_n(t)$ are the observations of a sample of n independent and identically distributed random functions $X_1(t), \ldots, X_n(t)$ that are assumed to be drawn from a continuous stochastic process $X=\{X(t),\ t \in J\}$, where J is a compact interval. It makes sense to interpret functional data as n realizations of the stochastic process X, often assumed with values in a Hilbert space $\mathcal{H}$, such as $L^2(J)$, the space of square integrable functions defined on the interval J. The associated inner product for such functions is $\langle x, y\rangle = \int x(t)y(t)dt$ and the most common type of norm, called L^2-norm, is related to the above inner product through the relation $\|x\|^2 = \langle x, x\rangle$. In a functional context, equivalence between norms fails and the choice of semi-metrics is driven by the shape of the functions, as noted in [2]. For instance, semi-metrics based on derivatives suppose that the functions are not too rough.

Let X be a square integrable functional variable with values in the separable Hilbert space $\mathcal{H}$. As noted in [7], we can define a few standard functional characteristics of the random function X, such as the theoretical mean function and the theoretical covariance function, for $s, t \in J$,

$$\mu(t) = \mathbf{E}\left[X(t)\right], \tag{1}$$

$$\sigma(s,t) = \mathbf{E}\left[X(s)X(t)\right] - \mathbf{E}\left[X(s)\right]\mathbf{E}\left[X(t)\right], \tag{2}$$

that play a crucial role in FPCA as we will see in Section IV. In the following, we will assume that X is centered, that is $\mu = 0$, otherwise, subsequent results refer to $X - \mu$. From (1) and (2), we can derive the equivalent empirical characteristics. Note that no notion of probability density exists in the infinite dimensional Hilbert space as mentioned in [8].

B. Trajectories smoothing

Usually, in practice, functional data, such as position and speed measurement, are observed discretely: we only observe a set of function values on a set of arguments that are not necessarily evenly space times or the same for all functions. Some preprocessing of the discretized data has to be made in order to recover the functional statistics setting, especially when observations are noisy. Most procedures developed in FDA are based on the use of interpolation or smoothing methods in order to estimate the functional data from noisy observations [3]. This problem can be solved by representing a trajectory as a linear combination of known basis function expansions such as a Fourier basis, wavelets or spline functions. Functional data are estimated by their projections onto a linear functional space spanned by K known basis functions $\psi_1, \ldots, \psi_K$ such as

$$\widetilde{x}_i(t) = \sum_{k=1}^{K} \theta_{ik}\psi_k(t) = \theta_i^T \psi(t), \tag{3}$$

where the unknown coefficient vectors $\theta_i = (\theta_{i1}, \ldots, \theta_{iK})^T$ have to be estimated from the data and $\psi(t)$ denotes the vector-valued function $(\psi_1(t), \ldots, \psi_K(t))^T$.

Let us consider a set of sampled trajectories $\{(y_{ij}, t_{ij}), i = 1, \ldots, n,\ j = 1, \ldots, N_i\}$ where y_{ij} and t_{ij} are the respective j-th sample position and time on the i-th trajectory. The argument values t_{ij} may be the same for each recorded trajectory or also vary from one trajectory to another one. For simplicity, we will assume that the functional data are observed on the same time grid $t_1, \ldots, t_N$, usually equally spaced. The expansion coefficient vector (θ_i) is the solution of the following least squares minimization problem

$$\min_{\theta_i} \sum_{j=1,\ldots,N} \left[y_{ij} - \theta_i^T \psi(t_j)\right]^2 = \|y_i - \Psi\theta_i\|^2, \tag{4}$$

where y_i is the vector of the observed functional data and Ψ is the $N \times K$ matrix containing the values $\psi_k(t_j)$.

Note that this representation in a truncated basis functions takes into account the functional nature of the data and makes it possible to discretize the infinite dimensional problem by replacing the functional data $x_i(t)$ by its coefficient vector θ_i, $i = 1, \ldots, n$. While a probability density notion on an infinite dimensional Hilbert space cannot be defined [8], the expansion of the curves on a truncated Hilbert basis allows to fit a distribution on the coefficient vectors. Usually, multivariate statistical procedures are next performed on the set of coefficients such as clustering techniques.

The choice of the number K of basis functions depends on the complexity of the curves. The larger is K in the expansion, the better is the fit but we then may capture undesirable noise. If K is too small, we may increase smoothness and some important characteristics of the functions may be vanished. Fixing the dimension of the model is not easy and a major drawback is due to the fact that the degree of smoothing is driven by the discrete choice of the parameter K. We can get better results by using roughly penalty approaches [3].

IV. A Principal Component Approach

Multivariate Principal Component Analysis is a powerful exploratory statistical method which synthesizes the quantity of data information by creating new descriptors in limited number [9] [10]. FPCA was one of the first methods of multivariate analysis that has been generalized to a functional setting. As for the covariance matrix in the multivariate standard case, the covariance function of functional variables are difficult to interpret and FPCA goals to analyze the variability of the functional data around the mean function in an understandable manner. By approximating infinite-dimensional random functions by a finite number of random score vectors, FPCA appears as a dimension reduction technique just as in the multivariate case and cuts down the complexity of the data. For this reason, this approach is commonly used in FDA.

A. *Generalization to the infinite-dimensional case*

Let $X_1, \dots, X_n$ be a sample of independent centered random functions. One wants to find weight functions γ_i that preserve the major variation of the original sample. The criterion is then the sample variance of the projections of the random functions $X_1, \dots, X_n$ into the weight functions, called *principal component functions*. These principal component functions are the solution of the maximizing problem:

$$\max_{\gamma_i \in \mathcal{H}} \frac{1}{n} \sum_{j=1}^{n} \langle X_j, \gamma_i \rangle^2, \tag{5}$$

under the constraint:

$$\langle \gamma_i, \gamma_k \rangle = \delta_{ik},\ k \le i, i = 1, \dots, n. \tag{6}$$

At each step, each principal component function represents the most important mode of variation in the random functions. The orthogonality constraint then provides an orthogonal basis for the linear subspace spanned by the random functions sample.

The solutions are obtained by solving the Fredholm functional eigenequation that can be expressed by means of the sample covariance operator $\widehat{\Gamma}$ induced by the sample covariance function $\widehat{\sigma}$:

$$\widehat{\Gamma}_n v(t) = \int_J \widehat{\sigma}_n(s,t) v(s) ds \tag{7}$$

$$= \frac{1}{n} \sum_{j=1}^{n} \langle X_j, v \rangle X_j(t), \quad v \in \mathcal{H}. \tag{8}$$

such that

$$\widehat{\Gamma} \gamma_i(s) = \lambda_i \gamma_i(s), \quad s \in J. \tag{9}$$

The principal component functions $\gamma_1, \dots, \gamma_n$ are then the eigenfunctions of $\widehat{\Gamma}_n$, ordered by the corresponding eigenvalues $\widehat{\lambda}_1 \ge \widehat{\lambda}_2 \ge \dots \ge \widehat{\lambda}_n \ge 0$. The projections $A_{ij} = \langle \gamma_i, X_j \rangle$, $j = 1, \dots, n$ are random variables, called *principal component scores* of X_j into the γ_i-direction [3]. These scores are centered, uncorrelated random variables accross j with variance equal to λ_i.

Another important property for FPCA involves the best L-term approximation property, meaning that the truncated expansion $\sum_{i=1}^{L} A_{ij} \gamma_i$ is the best approximation of X_j with a given number L of components in the sense of the mean integrated error. Because each functional variable X_j admits the empirical Karhunen-Loève decomposition,

$$X_j(t) = \sum_{i=1}^{n} A_{ij} \gamma_i(t), \quad j = 1 \dots, n, \tag{10}$$

the random scores $A_{ij} = \langle \gamma_i, X_j \rangle$ can be interpreted as proportionality factors that represent strengths of the representation of each individual trajectory by the ith principal component function. Furthermore, FPCA provides eigenfunction estimates that can be interpreted as "modes of variation". These modes have a direct interpretation and are of interest in their own right. They offer a visual tool to assess the main directions in which functional data vary. As in the multivariate case, pairwise scatterplots of one score against another may reveal patterns of interest and clusters in the data. In addition, these plots may also be used to detect outliers and explain individual behavior relatively to modes of variation.

As in the multivariate PCA, we can easily measure the quality of the representation by means of the eigenvalue estimators. The ith eigenvalue estimator $\widehat{\lambda}_i$ measures the variation of the scores into the $\widehat{\gamma}_i$-direction. The percentage of total variation τ_i explained by the ith principal component and the cumulative ratio of variation τ_L^C explained by the first L principal components are then computed from the following ratio

$$\tau_i = \frac{\widehat{\lambda}_i}{\sum_{i=1}^{n} \widehat{\lambda}_i}, \qquad \tau_L^C = \frac{\sum_{k=1}^{L} \widehat{\lambda}_k}{\sum_{i=1}^{n} \widehat{\lambda}_i}. \tag{11}$$

The amount of explained variation will decline on each step and we expect that a small number L of components will be sufficient to account for a large part of variation. Determining a reasonable number L of components is often a crucial issue in functional analysis. Indeed, choosing $L = n$ components may be inadequate and high values of L are associated with high frequency components which represent the sampling noise. A simple and fast method to choose the dimension L is the scree plot that plots the cumulated proportion of variance explained by the first L components against the number of included components L. Alternative procedures to estimate an optimal dimension can be found in [11] and [12].

B. *Estimation*

Several estimation methods of scores and principal component functions were developed for FPCA and asymptotic results was studied in [13]. The earliest method applied to discretized functional data to a fine grid of time arguments is based on numerical integration or quadrature rules [14] [15]. Numerical quadrature schemes can be used to involve a discrete approximation of the functional eigenequation (9)

$$\Sigma_n W \widetilde{\gamma}_m = \widetilde{\lambda}_m \widetilde{\gamma}_m, \tag{12}$$

where $\Sigma_n = (\widehat{\sigma}_n(t_i, t_j))_{i,j=1,\dots,N}$ is the sample covariance matrix evaluated at the quadrature points and W is a diagonal matrix with diagonal values being the quadrature weights. The solutions $\widetilde{\gamma}_m = (\widetilde{\gamma}_m(t_1), \ldots, \widetilde{\gamma}_m(t_N))$ are the eigenvectors associated with the eigenvalues λ_m of the matrix $\Sigma_n W$. The eigenvectors $\widetilde{\gamma}_m$ form an orthonormal system relatively to the metric defined by the weight matrix W. When the weight matrix W is not the identity matrix, an orthonormalization correction is needed using Gramm-Schmidt procedure. We can express the functional eigenequation in an equivalent symmetric eigenvalue problem

$$W^{1/2}\Sigma_n W^{1/2} u_m = \widetilde{\lambda}_m u_m \tag{13}$$

under the constraint:

$$u_l^T u_m = \delta_{lm}, \quad l, m = 1, \ldots, N. \tag{14}$$

where $u_m = W^{1/2}\widetilde{\gamma}_m$. Note that, if the discretization values t_j are closely spaced, the choice of the interpolation method should not have a great effect compared to sampling errors, even if the observations are corrupted by noise [3].

A more sophisticated method is based on expansion of functional data on known basis functions such as a Fourier basis or spline functions as described in Section III. This method takes into account the functional nature of the data and makes it possible to discretize the problem by replacing the functional data $x_i(t)$ by its coefficient vector θ_i, $i = 1, \ldots, n$. The sample covariance function of the projected data

$$\widetilde{\sigma}_n(s,t) = \frac{1}{n}\sum_{i=1}^{n} \widetilde{x}_i(s)\widetilde{x}_i(t) = \psi(s)^T \Theta \psi(t), \tag{15}$$

can be expressed by means of the $K \times K$ matrix $\Theta = \frac{1}{n}\sum_{i=1}^{n} \theta_i \theta_i^T$ which represents the covariance matrix of the coefficient vectors. Consider now the basis expansion of the eigenfunctions $\widetilde{\gamma}_m(s) = b_m^T \psi(s)$ where $b_m = (b_{m1}, \ldots, b_{mK})^T$ is the unknown coefficient vector to be determined. This yields the discretized eigenequation

$$\Theta W b_m = \widetilde{\lambda}_m b_m, \tag{16}$$

where $W = (\langle \psi_i, \psi_j \rangle)_{i,j=1,\ldots,K}$ is the matrix of the inner products $\langle \psi_i, \psi_j \rangle = \int \psi_i(t)\psi_j(t)dt$ of the basis functions. The solutions b_m are then the eigenvectors associated with the eigenvalues λ_m of the matrix ΘW. The orthonormality constraints on the principal components functions satisfy

$$b_l^T W b_m = \delta_{lm}, \quad l, m = 1, \ldots, K. \tag{17}$$

Note that this method looks like the discretization method for which the coefficient vectors $\theta_i = (\theta_{i1}, \ldots, \theta_{iK})^T$ play the role of the discretized functional data. FPCA is then equivalent to a standard multivariate PCA applied to the matrix of coefficients with the metric defined by the inner product matrix $W = (\langle \psi_i, \psi_j \rangle)_{i,j=1,\ldots,K}$.

C. The registration problem

The process of registration, well known in the field of functional data analysis [16] [17] [3], is an important preliminary step before further statistical analysis. Indeed, a serious drawback must be considered when functions are shifted, owing to time lags or general differences in dynamics. Phase variation due to time lags and amplitude variation due to intensity differences are mixed and it may be hard to identify what is due to each kind of variation. This problem due to such mixed variations can hinder even the simplest analysis of trajectories. Firstly, standard statistical tools such as pointwise mean, variance and covariance functions, may not be appropriate. For example, a sample mean function may badly summarize sample functions in the sense that it does not accurately capture typical characteristics. In addition, a FPCA procedure applied to the unregistered curves will produce too many principal components, some of them being not of interest for the analysis of the variability of the curves. In addition, phase variation may influence the shape of the principal component functions that may not be representative of the structure of the curves. Finally, the scores may present a kind of correlation.

A registration method consists in aligning features of a sample of functions by non decreasing monotone transformations of time arguments, often called *warping functions*. These time transformations have to capture phase variation in the original functions and transform the different individual time scales into a common time interval for each function. Generally speaking, a non decreasing smooth mapping $h_i \colon [a,b] \to [c_i, d_i]$, with $[c_i, d_i]$ the original time domain of the trajectory, is used to map each trajectory y_i to a reference trajectory x, usually called *target* or *template function*, already defined on $[a,b]$. In this way, remaining amplitude differences between registered (aligned) trajectories $y_i \circ h_i$ can be analyzed by standard statistical methods. The choice of a template function is sometimes tricky and it may be simply selected among the sample trajectories as a reference with which we want to synchronize all other trajectories. Note that warping functions h_i have to be invertible so that for the same sequence of events, time points on two different scales correspond to each other uniquely. Moreover, we require that these functions are smooth in the sense of being differentiable a certain number of times.

Most of literature deals with two kinds of registration methods: *landmark registration* and *goodness-of-fit based registration* methods. A classical procedure called *marker* or *landmark registration* aims to align curves by identifying locations $t_{i1}, \ldots, t_{iK}$ of certain structural features, such as local minima, maxima or inflexion points, which can be found in each curve [18] [19] [17]. Curves are then aligned by transforming time in such a way that marker events may occur at the same time $t_{01}, \ldots, t_{0K}$, giving $h_i(t_{0k}) = t_{ik}$, $k = 1, \ldots, K$. Complete warping functions h_i are then obtained by smooth monotonic interpolation. While this non-parametric method is able to estimate possibly non-linear warping functions, marker events may be missing in certain curves and feature location estimates can be hard to identify. Finally, phase variation may remain between too widely separated markers. An alternative method is based on goodness-of-fit by minimizing distance between registered trajectories and a template trajectory, with possible inclusion of a roughness penalty for h_i [20] [21]. Note that this latter registration method, as well as landmark registration are implemented in softwares R and Matlab [22] and can be downloaded through the website [23].

V. APPLICATION TO AIRCRAFT TRAJECTORIES

A. The aircraft trajectory dataset

We now apply the previously described FPCA technique to a 161 aircraft trajectory dataset. These data consist of radar tracks from Paris Charles de Gaulle (CDG) to Toulouse Blagnac airports recorded during two weeks. Most of the aircrafts are Airbus A319 (20%), A320 (18%) and A321 (33%), followed by Boeing B733 (15%), B463 (8%) a member of British Aerospace BAe 146 family and AT type (6%). Radar measurements are observed in the range of 4-6960 seconds at 4 seconds intervals. The assumption that all trajectories are

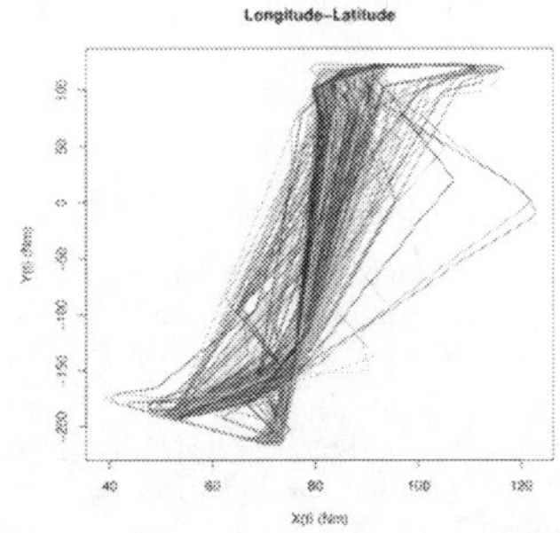

Figure 1. Trajectories from Paris CDG airport to Toulouse airport.

sample paths from a single stochastic process defined on a time interval is clearly not satisfied in the case of aircrafts: departure times are different, even on the same origin-destination pair and the time to destination is related to the aircraft type and the wind experienced along the flight. Without loss of generality, we will assign a common starting time 0 to the first radar measurement of the flights. Trajectories in Figure 1 exhibit high local variability and may be studied by using a FPCA approach. As observed raw data were passed through pre-processing filters, we get radar measurements at a fine grid of time arguments with few noise. We have then used the discretization method described in Section IV.

B. Multivariate FPCA

We now apply the FPCA procedure to multidimensional trajectories. Each trajectory data $f_i(t) = (x_i(t), y_i(t))$, $i = 1, \ldots, n$, collected over time are effectively producing two dimensional functions over the observed intervals $[0, T_i]$. Trajectories have been registered by using the landmarks used in [7] for the univariate altitude trajectories. Figure 2 displays the first four principal components for the latitude and longitude trajectories after the overall mean has been removed from each track. The first component in X and Y-coordinates

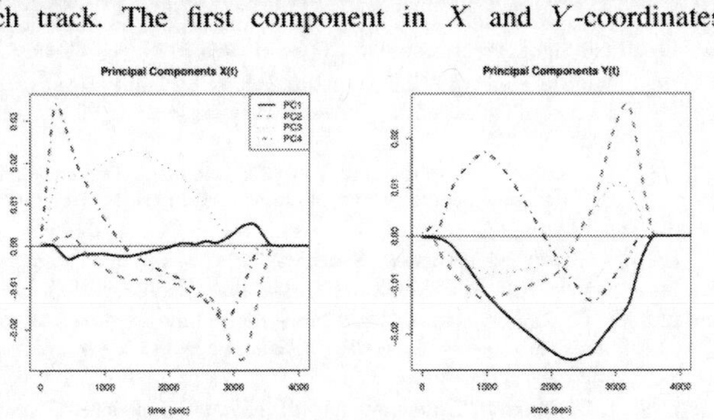

Figure 2. The first four principal component functions for the latitude trajectories $X(t)$ and the longitude trajectories $Y(t)$.

explain 58.7% of total variation whose 98% is due to the longitude trajectories $Y(t)$. We can visualize this effect on the overall mean function in Figure 3 by adding and subtracting a suitable multiple of the first principal component for each coordinate. This component quantifies an overall decrease in longitude that we can call *overall effect* (PC1) between the two different routes from Paris (CDG) to Toulouse airports, more and more important when one moves towards Toulouse airport. Aircrafts with high negative scores would show especially above-average tracks, mainly due to the Y-coordinate. As the

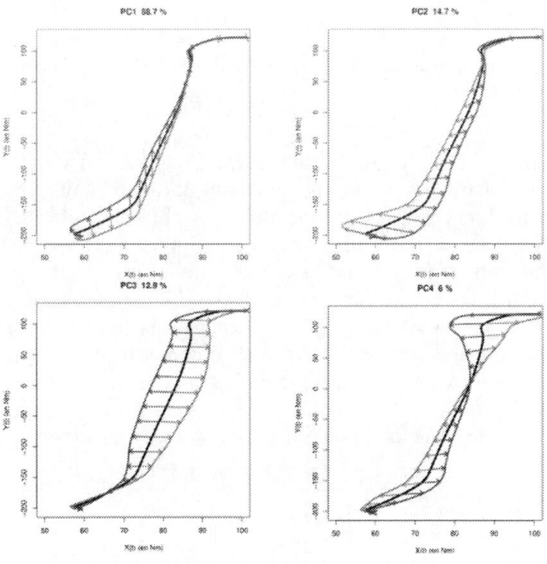

Figure 3. The effects on the mean aircraft trajectory (solid curve) of adding (red curves) and substracting (blue curves) a multiple of each of the first four principal components.

second principal component is orthogonal to the first one, the corresponding mode of variation is less important and accounts for 14.7% of total variation. The contributions of both coordinates are of the same importance, with 48% and 52% of total variation respectively explained by $X(t)$ and $Y(t)$. In Figure 2, we can observe an overall effect due to the $X(t)$ trajectories increasing with time and a distortion in the timing for the $Y(t)$ trajectories. In Figure 3, we can visualize that the closer we get to Toulouse airport, the more aircraft trajectories are separated relatively to the X-coordinate. Moreover, the separation between the arrivals at Toulouse airport are slightly inflated relatively to the Y-coordinate. We call this effect the *landing effect* (PC2). The third component accounts for 12.9% and the main contribution comes from the X-coordinate with 86%. This component depicts an overall effect relatively to the X-coordinate that separates the two routes, immediately after the take-off from Paris CDG airport. We call this effect the *separation effect* (PC3). Finally, the fourth principal component accounting for 6% of the total variation, whose 66% is explained by the X-coordinate, highlights an inversion of route, probably due to a change of take-off procedures at Paris CDG airport or landing procedures at Toulouse airport. We call this effect the *change effect* (PC4).

A k-means clustering is next performed on the score matrix. In Figure 4, we can visualize the mean cluster trajectories for three and five clusters. The first cluster (blue line) contains all aircraft types except the AT type while the third one (red line) is mainly composed of AT type. The mean trajectory of the first cluster displays the overall flight paths from Paris

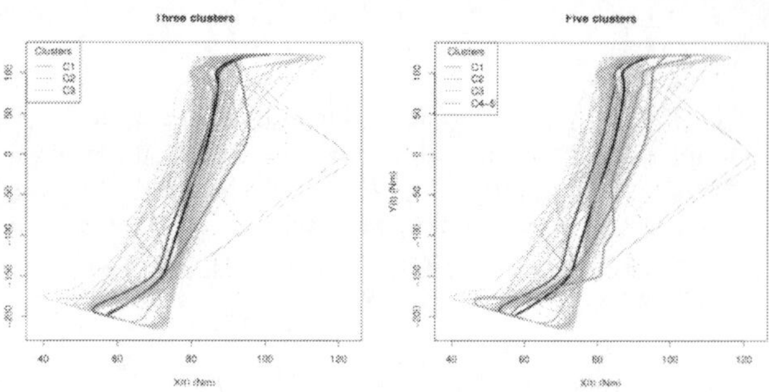

Figure 4. Mean cluster trajectories and the overall mean (black curve).

CDG airport to Toulouse airport. The second cluster (green line) displays a rerouting, probably due to a change in landing procedures at Toulouse airport. This cluster can be interpreted by means of the fourth principal component. The third cluster shows that AT type aircrafts flight along a very specific airway, far from the first two one, and may be explained by the third principal component. When clustering is performed with five clusters, the two last clusters are composed of atypical aircraft trajectories and the first three clusters are more representative.

TABLE I. CONTINGENCY TABLE OF THE COUNTS

Aircraft type	*Cluster 1*	*Cluster 2*	*Cluster 3*
A319	15	18	0
A320	14	14	1
A321	25	28	0
AT	2	0	8
B463	10	0	2
B733	22	1	2

TABLE II. CONTINGENCY TABLE OF THE COUNTS

Aircraft type	*Cluster 1*	*Cluster 2*	*Cluster 3*	*Cluster 4-5*
A319	9	16	0	8
A320	10	13	0	6
A321	18	13	0	6
AT	0	0	8	2
B463	10	0	2	0
B733	17	0	1	6

VI. Conclusion and Future Works

FPCA is a powerful tool to analyze and visualize the main directions in which trajectories vary. We have successfully applied this technique to analyze aircraft trajectories and it can be easily extended to the multivariate case. FPCA has many advantages. By characterizing individual trajectories through an empirical Karhunen-Loève decomposition, FPCA can be used as a dimension reduction technique. Moreover, rather than studying infinite-dimensional functional data, we can focus on a finite-dimensional vector of random scores that can be used into further statistical analysis such as cluster analysis.

The FPCA approach seems promising, as indicated by the results obtained on a real data set. However, the registration problem remains crucial because the assumption that all trajectories are sample paths from a single stochastic process is not satisfied and may be complex in the case of multidimensional aircraft trajectories. In this work, we have used a landmark registration technique. In future works, we will use more sophisticated procedures such as arclength parametrization. Moreover, we should add heading and velocity information by combining functional data and vector of data, inducing an extra level of complexity.

References

[1] A. Eckstein, "Data driven modeling for the simulation of converging runway operations," in Proceedings of the 4th International Conference on Research in Air Transportation (ICRAT) June 1–4, 2010, Budapest, Hungary, Jun. 2010, URL: http://www.icrat.org/.

[2] F. Ferraty and P. Vieu, Nonparametric Functional Data Analysis: Theory and Practice, ser. Springer Series in Statistics. Springer, 2006.

[3] J. O. Ramsay and B. Silverman, Functional Data Analysis, ser. Springer Series in Statistics. Springer, 2005.

[4] B. Gregorutti, B. Michel, and P. Saint-Pierre, "Grouped variable importance with random forests and application to multiple functional data analysis," Computational Statistics and Data Analysis, vol. 90, 2015, pp. 15 – 35.

[5] S. Puechmorel and F. Nicol, "Entropy Minimizing Curves with Application to Flight Path Design and Clustering," Entropy, vol. 18, no. 9, 2016, pp. 337–352.

[6] F. Nicol and S. Puechmorel, "Unsupervised curves clustering by minimizing entropy: implementation and application to air traffic," International Journal on Advances in Software, vol. 9, no. 3-4, 2016, pp. 260–271.

[7] F. Nicol, "Functional principal component analysis of aircraft trajectories," in 2nd International Conference on Interdisciplinary Science for Innovative Air Traffic Management (ISIATM) July 8–10, 2013, Toulouse, France, Jul. 2013, http://isiatm.enac.fr/.

[8] A. Delaigle and P. Hall, "Defining probability density for a distribution of random functions," The Annals of Statistics, vol. 38, no. 2, 2010, pp. 1171–1193.

[9] K. Pearson, "On lines and planes of closest fit to systems of points in space," Philosophical Magazine, vol. 2, no. 6, 1901, pp. 559–572.

[10] H. Hotelling, "Analysis of a complex of statistical variables into principal components," J. Educ. Psych., vol. 24, 1933, pp. 498–520.

[11] A. Kneip, "Nonparametric estimation of common regressors for similar curve data," Ann. Statist., no. 3, 09, pp. 1386–1427.

[12] P. Besse, "Pca stability and choice of dimensionality," Statistics and Probability Letters, vol. 13, no. 5, 1992, pp. 405 – 410.

[13] J. Dauxois, A. Pousse, and Y. Romain, "Asymptotic theory for the principal component analysis of a vector random function: Some applications to statistical inference," Journal of Multivariate Analysis, vol. 12, no. 1, 1982, pp. 136 – 154.

[14] C. R. Rao, "Some statistical methods for comparison of growth curves," Biometrics, vol. 14, no. 1, 1958, pp. 1–17.

[15] L. R. Tucker, "Determination of parameters of a functional relation by factor analysis," Psychometrika, vol. 23, no. 1, 1958, pp. 19–23.

[16] H. Sakoe and S. Chiba, "Dynamic programming algorithm optimization for spoken word recognition," IEEE Transactions on Acoustics, Speech, and Signal Processing, vol. 26, no. 1, Feb 1978, pp. 43–49.

[17] T. Gasser and A. Kneip, "Searching for structure in curve sample," Journal of the American Statistical Association, vol. 90, no. 432, 1995, pp. 1179–1188.

[18] F. Bookstein, Morphometric Tools for Landmark Data: Geometry and Biology, ser. Geometry and Biology. Cambridge University Press, 1997.

[19] A. Kneip and T. Gasser, "Statistical tools to analyze data representing a sample of curves," Ann. Statist., vol. 20, no. 3, 09 1992, pp. 1266–1305.

[20] J. O. Ramsay and X. Li, "Curve registration," Journal of the Royal Statistical Society: Series B (Statistical Methodology), vol. 60, no. 2, 1998, pp. 351–363.

[21] J. O. Ramsay, "Estimating smooth monotone functions," Journal of the Royal Statistical Society: Series B (Statistical Methodology), vol. 60, no. 2, 1998, pp. 365–375.

[22] J. O. Ramsay, G. Hooker, and S. Graves, Functional data analysis with R and Matlab, ser. Springer Series in Statistics. Springer, 2009.

[23] "Functional Data Analysis," URL: http://www.functionaldata.org/.

Analyzing Characteristics of Picture Books based on an Infant's Developmental Reactions in Reviews on Picture Books

Mizuho Baba
Graduate School of Systems and Information Engineering, University of Tsukuba
Tsukuba, 305-8573, JAPAN
e-mail: s1520811@u.tsukuba.ac.jp

Hiroshi Uehara
Graduate School of Systems and Information Engineering, University of Tsukuba
Tsukuba, 305-8573, JAPAN
e-mail: s1430193@u.tsukuba.ac.jp
Faculty of Systems Science and Technology, Akita Prefectural University
Yurihonjo, 015-0055, JAPAN

Miho Kasamatsu
Faculty of Engineering, Information and Systems, University of Tsukuba
Tsukuba, 305-8573, JAPAN
e-mail: s1311099@u.tsukuba.ac.jp

Takehito Utsuro
Chen Zhao
Graduate School of Systems and Information Engineering, University of Tsukuba
Tsukuba, 305-8573, JAPAN
e-mail: {utsuro.takehito.ge, s1630190}@ u.tsukuba.ac.jp

Abstract—**Parents or child-care personnel generally read aloud to an infant, when infants who are not able to read characters read a picture book. Infants are able to perceive the contents of the book by listening to the voice and watching the pictures. Therefore, reviews for picture books have different characteristics than general book reviews. There are descriptions of an infant's reactions as well as descriptions of reviewer's impressions in reviews. We focus on descriptions of an infant's reactions, and analyze those extracted from reviews. Especially, in this paper, we study the relation between the contents of picture books and an infant's developmental reactions. More specifically, we select six typical expressions representing an infant's developmental reactions. Then, we analyze characteristics of picture books which have sufficiently high frequency of those six expressions representing an infant's developmental reactions. Moreover, we further examine which characteristics of each picture book actually contribute to letting infants show developmental reactions.**

Keywords–picture books; review analysis; clustering; developmental reaction

I. INTRODUCTION

Educational books generally focus on a specific subject to be learned such as science and sociology. Picture books are, on the other hand, exceptional because they are efficient in infants' cognitive developments [1], having no intention on specific educational subject with their style of expressions, i.e., funny stories and pictures. Furthermore, readers of picture books are parents or child care personnel who make the book talk for infants who do not have sufficient literacy yet. Infants perceive and interpret incoming stimuli of the book talks and the pictures. Thus, considering such a situation, picture books are outstanding compared to other educational books, in that those who read them are separated from those who perceive them.

It is known in the research in the developmental psychology that infants express a variety of cognitive reactions to the external stimuli in accordance with their developmental stage. Supposing that picture books work as those kinds of stimuli, it is also expected that infants might express the cognitive reactions when the stimuli of picture books are perceived. Further considering that infants are free from understanding the printed letters of picture books, this tendency might be amplified to some extent.

In order to examine how the stimuli of picture books induces a variety of reactions in infants, we take an approach of applying a text mining technique to a large amount of the reviews on picture books written by their parents or the childcare personnel. Reviews for picture books have different characteristics compared to general book reviews. There are descriptions of an infant's reactions as well as descriptions of reviewers' impressions in reviews. We focus on descriptions of an infant's reactions, and analyze those ones extracted from reviews. Especially, in this paper, we study the relation between the contents of picture books and an infant's developmental reactions. More specifically, we select six types of expressions representing an infant's developmental reactions. Then, we classify picture books according to the frequency distribution of those types of expressions representing an infant's developmental reactions.

The results of the classification show there exist picture books drawing active children's reactions and those that are not. These facts imply picture book drawing active reactions might have some advantageous factors in their directions. We compare picture books drawing active reactions and those that are not so as to specify the factors affecting the degree of children's reactions.

Section II introduces the source Web site of the reviews on picture books we utilize in this paper. Section III describes infants' reactions to picture books we examine in this paper. Section IV describes how we select those picture books we analyze in this paper. Section V analyzes the characteristics

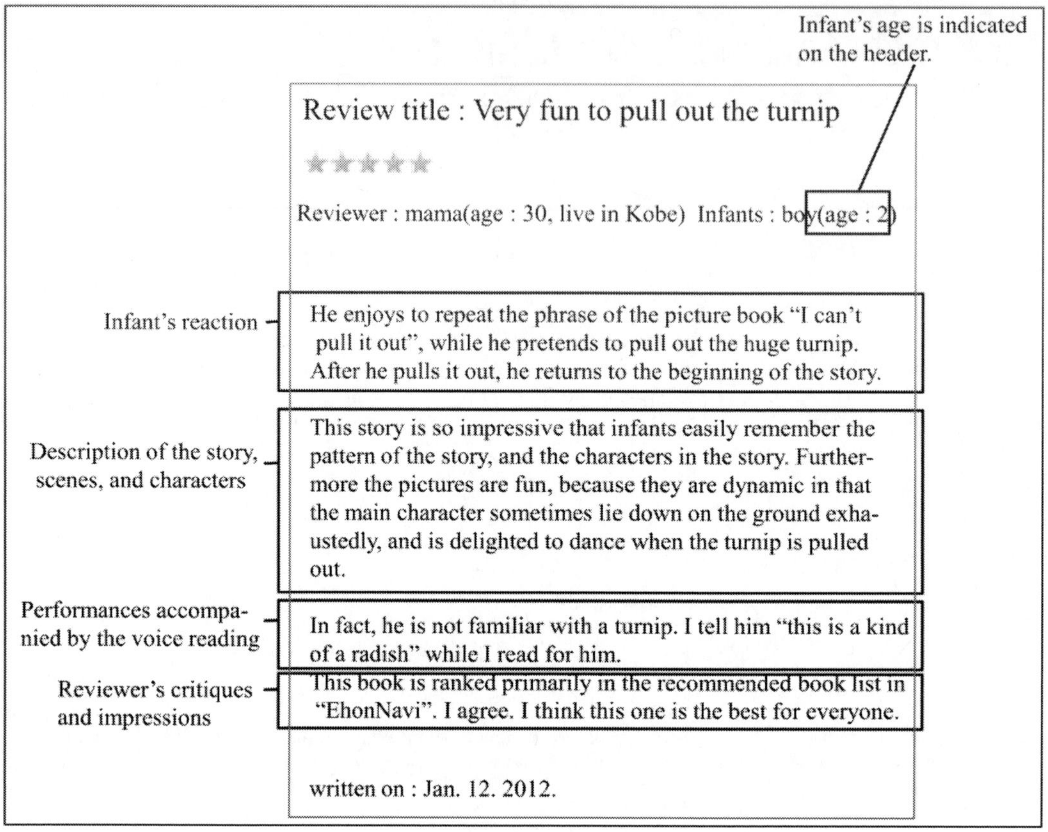

Figure 1. An Example of a Review of "The Giant Turnip"

of those picture books and finally Section VI concludes the paper.

II. The Web Site specialized in Picture Books

To analyze the infants' reactions, text data of reviews on picture books are collected from EhonNavi [2], a Web site specialized in picture books. EhonNavi provides information concerning picture books such as publishers, authors, outlines as well as a large amount of reviews written by the parents or child care personnel, where the numbers of the titles of the picture books included in EhonNavi amount to about 65,400. The number of the reviews amount to approximately 330,000 as of September 2016 (shown in Table I). Other than EhonNavi, popular Web sites with a large amount of book reviews include Amazon [3] and Booklog [4]. Out of them, EhonNavi has a unique characteristic in that its reviews tend to be elaborated, reflecting the reactions of those who make the books talk, as well as those who perceive them. Additionally, it is also the EhonNavi's characteristic that the age of the infant is attached to each review. All these characteristics are preferable for our work aiming at detecting the infants' reactions in accordance with their developmental stages. Therefore, we employ the reviews on EhonNavi for the analysis of this paper.

Figure shows an example of a review of EhonNavi. As shown in the figure, the header of each review includes the age of the infant to whom the reviewer reads the picture book. As described above, reviews on EhonNavi include descriptions of book readers' reactions, mixed with infants' reactions. Since reviewers are book readers in all the cases, infants' reactions described in reviews are those observed by reviewers.

III. Infants' Reactions Detected in Reviews on Picture Books

According to the theory of developmental psychology, infants express age specific reactions to incoming stimuli. We collect such infants' reactions that are specific to ages ranging from 0 to 3 from publications or papers concerning developmental psychology [5]–[8] and list them in Table II. In this table, we list those six types of reactions in the order from those observed in the early age 0 to those observed in the later age 3. This result indicates that infants at their very early age tend to react automatically with their physical expression, such as pointing the fingers, or grasping gestures, meanwhile, those at their later ages tend to react consecutively expressing their intention, such as game of make-believe, or asking why, though some reactions are common over multiple ages.

Then, in order to collect typical expressions representing each of the six types of infants' reactions listed in Table II, we randomly picked 345 reviews from 16 titles of picture books. We manually examine those randomly picked 345 reviews and

TABLE I. OVERVIEW OF EHONNAVI

(a) Principal Information

start date of the service	number of titles	number of unique users per month	number of members	number of reviews
Apr. 2002	65,400	1,100,000	420,000	332,000

(b) Distribution of the Numbers of Reviews according to Infants' Age

age of infants	0	1	2	3	4	5
number of reviews	7,820	14,802	24,794	29,538	26,123	21,585

collect typical expressions representing each of the six types of infants' reactions [9], [10]. In order to detect an infant's developmental reactions in reviews on picture books, Uehara et al. [9], [10] previously studied 10 expressions representing an infant's developmental reactions with frequency. Out of those 10 expressions, we focus on those that are more frequently observed, and allocate them to six types of infant's reactions as in the right hand side column of Table II.

According to the studies in developmental psychology [5]–[8], the infants' reaction *"gaze at / stare hard / listen hard"*, *"point fingers"*, and *"pretend"* are mostly observed around the age of 1, *"imitate"* around that of 2, *"game of make-believe"* around that of 2 to 3, and *"enter into"* and *empathy* around that of 3.

IV. SELECTING PICTURE BOOKS FOR ANALYSIS

Reviews including six expressions in Table II do not necessarily represent infants' reactions. Some of them represent their parents' reactions. In order to estimate the number of reviews which include six expressions representing infants' reactions only, we apply the following estimating procedure.

Let $f(b, a, e)$ be the frequency of an expression e out of the six expressions, in a title b and for an age a. Let $f_s(b, a, e)$ be the number of samples randomly selected from the reviews belonging to each $f(b, a, e)$. The maximum value of $f_s(b, a, e)$ is set to be 10. Out of them we manually count the number of reviews representing infants' reactions. Let $f_{sc}(b, a, e)$ be this number. Under these assumptions above, the estimated number of infants' reactions, $f_c(b, a, e)$ is expressed as the following formula.

$$f_c(b, a, e) = \frac{f_{sc}(b, a, e)}{f_s(b, a, e)} \times f(b, a, e)$$

We set a threshold on the outcome of the formula above to distinguish the picture books drawing active infants' reactions from the ones that are not. If applying formula above to any of six expressions belonging to a picture book results in the value ≥ 10, the threshold, the picture book is recognized as the one drawing active reactions. And those picture books fulfilling this condition are classified into the set $B_{\geq 10}$ as follows.

$$B_{\geq 10} = \left\{ b \,\middle|\, \sum_{a,e} f_c(b, a, e) \geq 10 \right\}$$

Meanwhile, picture books not fulfilling this condition are classified into the set $B_{<10}$ as follows.

$$B_{<10} = \left\{ b \,\middle|\, \sum_{a,e} f_c(b, a, e) < 10 \right\}$$

We rank picture books in descending order of the number of reviews and select the topmost 100 titles, where the total number of the reviews of those 100 titles amount to around 27,000 (as of December 2014). Out of them, we found 45 titles fulfill the condition of the set $B_{\geq 10}$. 22 titles are internationally published, and these are the ones for our analysis. Meanwhile, we found 19 titles belonging to the set $B_{<10}$. 6 titles are the ones for our analysis which are also internationally published.

V. ANALYZING CHARACTERISTICS OF PICTURE BOOKS

We found each picture book belonging to either set $B_{\geq 10}$ or $B_{<10}$ above, shows different distribution patterns of frequency of the expressions described in Table II. We classify picture books based on the distribution patterns, then make comparison between the picture books belonging to set $B_{\geq 10}$ and the ones belonging to set $B_{<10}$ both of which are in the same characteristics of developmental reaction in Table II. By this comparison, we try to specify the factors contributing to the contrast in children's reactions,

A. Representation of Picture Books

Table III shows two examples of picture books both of which belong to set $B_{\geq 10}$. Both of the expressions, *"enter into"* and *"empathy"* form one category, because they represent the same developmental reaction as mentioned in Table II. The distribution pattern of two examples shows obvious difference. Apparently infants' reactions concentrate on *"pointing fingers"* in the case of Table III(a). Meanwhile, Table III(b) shows diversities in expressions. In order to specify an infant's expressions of each picture book, we set the threshold as below.

<u>Threshold for specifying an infant's expressions:</u>

The expressions with frequencies over 60 % of the number of most frequent expressions.

Taking Table III(b) as an example, the most frequent reaction is *"pointing fingers"*. Frequencies of both of reactions *"gaze at"* and *"imitate"* are over 60% of the number of *"pointing fingers"*, while frequencies of both of *"pretend"* and *"game of make-believe"* are under the value. Then, an infant's expressions are *"pointing fingers"*, *"gaze at"*, and *"imitate"*.

Meanwhile in the case of the picture books belonging to set $B_{<10}$, only the most frequent expression are used as an infant's expression.

B. Classifying Picture Books based on an Infant's Developmental Reactions in Reviews on Picture Books

Table IV shows the result of the classification based on an infant's expressions defined as above. Picture books with

TABLE II. INFANTS' REACTIONS BASED ON THE THEORY OF DEVELOPMENTAL PSYCHOLOGY AND TYPICAL EXPRESSIONS

characteristics of developmental reactions	explanations and examples	typical expressions	
		ID	expression
reactions to visual stimuli	Showing an interest in the pictures especially the ones of foods. / Enjoy to find something in the pictures that are familiar to the infants.	1.	gaze at / stare hard / listen hard
physical expressions mixed with verbal expressions	pointing fingers and making gestures in the case the infants are not able to express verbally. / Reaching for the things on the picture book as if they were the real things.	2.	pointing fingers
pretend play	An example: If the infant is asked to hand something to his or her parents, he or she pretends to hand it to them even though it does not exist.	3.	pretend
imitate	Imitating various things such as the persons, things, and the events surrounding the infant.	4.	imitate
game of make-believe	Reproducing the story of the picture book based on such activities that the infant imagines himself/herself to be in the place in the picture book.	5.	game of make-believe
empathy for the story	Emotionally being involved in the world depicted by the picture book. / An example: "If I could enter into the picture book, I would save the cat."	6.	enter into or empathy

TABLE III. REPRESENTATION OF PICTURE BOOKS

(a) Where's the Fish ?

age	gaze at	pointing fingers	pretend	imitate	game of make-believe	enter into + empathy	total
0	2	4	0	0	0	0	0
1	6	81	1	2	0	0	1
2	1	31.5	0	1	0	0	0
3	1	12	1	0	0	0	0
4	0	8.4	0	0	0	0	0
5	1	8.4	0	0	0	0	0
over 6	1	12	0	0	0	0	0
Total	11	148.9	2	3	0	0	1

(b) The Very Hungry Caterpillar

age	gaze at	pointing fingers	pretend	imitate	game of make-believe	enter into + empathy	total
0	**9.9**	1	0	0	0	0	10.9
1	4	**12**	0	4	0	0	20
2	2	6	2	**8**	1	0	19
3	2	2	0	1	1	0	6
4	0	1	0	1	0	0	2
5	0	0	1	4	0	2	7
over 6	1	1	0	1	0	0	3
total	18.9	23	2	15	2	0	60.9

multiple infant's expressions belonging to set $B_{\geq 10}$ are classified into multiple categories. In such a case, the titles are attached with hyphenated number, as in the column "Picture Books Effective for the Reactions".

Additionally, we make sub-categories under each expression as the column "The Intentions of Reactions" by manually interpreting contexts surrounding the expressions in the reviews. Followings are the explanations of each sub-category.

(a) *"gaze at"*

- onomatopoeia or simple illustration ··· Infants are interested in Onomatopoeia or simple illustration.
- gazing at faces ··· Infants are interested in faces on the picture books.
- colorful illustration ··· Infants are interested in colorful illustrations.

(b) *"pointing fingers"*

- exploration ··· Infants explore something by pointing fingers.
- finding correspondence ··· Infants detect correspondence between narrations and the illustrations.
- selecting preference ··· Infants point to their preference out from various kinds of illustrations.

(c) *"imitate"*

- imitating to eat ··· Infants imitate to eat printed foods on the picture books.
- imitating character's actions ··· Infants imitate characters performance on the picture books.

(d) *"game of make-believe"*

- reproduction of the story ··· Infants reproduce the story after he/she listened to picture book readings.

(e) *"enter into, empathy"*

- care about character's situation ··· Infants express their empathy for the characters' painful situations.

"Ages" on the 3rd column represents the range of ages at which the frequency of each expression exceed 10, the threshold introduced in the previous section. The last column "Picture Books Ineffective for the Reactions" in Table IV are allocated ones from set $B_{<10}$ which evoke weak reactions. If there is no such picture book at all, the space is left blank.

TABLE IV. CLASSIFICATION BASED ON INFANTS' DEVELOPMENTAL REACTIONS

an infant's reaction	intentions of re-action	ages	picture books effective for the reactions	picture books ineffective for the reactions
gaze at	onomatopoeia or simple illustra-tion	0~1	Chug-chug Train-1	
	gazing at faces	0~1	Smiley face-1 Peek-a-boo	Playing Peek-a-Boo
	colorful illustra-tion	0~1	Little Blue and Little Yellow Good Evening Dear Moon-1 Won't Go to Bed?-1 Very Hungry Caterpillar-1	
	others	0~1	The family of Fourteen Fix Breakfast-1	
pointing fingers	exploration	1~2	Quin and Peep Play Hide and Seek Where's the Fish? Who Ate it? Miki's First Errand-1	
	finding correspon-dence	1~2	Goodnight moon Where the Wild Things Are-1 Chug-chug Train-2 Very Hungry Caterpillar-2	Little Gorilla
	selecting preference	2	The family of Fourteen Fix Breakfast-2	The Blue Seed
imitate	imitating to eat	1~3	Smiley Face-2 Strawberries Guri and Gura Very Hungry Caterpillar-3	Guest of Guri and Gura Ghost Tempura
	imitating character's actions	1~2	Won't go to Bed?-2	
	others	1~3	The family of Fourteen Fix Breakfast-3 Good Evening Dear Moon-2 Blackie, the Crayon-1 The Magic Grove-1	
game of make-believe	reproduction of the story	2~4	The Gigantic Turnip The Magic Grove-2 The Three Billy Goats Gruff	I love to Take a Bath
	others	2~4	Blackie, the Crayon-2 Chug-chug Train-3 Won't go to Bed?-3	
enter into empathy	care about charac-ter's situation	2~	Finding Little Sister Amy and Ken Visit Grandma Miki's First Errand-2	
	others	2~	Where the Wild Things Are-2 Blackie, the Crayon-2	

C. *Characteristics of Picture Books with Frequent Developmental Reactions of Infants*

The fact that there are picture books in each sub-category in Table IV indicates that there exist types of picture books effective for infants' reactions and types that are not so effective. We compare effective picture books and ineffective ones by each sub-category in Table IV to specify the features which might realize the gap of infants' reactions. The comparison is limited to the sub-categories for which the column space "Picture Books Ineffective for the Reactions" is not blank. Followings are the results.

1) gazing at faces:
   Effective picture books have a very simple style. For example, they contain scenes with repetitive peek-a-boo gestures. Meanwhile, an example of ineffective picture book has a pop-up that might draw the infants' attentions on the pop-ups themselves. That is, the infants' interests on the peek-a-boo might be interrupted by the pop-ups.
2) finding correspondence:
   Picture books effective for this reaction tend to illustrate objects with the straight forward styles, and corresponding texts appear with large and clear fonts. These styles might make it easier for infants to be aware of correspondence between illustration and the texts.
3) selecting preference:
   In the case of effective picture books, a variety of characters and their actions seem to draw the infants' attention, thereby encouraging them to express their preference by pointing fingers. Ineffective picture books tend to use the same characters and conventional actions throughout the story.
4) imitating to eat:
   Picture books effective for this reaction are a kind of food entertainment.Taking *Guri and Gura* as an example, scene of baking sponge cake are effective for raising infants' expectations for eating. Also,next scene of sharing sponge cake among lots of animals depict deliciousness of sponge cake. Picture books

not effective for this reaction do not have any kind of entertainment.

5) reproduction of the story:
Effective picture books in this sub-category comprise of scenes with repetitive rhythmical narration. This simple rhythm seems to help infants understanding stories impressively. On the contrary, ineffective picture books have been found to be composed of changing narrations with each scene without any rhythm.

VI. Conclusion

In this research, we classify picture books based on the types of infants' developmental reactions and try to specify the factors contributing to each active reaction. Analysis implies that infants' reactions vary depending on various features of picture books, such as clarity, rhythm, simplicity etc. Although the research samples are limited, these findings will contribute to constituting picture books so as to purposely draw specific reactions. To establish this knowledge, we will expand our analysis.

References

[1] J. Pardeck, Books for Early Childhood:A Developmental Perspective. Greenwood Pub Group, 1986.

[2] URL: http://www.ehonnavi [accessed: 2017-04-15].

[3] URL: http://www.amazon.co.jp [accessed: 2017-04-15].

[4] URL: http://booklog.jp [accessed: 2017-04-15].

[5] J. Sully, Studies of Childhood. Free Association Books, 2000.

[6] J. Piaget, Play, Dreams, and Imitation in Childhood. WW Norton & Co Inc,, 1962.

[7] A. M. Leslie, "Pretense and representation:the origins of theory of mind," Psychological Review, vol. 94(4), 1987, pp. 412–426.

[8] A. S. Walker-Andrews and R. Kahana-Kalman, "The understanding of pretence across the second year of life," British Journal of Developmental Psychology, vol. 17(4), 1999, pp. 523–546.

[9] H. Uehara, M. Baba, and T. Utsuro, "Detecting an infant's developmental reactions in reviews on picture books," in Proc. 29th PACLIC, 2015, pp. 64–71.

[10] H.Uehara, M. Baba, and T.Utsuro, "Analyzing an Infant's Reactions in Reviews on Picture Books based on Developmental Psychology," International Journal of Signal Processing Systems, vol. 4, no. 4, 2016, pp. 311–317.

A Rule-based Named Entity Extraction Method and Syntactico-Semantic Annotation for Arabic Language

Lhioui Chahira
LaTICE Laboratory
ISI, Sousse University
Medenine, Tunisia
chahira.lhioui@ieee.org

Zouaghi Anis
LaTICE Laboratory
ISSAT, Sousse University
Sousse, Tunisia
anis.zouaghi@gmail.com

Zrigui Mounir
LaTICE Laboratory
FSM, Monastir University
Monastir, Tunisia
mounir.zrigui@fsm.rnu.tn

Abstract— **There is a widely held belief in the natural language processing (NLP) and computational linguistics communities that knowledge recognition such us Named Entities (NE) recognition is a significant step toward improving important applications, e.g., question answering and natural language understanding (NLU). In this paper, we present an NE recognition system for Modern Standard Arabic using the NooJ platform. This system exploits many aspects of the rich morphological features of the language. The experiments on the pilot Arabic Propbank data show that our system based on linguistic rules produces a global NE recognition F-measure score of 87%, which improves the current state of the art in Arabic NE recognition.**

Keywords- Named Entity Extraction; Semantic annotation; NooJ platform.

I. Introduction

The extraction and automatic recognition of named entities (NE) is a part of a syntactico-semantic analysis, which is a step that follows the morpho-lexical analysis during the automatic processing of a text or a corpus. This extraction consists in exhibiting certain grammatical concepts or syntactic structures, checking their validity and attesting their belonging to particular grammatical classes such as "proper names", "temporal expressions", "numerical expressions", "abbreviations" , etc.

From the beginning, the implementation of the lexicographical solution, subsisting of electronic dictionaries enumerating all the named entities, has proven to be impossible. In particular, this is due to the problems of multiple writing and the lack of standard writing or transcription of NE, especially those of foreign origin, to the target language. Indeed, it is impossible to enumerate all the proper names in lists, as well as to collect and to maintain them. It is also impossible to treat all spelling variants and to resolve the resulting ambiguity.

Three fundamental approaches have been used for the extraction of NE issue in literature. These approaches are: rule-based approach, learning-based approach and hybrid approach. However, the most commonly used methods for NE recognition are often machine learning-based methods. In the last two decades, rule-based methods for NER (Named Entity Recognition) have progressively been abandoned. Nevertheless, these methods are robust and their results are accurate. They are generally based on non-contextual grammars. Thus, our major concern in this study is to examine a rule-based NE extraction and syntactico-semantic annotation of such important knowledge. For this purpose, we use the non-contextual grammars offered in the NooJ language development platform [10] where they are called local grammars that are used to locate in a very precise way local phenomena very precisely in texts, such as dates, numerical determinants, proper names, names of places and organisms, etc. These grammars are lexicalized graphs [10], which use dictionaries of simple and compound words. They are equivalent to recursive networks of transitions (RTN) or even networks of increased transitions (ATNs). In practical, local grammars are graphs that can call independent sub-graphs. Among the advantages of such a structure are the effectiveness of its direct application to texts, the recognition of complex linguistic concepts as well as transformational analysis and annotations production.

The choice of NooJ platform is guided by the fact that NooJ is a freely available linguistic development environment for many languages [1]. It allows developers to construct, test and maintain large coverage lexical resources as well as to apply morphological morpho-syntactic tools for Arabic processing [1]. NooJ can recognize rules written in finite-state form or context-free grammar form, facilitating the development of rule-based NER systems. Nooj provides a disambiguation technique based on grammars to resolve duplicate annotations [1]. Arabic is one of the languages that are supported by NooJ; there are free Arabic resources for use within the NooJ environment on the NooJ official Web site [1]. Mesfar [5] and Lhioui [3][15] have also used NooJ in their Arabic NER research..

In this paper, we suggest a Named Entities extraction system for Modern Standard Arabic (MSA) that exploits many aspects of the rich morphological features of the language. It is based on a linguistic approach that uses NooJ technology for the detection of such knowledge. Given the lack of a reliable electronic Arabic dictionaries, and thanks to their coverage, our strategy uses the EL-DicAr dictionary [2] developed by the NooJ platform and its extension developed in [3] for the step of morphological analysis.

In this article, we begin by presenting some of the existing work on Arabic NE extraction. Then, we describe the difficulties inherent in the recognition of NE. After that, we explain with more details our preconized approach. Finally, we check and evaluate our proposed approach.

This paper is laid out as follows: Section 2 presents the definition of named entity concept and its categorizations; Section 3 outlines different approaches that treat this problematic and some related works; Section 4 reveals some difficulties that inhibit the extraction of NE in texts written in Arabic language; Section 5 describes and argue the approach and system adopted for this work; Section 6 gives the experimental setup, results and discussion. Finally, Section 7 draws our conclusions.

II. THE NAMED ENTITY CONCEPT DEFINITION AND CATEGORIZATIONS

The extraction of NE is one of the most popular areas in recent years. According to MUC (Message Understanding Conference) [4], we distinguish at least three types of entities to be recognized and classified by category [2][3]:

- ENAMEX: This class groups the proper names. Indeed, proper names are very common in electronic texts, especially journalistic articles. However, in spite of the frequency of their appearances and the importance of the information they encapsulate in particular for the semantic interpretation of the texts, the proper names remain inadequately illustrated in the electronic lexical resources and their automatic extraction is just only a relatively young field. This class contains at least three subcategories:
    - Person: Names of persons such as names of politicians, poets, athletes, etc.
    - Organization: refers to the names of companies, banks, associations, universities, research centers, pharmacies, clinics, etc.
    - Event: such as sporting events, political events, war and crime event, etc.
- NUMEX: This class groups numeric expressions of percentages, size, currency expressions, etc.
- TIMEX: This class refers to temporal expressions of date or duration.

III. RELATED WORK

Numerous studies have been conducted on the Latin languages as well as the Arabic language to automatically extract knowledge. Looking over the state of the art, we have found that there are three main types of extraction systems of named entities. These systems are based on three types of approaches, which are, respectively:

- Rule-based approach: Most systems use this approach. Typical rule-based systems use both internal and external evidence, as well as word-trigger dictionaries for locating help. The rules are manually built by an expert linguist. The advantages of such approach are principally the accuracy, the robustness and the coverage of the obtained results. In brief, this kind of approach is has been well appreciated so far in literature [3][5]-[7].
- Learning approach: Systems based on this approach use stochastic techniques and learn specific knowledge on a large learning corpus where target NEs are labeled. Learning algorithms are then applied automatically to develop a NE base using several statistical models (such as Hidden Markov Model (HMM), Support Vector Machine (SVM), Conditional Random Fields (CRF), etc.) [8][9]. Nevertheless, this approach requires a huge amount of learning data for its learning algorithm, which is quasi-absent for some scientific research neglected languages, such as Arabic [1].
- Hybrid approach: This approach combines the two above-mentioned approaches for their complementarity. This approach leads to systems based on the use of both manually-written and rules that are constructed automatically using syntactic and contextual information derived from training data to learning algorithms and decision trees [11][12].

The adequacy of rule-based systems was recognized at the MUC conference. It is this same technique that we advocate for the development of a recognition component of named entities. This component is based on rules written by hand and represented in the form of local grammars that are constructed using the syntactic module of NooJ. These rules were based on internal and external evidence in order to identify and categorize named entities where:

- Internal evidence: is provided by the constituents of the named entity. The constituents can be contained in lists of triggering words or proper names called gazetteers.
- External evidence: is provided by the context in which, a named entity appears. They are based on the syntactic relations within a sentence to assign the category of such an entity. This categorization uses the morpho-syntactic information provided by the previous morphological analysis stage.

The use of this evidence is indispensable because of the absence of obvious indications to detect the presence of a proper name, such as the presence of capital letters at the beginning of such names in the Romance languages. This imposes a rather thorough understanding of the morphological nature of each form of the text, particularly its grammatical categories and semantic information (e.g., + Person, + Country, + Housing, + Money, etc.).

IV. ISSUES IN NAMED ENTITY RECOGNITION

According to the state of the art overfished by [3][5] [13], the recognition of the TIMEX and NUMEX in Arabic poses no problem, this can be challenging in the case of the ENAMEX. This can be explained by the lack of structural or contextual indices. In fact, all temporal and numerical expressions are identifiable by a list of lexical markers (day names, month names, currencies, units of measure, etc.). On the other hand, ENAMEX suffers from a lack of structural or contextual clues to be recognized.

Moreover, in addition to the absence of capital letters as a naïve index for recognition in Latin languages, Arabic ENAMEX requires linguistic information to be dynamically generated by a prior semantic annotation step.

Other problems specific to the recognition of the NE in Arabic arise also in the identification and delimitation as in the semantic annotation of these NE. In what follows, we depict the repercussion of the absence of voyellation and the problem of delimitation of the Arabic NE.

A. *The absence of vowels*

The absence of diacritical marks may affect the recognition systems of named entities. This is mainly due to the semantic ambiguity that arises from the set of potential vocalizations that can be attributed to any partial vowel or unvoiced form. Indeed, vocalizations accepted for any form of text can lead to the absence of diacritical signs and it can affect the recognition systems of named entities. This is mainly traceable to the semantic ambiguity that arises from the set of potential vocalizations that can be attributable to any partial vowel or unvoiced form. Indeed, vocalizations accepted for some form of text can lead to different triggers of NE. For example, the unbounded form معلم (m'llm) can accept, among other things, the two following vocalizations: in different senses the triggers of the NE.

- مُعَلِّمُ (mu'allimu) : Word trigger for a teacher
- مَعْلَمُ (ma.'alamu) : Word trigger for a museum of monuments

This example illustrates the implications of the absence of vowels in the text words on the annotation step of the named entities.

B. *Morphological complexity*

Arabic is a highly-inflected language. It uses an agglutinative strategy to form a word. If NE appears in its agglutinative form, then this poses a difficulty for the identification and hence the recognition of this entity [3]. For example, if we take the simple word بَلْدَتُنَا <baldatunA>, which means "our town", this Arabic word is composed from two sub-words: the lemma بلد <balda> "town" and the suffix تنا <tunA> "our". Hence, it would be difficult and ambiguous in Arabic processing to treat agglutinative words. Many works focus on this phenomenon. However, NooJ gives the possibility to treat agglutination problem by the use of flexional and derivational rules [10]. Hence, the choice of NooJ linguistic tool, in our work, is justified.

V. OUR RULE-BASED METHOD FOR NE RECOGNITION AND SEMANTIC ANNOTATION

To remedy all these problems, we construct a system of recognition and extraction of Arabic entities. According to Figure 1, we proceed:

- A morphological analysis: to collect the maximum information for all the words of the text. This is done with a consultation of the electronic dictionary El-DicAr of [2] and the Arabic touristic dictionary developed by [3].
- Subsequently, this information will be used in local syntactico-semantic grammars in order to locate the relevant sequences.

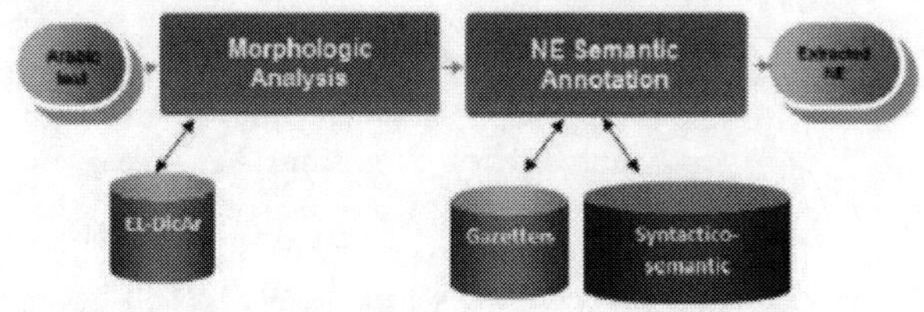

Figure 1. General architecture of the recognition of the Arab NE

A. *Morphological Analysis*

Given the agglutinating structure of the majority of Arabic words, our morphological analyzer makes it possible to separate and identify the morphemes of the input forms and to associate them with the set of information necessary for the current processing. These forms are decomposed to recognize the affixes (conjunctions, prepositions, personal pronouns, etc.) attached to them. These morphological possibilities in NooJ facilitate the identification of triggering words, names of persons or localities even when they are agglutinated.

Each of these forms is associated, by morphological analysis, with a set of linguistic information useful for the next step: lemma, grammatical label, gender and number, syntactic information (+ Transitive), semantic information (+ Person), etc.

Consequently, instead of enumerating all the inflected forms (singular, dual, plural, masculine, feminine) of the occupational names considered as lexical markers of person names (e.g., مهندس <engineer>), we use the syntax of the regular expressions of NooJ where the grammatical symbol مهندس (<mhnds>, <engineer>) refers to all vocalized, partially vocalized, and unvoiced bent forms attached to this lemma. Our morphological analysis is based on two Arabic dictionaries described in table III:

TABLE I. RESOURCES USED IN MORPHOLOGICAL ANALYSIS.

	EL-DicAr [2]	'Touristic Arabic DICtionary [3]
Nouns	19504	8789
Verbs	10162	345
NE	3686 localizations +11860 Proper names	622 500 (Organisations +Localizations+Events)

The two dictionaries are also used and detailed in [16].

B. NE Semantic Annotation

The information provided by morphological analysis is directly used by our recognition system of named entities. In addition to its morpho-syntactic information gathered, this system is based on the use of two types of linguistic resources:

- Gazetteers: these are lexical markers previously recognized as potential members of properly named and properly classified entities. Among these, we perceive:
  - Names of persons
  - Names of places: countries, cities, regions, states, names of roads, seas, oceans, mountains, rivers, etc.
  - Names of organizations: associations (regional, national and international), universities, televisions, banks, etc.
  - Currency expressions: cost, money, etc.
  - Temporal expressions: the names of the days of the week, months, etc.
- Local Grammars: These are represented in the form of Augmented Transition Network-ATNs. They are used to represent sequences of words. These sequences are described by manually written rules and consequently produce certain linguistic information such as the type of the identified named entity (person name, organization, location, etc.).

Figure 2 shows the main graph of NE represented with NooJ linguistic platform. The same graph contains embedded sub-graphs.

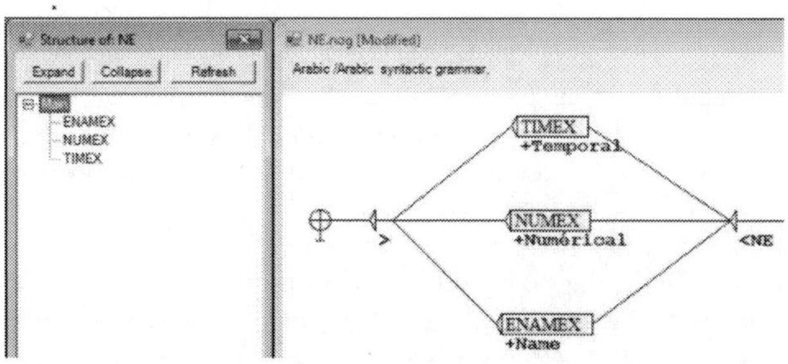

Figure 2. Main graph embedded the three types of NE: TIMEX, NUMEX and ENAMEX

1) Local grammars for the extraction and annotation of NUMEX: The problem of automatic recognition of numerical determinants in a text is part of the more or less complex linguistic phenomena. Generally, they can not be processed at the level of lexical analysis. They require very redundant descriptions that would be very tedious, if not impossible, to describe them manually in electronic dictionaries compiled in the form of finite automata.

We have classified numerical expressions into four categories: percentage expressions, weight expressions, measurement expressions, and monetary expressions (see Figure 3).

Then, we focused on the extraction of numerical values.

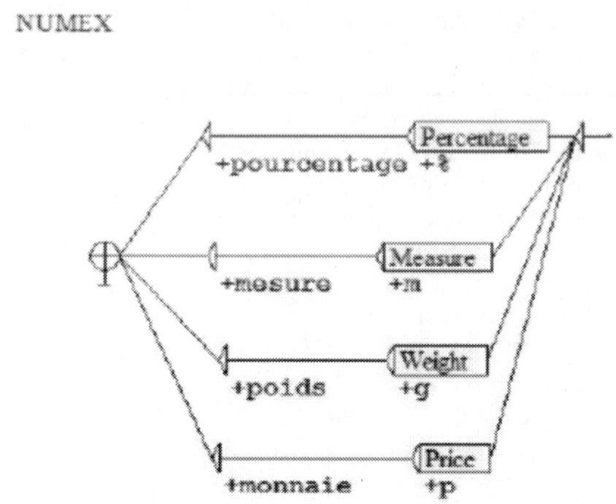

Figure 3. Main sub-graphs of the different types of NE.

Figure 4 shows the main recognition graph of these values. This is restricted to call to sub-graphs relating to the identification of numerals representing units, tens, hundreds and thousands. As outputs, we attribute the grammatical category "DET" (a determinant), the semantic information "+NUM" (numerical) as well as the arithmetic value that it represents "+Val". Thus, each recognized numeral occurs with its equivalent written in numbers.

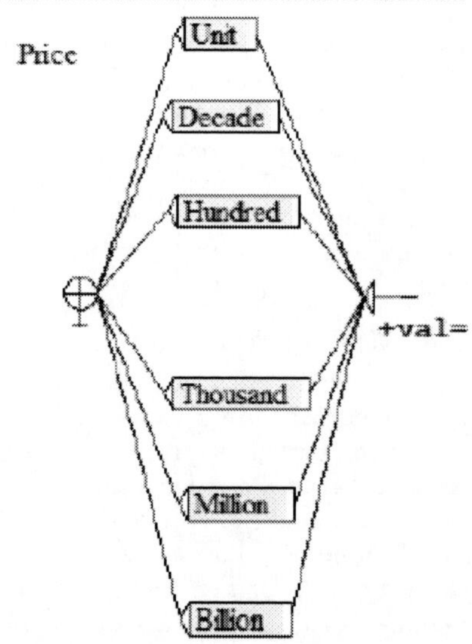

Figure 4. Main sub-graph describing the local grammar responsible for the extraction of numerical values

2) Local grammars for extraction and annotation of TIMEX: Temporal expressions, TIMEX, are as important as numerical expressions in syntactic or information extraction systems. Indeed, a user can query our system to get information about an event. Usually, any event is linked to a date or time represented as a time expression. As a result, according to Figure 5, our rule-based system allows the extraction of ages, hours, dates and periods.

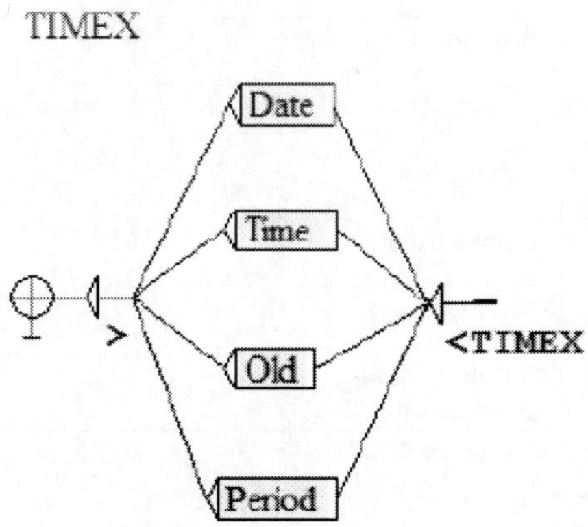

Figure 5. Main sub-graph describing the local grammar responsible for the extraction of TIMEX

3) Local grammars for extraction and annotation of ENAMEX: In our work, the ENAMEX extraction means the extraction of proper names , localizations and organizations. Figure 6 shows the NooJ local grammar [10], which is responsible for the syntaxic-semantic annotation of different ENAMEX type.

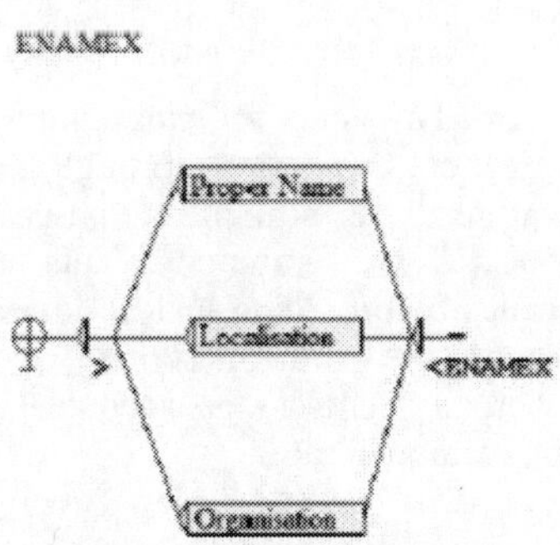

Figure 6. Main graph describing the local grammar responsible for extracting expressions associated with ENAMEX

For the names of places, we began by developing a grammar of internal proofs associated to the cities name, regions, hotels, itineraries, avenues, rivers, seas, oceans, etc. Thus, we identified the triggering words as مدينة (<mdiynT>, <city>), جبل (<jbl>, < mountain >), جزيرة (<jzIrT>, <island>),دولة (<dwlT>, <country>), نهج (<nhj>, <avenue>). These lexical (triggers) markers are used to describe recognition rules in local grammars. Figure 7 shows the main graph of local grammar responsible for the extraction of localization expressions. In the same manner, this grammar is implemented with linguistic NooJ platform.

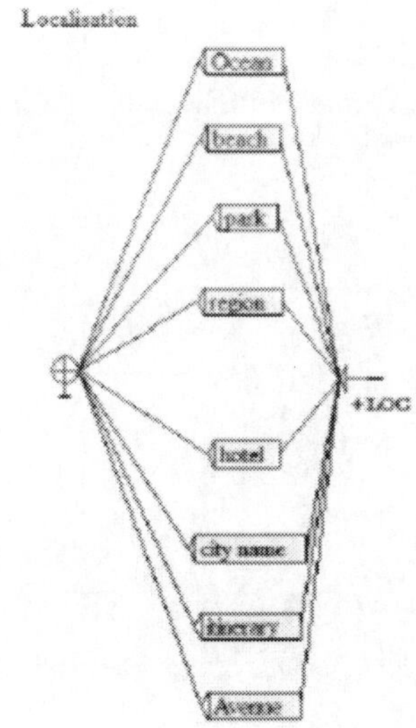

Figure 7. Main sub-graph describing the local grammar responsible for extracting location expressions

Besides the places name, we made the recognition grammar of people names. Figure 8 below shows a graphical implementation of proper names grammar in NooJ platform.

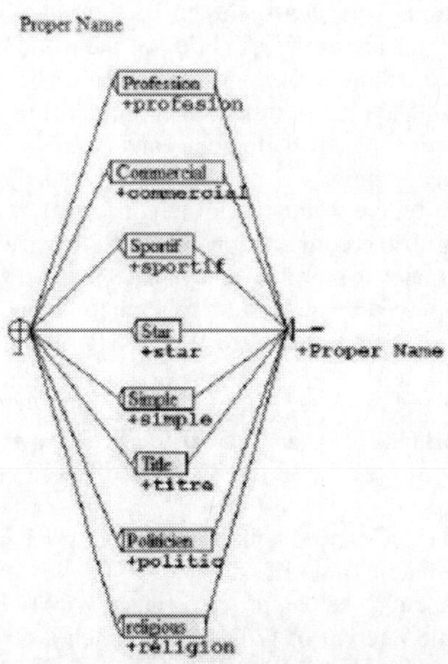

Figure 8. Main sub-graph describing the local grammar responsible for extracting proper names expressions

The identification of organizations names began with the elaboration of a dictionary, which contains 959 organizations names such as: يونسكو (<yUnskw>, Unesco) recognized by the mean of (N + Org) syntactico-semantic annotation or what we call lexical markers. We note that the majority of entries are compound and abbreviated words. Then, we have a list of 626 trigger words like مؤسسة (<m'wssasT>, company), جمعية (<jm'yT>, association), and so on. These lexical markers are used to describe recognition rules in local grammars. In total, we have ten sub-graphs that implement recognition global grammar of organizations name (cf. Figure 9)

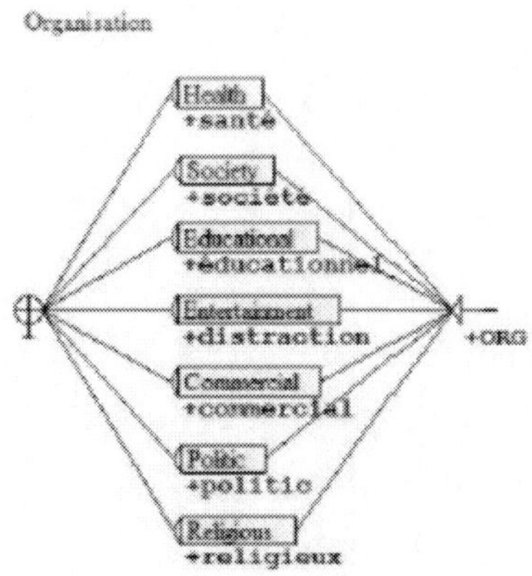

Figure 9. Main sub-graph describing the local grammar responsible to extracting names and abbreviations for organizations

VI. EVALUATION OF THE NE EXTRACTION SYSTEM

After collecting the corpus, we had to go to experimentation. This step seems to be the most important one because it measures the reliability of the work.

The experimentation of our resources was done with NooJ concordance [10]. As mentioned before, this platform uses (syntactical, morphological and semantic) local grammars already built.

Traditionally, the evaluation of any information retrieval system relies on the computation of a set of metrics. These calculations make it possible to evaluate the proportion of the errors displayed by the system relative to the ideal result.

The metrics usually used are: Recall (R), Accuracy (P), F-Measure (F).

We evaluate our recognition system on 70% of the Arabic PropBank [14] and a 70% of our own corpus described in [3] (see Table II). The rest of these corpora is used for the test.

An evaluation carried out on these corpora gives the results presented in Table III.

Our syntactico semantic recognizer yields F-scores included in the interval of [76%-96%] which are satisfying measures compared to [8], [12] and [14].

TABLE II. RTRH [3] TOURISTIQUE CORPUS

Corpus dialogue number	4000
Cities and towns	3120
Restaurants	9130
Itineraries appellations	3100
Locations	6125
Organizations	9125
Persons names	4125
Entertainments	6150
Localizations	8125
Transport fields	6120
Specialties	1130
Hotel and restaurant categories	1125
Contacts	6125

TABLE III. EVALUATION OF NE SYSTEM

		Precision	Record	F-Measure
TIMEX		97%	95%	96%
NUMEX		97%	94%	95.5%
ENAMEX	Proper Names	92%	79%	85%
	Organisation Names	90%	78%	84%
	Location Names	82%	71%	76%

VII. CONCLUSION

We have described a system for extracting proper nouns, temporal and numerical expressions through a combination of morphological analyzer and a rule-based recognition system using local NooJ grammars. This permitted to achieve performance by providing lexical coverage in more than 87%. Despite the above-described problems, the recommended method seems to be adequate and exhibits very encouraging extraction rates.

REFERENCES

[1] K. Shaalan, "A Survey of Arabic Named Entity Recognition and Classification," Computational Linguistics, 40 (2), pp. 496-510 , 2014.

[2] S. Mesfar, "Analyse Morpho-syntaxique automatique et reconnaissance des entits nommes en arabe standard," A Doctorat thesis, vol. Franche- Compt University, 2008.

[3] L. Chahira, Z. Anis, and Z. Mounir, "Knowledge Extraction with NooJ Using a syntactico-Semantic Approach for the Arabic Utterances Understanding," CICLing, Konya, 2016.

[4] "MUC," 2014, URL: http://en.wikipedia.org/wiki/Message Understanding Conference [retrived: 10, 2016].

[5] S. Mesfar, "Named entity recognition for Arabic using syntactic grammars," In Proceedings of the 12th International Conference on Applications of Natural Language to Information Systems pages pp. 305-316, Berlin, 2007.

[6] B. Siham, T. Meryem, and A. Driss, "Named Entity Recognition using a A rule based approach," Computer Systems and Applications (AICCSA), 2014 IEEE/ACS 11th International Conference on, pp. 478-484, DOI 10.1109/AICCSA.2014.7073237, 2014.

[7] A. Sherief, K. Shaalan, and M. Shoaib, "Integrating rule-based system with classification for Arabic named entity recognition," In Alexander Gelbukh, editor, Computational Linguistics and Intelligent Text Processing, volume 7181 of Lecture Notes in Computer Science, vol. Springer, Berlin Heidelberg, 2012, pp. 311-322.

[8] B. Mohit, S. Nathan, B. Rishav, K. Oflazer, and S. Noah, "Recalloriented learning of named entities in Arabic wikipedia," In Proceedings of the 13th Conference of the European Chapter of the Association for Computational Linguistics (EACL), 2012.

[9] R. P. Valetta-Malta. Y. Benajiba, M. Diab, "Using Language Independent and Language Specific Features to Enhance Arabic Named Entity Recognition," The International Arab Journal of Information Technology, Vol. 6, No. 5, November 2009, pp. 464-472, 2009.

[10] M. Silberztein, Ed., Formalizing Natural Languages: The NooJ Approach. Wiley-ISTE, Jan. 2016, ISBN: 978-1-84821-902-1.

[11] Z. Ins, H. Souha, Mezghani, and B. Lamia, Hadrich, " The contribution of a hybrid approach to the recognition of Arabic-language entities," TALN Montral, 19-23 juillet, 2010.

[12] S. Abuleil, "Hybrid System for Extracting and Classifying Arabic Proper Names," Proceedings of the WSEAS Int.Conf. on Artificial Intelligence, Knowledge Engineering and Data Bases, Madrid-Spain, pp. 205-210, 2006.

[13] H. Fehri, K. Haddar, and A. Ben Hamadou, "Recognition and translation of Arabic named entities with NooJ using a new representation model, In Proceedings of the 9th International Workshop on Finite State Methods and Natural Language Processing (pp. 134-142). Association for Computational Linguistics. July, 2011.

[14] Palmer, M., Babko-Malaya, O., Bies, A., Diab, M. T., Maamouri, M., Mansouri, A., & Zaghouani, W. (2008). A Pilot Arabic Propbank. In *LREC*.

[15] L. Chahira, " Development of an automatic spoken language understanding system of spontaneous Arabic speech based on an hybrid approach, linguistic and stochastic approach," A Doctorat thesis, vol. Faculty of Economics and Management of Sfax University, LaTICE Laboratory, Tunis 2017.

[16] L. Chahira, Z. Anis, and Z. Mounir, "Knowledge Extraction with NooJ Using a syntactico-Semantic Approach for the Arabic Utterances Understanding," CICLing, Konya, 2016.

iTweet about #Privacy
Mapping Privacy Frames in Twitter Conversation

Federica Fornaciari
Department of Arts and Humanities
National University
La Jolla, CA, USA
e-mail: ffornaciari@nu.edu

***Abstract*— Adopting a pragmatic bottom-up approach, the current study applies semantic network analysis and discourse analysis to unfold individual frames of privacy emerging in Twitter. To do so, the author collected and analyzed 100,000 publicly available Tweets selected using the word "privacy." The following two overarching questions guided the study: What are the frames that emerge in relation to privacy on Twitter? How are these frames discussed? Through a mixed method approach, the author identified the following nine frames of privacy: Privacy and Technology, Personal Privacy, Legal Privacy, Fundamental Privacy, Privacy Concerns, Spatial Privacy, Gossip, Trading Privacy, and Expected Flow of Information. The author also developed robust dictionaries to automate frame detection. In a future step, the author plans to use these dictionaries of privacy to analyze larger corpora of text and reach a meaningful understanding of how individuals frame privacy in everyday conversation.**

Keywords-network analysis; discourse analysis; framing theory; privacy; Twitter

I. Introduction

In a technologically driven communication environment, privacy is undoubtedly a major concern influencing how we share or withhold information – and how we think about personal data. Perhaps paradoxically, many voice their privacy concerns in rather public venues, such as social media. These public platforms facilitate researchers who wish to explore, unobtrusively, the textures and patterns of user's casual discussions – and thereby observe how individuals understand and frame reality [1]. Based on the assumption that Twitter discussion mimics an online word-of-mouth [2], the author suggests combining semantic network analysis and discourse analysis to explore the frames of privacy emerging on Twitter, and to develop dictionaries that facilitate frame detection. The results of such study begin to shed light upon how individuals discuss privacy in everyday conversation.

Privacy is an increasingly relevant issue in today's computing era. Currently, many individuals store personal data in the Cloud, a virtual data storage where users can archive and remotely access information [3]. For many, accessing the Internet and sharing information online has become a routine activity. Yet – partly due to the gained popularity of online-networked platforms – privacy increasingly becomes a concern for users who desire to protect their data. Belonging in this category of networked environments, social media too are platforms where users share information becoming potential victims of privacy loss. However, social media are also possible vehicles for discussing concerns and solutions related to privacy.

Section two provides a short review of relevant literature to contextualize framing theory, semantic network analysis, and discourse analysis. Section three presents the research questions and describes the methodological approach adopted in the current study. Section four introduces some preliminary findings. Finally, section five discusses findings and limitations.

II. Literature Review

A. *Framing theory*

Goffman [4] explained that individuals approach the complexity of reality developing or borrowing primary frames, or "schemata of interpretations," based on abstract principles that organize, untangle, and simplify reality. Frames emerge through symbolic forms of expression and provide structures that enforce preferred interpretations of the social world. Frames may be individual or collective [5], and emerge within different occurrences of the communication process: the communicator, the text, the receiver, and the culture itself [6]. Available frames are either consciously recognized or unconsciously processed, often influencing how people understand, assess, remember and discuss issues [7].

B. *Semantic Network Analysis and Discourse Analysis*

Semantic network analysis is a specific type of automated content analysis that investigates text to explore the networks that emerge from the occurrences and co-occurrences of concepts [8]. In such a way, semantic network analysis allows drawing conceptual maps as they emerge in text.

Discourse analysis, on the other hand, is a qualitative process seeking to provide deeper explanation of meaning through the analysis of themes and patterns that emerge from texts [9] [10]. It also takes into account the role of context in developing the semantic networks of "privacy." Such a qualitative approach may be used to strengthen the findings obtained in the quantitative steps of this research project.

The current study combined quantitative semantic network analysis [11]–[13] with qualitative discourse analysis [9] [10]. Such mixed method approach enabled the author to validate, contextualize, and strengthen the results obtained through each method of analysis [14].

III. Method And Research Questions

The current study is twofold. First, the author combined semantic network analysis and discourse analysis to map and explore the frames of privacy emerged in Twitter using a bottom-up approach [15]. Then, the author developed robust dictionaries to automate frame detection in large corpora of text. In a future step, the author plans to use these dictionaries to analyze larger samples of tweets and thereby develop a more robust understanding of existing *individual frames* of privacy, which refer to our cognitive understanding of privacy [4].

In the current study, the author analyzed 100,000 publicly available tweets collected using the keyword "privacy" between July 1st 2016 and July 25th 2016 (the software HootSuite facilitated the collection of tweets). Considering the nature of the current study, the author did not distinguish between tweets and re-tweets, as both were considered equally useful and meaningful in frame implementation. After collection, the author used the software Automap [11] to generate frequency lists and begin the analysis.

The following two overarching questions guided the study:

RQ1 – *What are the frames that emerge in relation to privacy on Twitter?*

RQ2 – How are these frames discussed?

The quantitative analysis, implemented to address RQ1 included three steps.

To address RQ1, the author implemented several steps. First, the author imputed the tweets in the software Automap to generate frequency lists. This resulted in almost 10,000 item recorded in a frequency list. Using Automap, the frequency list was refined by deleting non-content bearing elements such as articles, conjunctions, and other noise from the text [11].

Second, the author manually processed the frequency list to qualitatively assess the contexts of use of each word. To undertake this second step, the author read and reread carefully the frequency list. During each reading, and informed by existing literature, the author added new themes as they emerged from the words in the list. For instance, keywords referring to legislations – such as the Health Insurance Portability and Accountability Act (HIPAA) and the Family Educational Rights and Privacy Act (FERPA) were included in a "legal privacy" dictionary.

As a result, the author developed lists of recurring terms and expressions, and clustered these into overarching sub-themes and groups that co-occurred with the word "privacy" in Twitter conversation. The words in the frequency list were sorted into 40 sub-themes. These themes were then combined into nine overarching frames including the following: privacy and technology, personal privacy, legal privacy, fundamental privacy, privacy concerns, spatial privacy, gossip, trading privacy, and expected flow of information. Each frame was subsequently analyzed through qualitative discourse analysis to allow a deeper, qualitative understanding of how privacy was discussed within each category.

Third, the author and a coder manually processed the list of the frequencies and placed each word in the corresponding category. Agreement between the two researchers was then calculated to gauge the reliability of the third step. Intercoder reliability scored between .88 and .95 [16]. These three phases enabled the author to map the semantic networks of privacy as they emerged from the 100,000 tweets collected. It also allowed the author to start developing robust dictionaries of the individual frames of privacy.

To address RQ2, the author used the keyword in the dictionaries to select sub-samples of tweets belonging in each theme emerged from the semantic network analysis. For example, the theme "privacy is a fundamental human right" emerged from words such as: human right, sacred, freedom, liberty, and universal. These keywords were used to retrieve a sub-sample of tweets from the original sample. Each sub-sample consisted of 20 tweets randomly selected. The author further analyzed each sub-sample through discourse analysis to understand and clarify how each theme was discussed in the tweets.

IV. Preliminary Findings

After a preliminary analysis, eight frames emerged. The frames were labeled as follow: privacy and technology, personal privacy, privacy concerns, legal privacy, fundamental privacy, spatial privacy, gossip, and trading privacy.

The frame "Privacy and Technology" implies that when new technology is introduced, new privacy concerns develop.

"Personal Privacy" suggests that privacy is related to sociality, social roles, relationships, and personal feelings.

"Privacy Concerns" emerges from tweets suggesting that privacy infringements generate problems and that the tradeoff is often unfair.

"Legal Privacy" emphasizes that the government, regulations, contextual norms, permission, and transparency are fundamentally related to privacy.

"Fundamental Privacy" emerges when users frame privacy as a fundamental human right suggesting that, as such, it should be protected.

"Spatial Privacy" emerges in tweets that describe privacy in terms of access or boundary control.

"Gossip" is implemented when users describe gossip as an invasion of someone's privacy.

Finally, "Trading Privacy" emerges when tweets focus upon the economic value of information, implying that personal data are commodities that can be stolen or sold.

Table 1, in the next page, summarizes the eight frames identified providing examples of the dictionaries used for frame detection. It also delivers data on the cumulative frequencies to provide an overview of frame implementation in the sample analyzed.

TABLE I. CUMULATIVE FREQUENCIES OF FRAMES

Frame	Example of Keywords	Cumul. Freq.
Privacy and Technology	Cellphone, Pokemon Go, Google, Facebook, cameras...	81,812
Personal Privacy	Boyfriend, relationship, girlfriend, angry, annoying...	51,697
Privacy Concerns	Data, concerns, dossiers, spy, cookie, surveillance, war, security	35,232
Legal Privacy	Laws, setting, bill, banned, transparency, setting, court, Obama, permission, health, education...	34,408
Fundamental Privacy	Right, need, important, respect, essential, hope, human...	32,028
Spatial Privacy	Border, gates, space, location, bedroom, bar, wall, cars...	12,719
Gossip	Paparazzi, famous, popstar, vanityfair, popularity...	8,104
Trading Privacy	Business, consumers, property, buy, marketing, commercial	5,822

V. DISCUSSION

In Twitter discussion, privacy surfaces as multifaceted and complex. Users discuss privacy as a social construct that entails a variety of components and perspectives.

Not surprisingly "privacy and technology" was the most frequent frame adopted in Twitter discussion. People often express their concerns about personal data stored in networked environments, such as Facebook and Google. When voicing these concerns, users also criticize the obscurity and scarce usability of existing privacy policies. Strong privacy concerns are frequently channeled to new technologies such as face recognition software, drones, and Pokemon Go. These concerns develop a very typical pattern of reactions to the introduction of new technological devices that emerge as powerful, unexpected, and often intimidating due to their potential for information collection, processing, and shareability.

Current research on social capital emphasizes that privacy is fundamentally related to publicity and sociality. In fact, needs for connection and sociality often encourage individuals to share personal information [17]. As a social media, Twitter could be considered a preferred platform for discussing the importance of relationships and sociality, and the risks that privacy infringement may cause in this respect. The high frequency of tweets referring to "personal privacy" reflects that privacy, sociality, and publicity meaningfully intersect in individuals' frames of privacy as well.

The predominance of the frame "legal privacy" emphasizes that Twitter users are often adopting a legal or ethical framework to understand and discuss privacy. They emphasize the role of government in the protection of privacy, while highlighting the role of contextual norms of information flow [18].

As shown in the frequency of "fundamental privacy", Twitter users understand privacy as a sacred and fundamental human right that should always be protected. Moving forward, the author believes that the frame "Gossip" should be included as a sub-theme of "fundamental privacy." In fact, the frame "gossip" suggests that celebrities are human beings and – as such – deserve privacy.

Due to the nature of the current contribution (i.e., short paper), the author emphasizes the need to further refine the methodology and to more closely interpret the findings. Moving forward, the author intends to use software for Natural Language Processing such as Nooj [19] in order to automatically distinguish between orthographical sequences of letters and relevant linguistic units. Moreover, the author will use the dictionaries of privacy developed during the current study to facilitate extracting semantic information from text [as suggested in 20]. The dictionaries will prove particularly useful in analyzing tweets collected over a longer and therefore more representative timeframe. Despite its limitation, the author believes that the current study provides valuable toolkits to automate the detection of individual frames of privacy in Twitter conversation.

REFERENCES

[1] A. Jalal, and M. Zaidieh, "The use of social networking in education: Challenges and opportunities," World of Computer Science and Information Technology Journal, vol. 2, pp. 18-21, 2012.

[2] B. J. Jansen, M. Zhang, K. Sobel, and A. Chowdury, "Twitter power: Tweets as electronic word of mouth," *Journal of the American Society for Information Science and Technology*, vol. 60, pp. 2169–2188, 2009.

[3] E. A. Aldakheel, "A Cloud Computing Framework for Computer Science," Education. Master's Thesis, Bowling Green State University, United State of America, 2011.

[4] E. Goffman, "Frame analysis: An essay in the organization of experience," Northeastern University Press, Boston, 1974.

[5] S. D. Reese, "Prologue: Framing public life, a bridging model for media research," in Reese, S.D, Gandy, O.H., and Grant, A.E. (Eds.), Framing public life: Perspectives on media and our understanding of the social world, Erlbaum, Mahwah, NJ, 2001.

[6] Z. Papacharissi and M. de Fatima Oliveira, "News Frames Terrorism: A Comparative Analysis of Frames Employed in Terrorism Coverage in U.S. and U.K. Newspapers," *The International Journal of Press/Politics*, vol. 13, pp. 52–74, January 2008.

[7] W. Gamson, and A. Modigliani, "Media discourse and public opinion on nuclear power," *American Journal of Sociology*, vol. 95, pp. 1-37, 1989.

[8] W. van Atteveldt, J. Kleinnijenhuis, and N. Ruigrok, "Parsing, semantic networks, and political authority using syntactic analysis to extract semantic relations from Dutch newspaper articles," *Political Analysis*, vol. 16, pp. 428–446, October 2008.

[9] N. Fairclough, "Critical analysis of media discourse," in: Marris, P., Thornham, S., (Eds.), Media studies. New York University Press, New York, pp. 308–325, 2000.

[10] T. vanDijk, "The study of discourse," in: Treun A., van Dijk (Eds.), Discourse as structure and process. Sage, London, pp. 1-34, 1997.

[11] K. M. Carley, D. Columbus, and A. Azoulay, "Automap user's guide 2012," CASOS technical report Carnegie Mellon University, Pittsburgh, PA, 2012.

[12] A. E. Smith and M. S. Humphreys, "Evaluation of unsupervised semantic .mapping of natural language with Leximancer concept mapping," *Behavior Research Methods*, vol. 38, pp. 262–279, 2006.

[13] M. Stubbs, "Text and Corpus Analysis," Computer-Assisted Studies of Language and Culture. Cambridge, MA, Blackwell, 1996.

[14] A. Tashakkori, and C. Teddlie, "Handbook of mixed methods in social and behavioral research." Thousand Oaks, CA: Sage, 2003.

[15] D. J. Solove, "Conceptualizing privacy," *California Law Review*, pp. 1087–1155, 2002.

[16] W. Perreault, and L. Leigh, "Reliability of nominal data based on qualitative judgments," *Journal of Marketing Research,* vol. 26, pp. 135–148, 1989.

[17] N. B. Ellison, J. Vitak, C. Steinfield, R. Gray, and C. Lampe, "Negotiating privacy concerns and social capital needs in a social media environment," in Trepte, S. and Reinecke, L. (eds.*) Privacy Online,* Berlin: Heidelberg, 2011.

[18] H. Nissenbaum, "Privacy in context. technology, policy, and the integrity of social life," Stanford: Stanford Law Books, 2010.

[19] M. Monteleone, and S. Vietri, "The NooJ English dictionary. Formalising natural languages with NooJ 2013," Selected Papers from the NooJ 2013 International Conference, pp. 69-84, 2014.

[20] M. P. di Buono, A. Maisto, and D. Pelosi, "From linguistic resources to medical entity recognition: a supervised morpho-syntactic approach," The First International Conference on Big Data, Small Data, Linked Data and Open Data (ALLDATA 2015), IARIA, pp. 81-86, Apr. 2015.

Industry Experience: Chinese Names Duplicate Records Detection

Thong Tong Khin and Badrul Affandy Ahmad
Software Development Lab,
Mimos Bhd,
Kuala Lumpur, Malaysia.
e-mail: {thong.tkin, badrul.affandy}@mimos.my

Wang Xiaomei
Xiamen University Malaysia,
Sepang, Malaysia.
e-mail: xmwang@xmu.edu.my

Kandiah Arichandran
Kuala Lumpur, Malaysia.
e-mail: arichandran@gmail.com

Abstract— **The Soundex method is the preferred method for duplicate detection process on Malaysian Chinese names. The names are written in English text, but are phonetically translated from various Chinese dialects. When using the Russell Soundex method, it is found that the number of duplicates is high and the number of false positives is also high. The adaptive nature of Soundex method provides an avenue to optimize it for foreign language names, such as Chinese names. Through a series of tests, this study has optimized the Soundex codes for general Malaysian Chinese names. The test results have shown that a few short Chinese surnames contribute to false positives.**

Keywords: duplicate detection; Chinese names; Soundex; false positive.

I. INTRODUCTION

Normally, during data cleansing projects, duplicate detection of foreign language names is done by using the Soundex method [1]. When using the original Soundex method for Malaysian Chinese names, it is found that it produces a large number of duplicates and false positives. Be it in the government or private office use, Chinese names are written in English text, but they actually come from various phonetics of respective dialects. It is possible that the same Chinese character names are being translated into different spelling names (Romanized) due to different phonetics systems of Chinese dialects. Chinese names are normally written either as three words or two words. Sometimes, English names are also prefixed to the names. The different name formats would affect the matching results with Soundex codes. Emma Woo [4] described ten most popular Chinese format names in America. Some of the Chinese American formats also apply in Malaysia. This study excludes other ethnicities including Malay, Indian, and Kadazan, because their names are suitable for string matching algorithm application.

There is a large number of duplicate detections approaches such as Levenshtein [13], edit distance [3] and Soundex. In the Levenshtein method, edit distance and name comparison methods match results based on substitution, deletion, insertion or transposition of characters. In this study, we selected the Soundex method because it can process phonetic data effectively with its matching Soundex codes. The Russell Soundex method was invented by Robert Russell and O'Dell in 1918 [2]. A large number of studies have been conducted to optimize Soundex rules [5] [6] [7] [8]. A cross-language algorithm was developed to measure the similarity of Asian words phonetically [9]. The algorithm showed positive results for Asian names but it had limited success when using Chinese names. Soundex-Pinyin is a spelling correction system to detect Chinese strings, but this system requires Pinyin input [10]. In this study, a newly improved algorithm based on the existing Soundex algorithm is proposed to optimize the detection results of names. An investigation is also done to improve the algorithm on Chinese names detection while it is developed as a plugin component applicable to any data cleansing or ETL (Extract Transform Loading) process workbench. The duplicate detection process reads Malaysian Chinese names as input and then applies the Soundex method. The matching records are written to a duplicate list, while the non-matching records are written to a non-matching list. The matching list is further analyzed by a subject matter expert to determine Chinese word relevance. If it is relevant and matched, the outcome is true positive, otherwise it is considered false positive, for example Chan and Chin surnames.

The results of this study are supported through the use of a confusion matrix, which provides false positives and accuracy readings [12]. False positive readings provide information on the ability of the Soundex method to detect the correct duplicates. The accuracy reading provides to the user the confidence level of the Soundex method in general.

The rest of the paper is structured as follows. In Section II, the problem statement is formulated. In Section III, the method to customize Soundex rules is described. In Section IV, the results using the new Soundex are presented and discussed. Finally, in Section V, this paper concludes with a summary and ideas for future enhancement.

II. PROBLEM STATEMENT

A. English text based Soundex method

This study uses the Soundex method for duplicate name detection; thus, the matching is done on the Soundex codes. The Russell Soundex method was developed with the following rules, to produce a four-digit alphanumeric code:

- Step 1: The first letter of the name is selected as the first digit of code, but all occurrences of characters A,E,H,I,O,U,W,Y are omitted.
- Step 2. Assign the codes to the letters as in Table I.
- Step 3. If two or more letters with the code were adjacent in the original name, omit all but the first.
- Step 4. Convert to the four-digit format by adding training zeros if there are less than three digits, or by dropping the right most digits if there are more than three.

TABLE I. RUSSELL SOUNDEX

Letters	Code
B, F, P, V	1
C,G,J,K,Q,S,X,Z	2
D,T	3
L	4
M,N	5
R	6
A,E,H,I,O,U,W,Y	Omitted

The Russell Soundex is accurate to detect character similarities between names after vowels and coded characters are dropped. It is suitable to detect duplicate names due to its nature to detect names based on closest phonetic sounds. The Soundex was originally developed to uncover specific relative's names in American history journals, but in recent time, it is used in record linkage analytics [11]. The major problem was that the English based Soundex did not produce good results when it was applied for Chinese names. The original Soundex's rules were not suitable for detecting Chinese names. In the first duplicate detection test with Russell Soundex code, the result was not encouraging because there was a high a number of duplicates and false positives.

B. Multiple formats of Chinese names

The collection of 300 and 527 names from our experiment data also provides us with some information on how the actual scenario might be found in government or private agencies when processing Chinese names. There are a few name formats to consider in the Soundex process that might affect the accuracy. In particular, when working with 4 digit codes, the prefix with English name, for example Franky Cheah, and double names with alias symbol for example Chin@Ah Kow, have very limited success in producing true positive duplicates. The name formats encountered in our sample data for testing are described below.

1. Chinese name with surname first: Lou Sheng, Lin Hui Ling.
2. Chinese name composed of three or more separate words: Kwai Yung Chui Ja
3. Hyphenated Chinese disyllabic name, with an uppercased second syllable: Han-Sheng Lin
4. Combination of an American given name and a Chinese middle name: Jean Yun-Hua King
5. Family name in the middle of the name: Abraham Ng Kamsat
6. Chinese name with alias of second name: Ngoh Swee Lan @ Ng Swee Lan

III. METHODS

A. Customize Soundex rules

In this study, we present three rules, namely Soundex 13, Soundex 20 and Soundex 21, that show significant results. By using data integration tool, such as Pentaho or Talend, the Soundex script is applied to an ETL flow. Matching the duplicates was done by comparing the four-digit alphanumeric codes against duplicate items. The duplicate matching result is further examined manually in order to determine the number of duplicates and false positives. We tested two sets of names (300 and 527) and the results of the Russell Soundex test is given in Table IV. Apparently, there was a high number of false positives in the duplicates results. The duplicate items, in general, were closely spelled names.

In Table II, the Soundex 21's rules are described as follows:

1) Vowels are considered for Chinese names due to the fact that vowels are the core in Chinese syllabic structure. Vowels cannot be omitted in any Chinese syllables and the simplest Chinese syllabic structure is composed of a vowel and a tone, for instance, "I" in International Phonetic Alphabet (IPA) or *yi* in Hanyu (Pinyin). There are two values for vowels, 6 for "I" and 7 for "U". The two characters "Y" and "W" (value 8) are also included in the matrix as these two glides are regarded as allophones of the high vowels /i/ and /u/ under certain conditions in Chinese.

TABLE II. CUSTOM SOUNDEX RULES

Code	Soundex 13	Soundex 20	Soundex 21
1	P,F,B,V,M	P,F,B,V,M	B,F,P,V
2	D,T,L	D,T,L	D,T,L
3	J,Q,X,K,G	J,Q,X	J, Q,X
4	Z,C,S,R	Z,C,S,R	Z,C,S,R
5		K,G	K,G
6	I	I	I
7	U	U	U
8	W,Y	W,Y	W,Y
Omitted	A,E,H,O,N	A,E,H,O,N	A,E,H,O,N, M

2) For consonants, we grouped them according to the place of articulation. For instance, value 1 is for labial consonants " B, P, F, V"; value 2 is for denti-alveolar consonants "D, T, L"; value 3 is for alveolo-palatal consonants " J, Q, X"; value 4 is for denti-alveolar consonants " Z, C, S" and fricative "R"; value 5 is for velar consonants "G, K". Among these consonants, "V" is a special one as it is used by Malaysian Chinese names due to the fact that many names are spelled in dialects. However, the pronunciation of "V" is not used in Mandarin.

3) The three vowels A, E, O and two other letters M,N are omitted due to their high frequency in word histogram (Table V).

In Soundex 13, the main difference from Soundex 21 is the labial consonants "B,P,F,V,M" that include the M for Chinese phonology nasal sound. Value 5 is left blank for consistency. The omitted letters are "A,E,H,O,N". In Soundex 20, the main difference from Soundex 21 is the labial consonants "B,P,F,V,M" in which there is the additional M for Chinese phonology nasal sound. The omitted letters are "A,E,H,O,N". After many test iterations, it was found that Soundex 21 produces better results than Soundex 13 and Soundex 20.

IV. RESULTS

Given the experimental data from two data sets, namely 300 name lists and 527 name lists, four tests were conducted using Russell Soundex and the customized Soundex versions 13, 20 and 21.

The result data is divided into actual and predicted output in order to calculate true positives (TP), true negatives (TN) and false positives (FP) readings. The accuracy and false positives formulas are given in Table IV. With the help of a Chinese language expert, we identified the duplicates by taking into consideration at least two words and also close spelling which should represent the same Chinese character in reality. Actual duplicates are recorded in a data matrix. After the Soundex tests, prediction observation is recorded such as TP, TN, FP. The prediction data is either yes or no. Thus, each set of data then has the confusion data matrix ready for examination.

A. Duplicate detections with Russell Soundex

The results in Table IV show duplicates, accuracy, and false positives. The non-duplicate list shows false negatives, whereby supposedly matched names are not detected.

The number of duplicates found for 300 and 527 names are 45 and 85, respectively. The false positives percentage was 46.3% for the first set of 300 names. The family name Chong and Cheong were close, but they did not represent the same Chinese character, similarly Lai and Lee, also Chin and Chan. The family names heavy with vowels and short in length would likely cause false positives if their first names were the same or similar in spelling.

Referring to Table III, the names Lim Jing, Tan Sin Yee, Wong Meow Fah, were given the respective codes L525, T525 and W525. However, the algorithm also gave the same codes for Lim He Jian, Tan Jenny and Wong Nyet Yin which were not related in reality. The names were detected as closely matched because Russell Soundex omitted many characters that Chinese names usually have.

TABLE III. EXAMPLE FALSE POSITIVES WITH RUSSELL SOUNDEX

Set	Code	Name	Chinese Characters
1	L525	Lim Jing	林静
	L525	Lim He Jian	林 何 健
2	T525	Tan Sin Yee	陈 欣 宜
	T525	Tan Jenny	陈 珍 妮
3	W525	Wong Meow Fah	黄 妙 花
	W525	Wong Nyet Yin	黄 月 英

B. Duplicate detections with customized Soundex rules

For the first stage of the project, we had our Soundex method testing on the names using a revised phonetic algorithm. For the 300 names list, Russell Soundex detected a higher number of duplicates and accuracy readings as compared to Soundex 13, Soundex 20 and Soundex 21. It is also noticed that, in the set of 300 names, the false positives of Soundex 21 were fewer than Soundex 20. For the 527 names list, the Soundex 13 had the most number of duplicates. For the 527 names list, the Soundex 13 had 38.3% of false positives and that was higher than Soundex 20 and 21. Both Soundex 20 and 21 had almost the same number false positives. In general, the customized Soundex results had lower false positives and number of duplicates than the results from Russell Soundex. The accuracy of custom rules is also generally higher than using Russell Soundex. The number of false positives for Soundex 20 and Soundex 21 was almost the same. The effect of letter M was not significant. The Soundex 21 was far better than Soundex 20 in accuracy readings of the 300 names list, but both had the same accuracy for the 527 names list.

TABLE IV. SOUNDEX WITH 4 DIGIT RESULTS

Soundex Type	Number of Names	Number of Duplicates	Accuracy % ((TP+TN)/ Total)	False Positive % (FP/(FP+ TN))
Russell	300	45	57	46.3
	527	85	46	64.8
13	300	24	79	18
	527	86	65	38.3
20	300	32	78	23.8
	527	75	69	31.7
21	300	32	83	19.4
	527	75	69	31.8

TABLE V. WORD HISTOGRAM OF 5 CHARACTERS IN THE 527 NAME LIST

Characters	6 digits	7 digits	8 digits
A	276	330	357
E	255	320	360
H	251	285	311
O	196	216	230
N	242	317	396

There were false positive results due to the presence of English names prefix, the closely matched spelling of different family names, such as between Chia and Chai, and the dissimilarities between first names (second and third) of the same family name (first).

When applied to Chinese names, the Soundex result had a few false positives because of misspelled names and English name prefixes and closely matched name consonants. The closely matched name occurred when all vowels and other omitted characters were removed, such as, in Soundex 13, Tee Yan Qi and Tan Hwa Jie revealed a similar code, namely T735.

C. Conclusions

Soundex 21 was generally far better than Russell Soundex in producing fewer duplicates and false positives. The false positives of Soundex 21 were slightly fewer than Soundex 13, but almost the same as Soundex 20. The Soundex 21 had higher accuracy reading than Soundex 20. This result gave confidence that the Soundex 21 was able to produce a good duplicate detection result.

V. CONCLUSION

When using Russell Soundex in the duplicate detection, the result produced a high number of false positives. The number of false positives is reduced while the percentage of accuracy is increased when the code rules are customized and improved in Soundex 13, Soundex 20 and Soundex 21. As a result, the duplicate detection, especially with Soundex 21, produced an acceptable result. Future research is needed on automating the intelligence to detect and verify Chinese names as part of a duplicate error correction system.

ACKNOWLEDGMENT

The authors of this paper would like to thank MIMOS Bhd for their involvement in ETL project at a commercial bank.

REFERENCES

[1] J. Soo, O. Frieder, "On foreign name search" European Conference on Information Retrieval, pp. 483-494, Springer Berlin Heidelberg. 2010.

[2] R. Russell and M. Odell. "Soundex." US Patent 1, 1918.

[3] K. Rieck and C. Wressnegger, "Harry: A Tool for Measuring String Similarity" Journal of Machine Learning Research 17, pp. 1-5, 2016.

[4] E. W. Louie, "Chinese American Names: Tradition and Transition" McFarland, 1998.

[5] R. Shah, "Improvement of soundex algorithm for indian language based on phonetic matching." International Journal of Computer Science, Engineering and Applications 4, No. 3, pp. 31-39, 2014.

[6] D. Holmes and M. C. McCabe, "Improving precision and recall for soundex retrieval." International Conference on Information Technology: Coding and Computing 2002, pp. 22-26, IEEE Press, 2002.

[7] A. H. Yousef, "Cross-language personal name mapping." International Journal of Computational linguitics Research, vol 4, issue 4 , 2013.

[8] D. Pinto, D. Vilarino, Y. Aleman, H. Gomez, N. Loya and H. Jimenez-Salazar, "The Soundex phonetic algorithm revisited for SMS text representation." International Conference on Text, Speech and Dialogue, Springer Berlin Heidelberg, 2012.

[9] O. Iltun, S. Kodama, and Y. Mikami, "Cross-language phonetic similarity measure on terms appeared in asian languages." International Journal of Intelligent Information Processing 2.2, pp. 9-21, 2011.

[10] D. H. Li and D. W. Peng, "Spelling Correction for Chinese Language Based on Pinyin-Soundex Algorithm," International Conference on Internet Technology and Applications, Wuhan, pp. 1-3, IEEE Press, 2011.

[11] A. Karakasidis and V. S. Verykios, "Privacy Preserving Record Linkage Using Phonetic Codes." Fourth Balkan Conference in Informatics 2009, pp. 101-106, IEEE Press, 2009.

[12] V.A. Narayana, P. Premchand, A. Govardhan, "Performance and Comparative Analysis of the Two Contrary Approaches for Detecting Near Duplicate Web Documents in Web Crawling" International Journal of Computer Applications (0975-8887), Vol 59, No. 3, 2012.

[13] I. Levenshtein, "Binary codes capable of correcting deletions, insertions, and reversals" Doklady Akademii Nauk SSSR, 163(4), pp. 845–848, 1966.

Topic Models to Contextualize and Enhance Text-Based Discourses Using Ontologies

Dimitris Gkoumas
Future Internet Living Lab Budapest
Budapest, Hungary
e-mail: dgoumas@corvinno.com

Réka Vas
Department of Information Systems
Corvinus University of Budapest
Budapest, Hungary
e-mail: reka.vas@uni-corvinus.hu

***Abstract*—Public policy-making has a clear and unique purpose: achieve a desired goal that supports the best interest of all members of the society by providing guidance for addressing selected public concerns. Examples include clean air, healthcare, waste management etc. The identification of social targets and pathways – by which these targets could be reached – are at the core of policy-making. This paper is part of an ongoing research aiming at enhancing public policy-making in the field of waste management by contextualizing and enriching text-based, Web forum discourses on waste management. For that purpose, an ontology model describing the waste management domain has been created. In the next step, the actual forum discussions are connected to one or more subdomains of the ontology by determining what proportion of the sub-domain is covered by that discourse. Finally, applying text mining techniques semantically enriched domain concepts are assigned to the discourse. This paper also provides a critical discussion on two text mining approaches that could be applied for this purpose, also highlighting points that deserve further investigation.**

Keywords-Discourse contextualization; discourse enhancement; clustering topic model; probabilistic topic model; ontologies in NLP.

I. INTRODUCTION

Humans interact with the *real world* and they observe it from different perspectives trying to give an interpretation of it by creating mental concepts. Different people look at the world from different angles, paying attention to different things. Even the same person might also pay attention to different aspects of the world in different periods of time. This is called *reflected world* and is different from the real world because the perspective a person takes or has taken is often biased. The reflected world is mainly represented by speech or writing using a natural language, and in most cases the result is textual data.

Textual data plays a major role in conveying knowledge and information about the reflected world, which could be further used for problem solving or decision making as a result of public policy. However, the rapid increase in the amount of the textual data and its unstructured format make information extraction (IE) a challenging task. Additionally, acquiring knowledge from textual information is not always a straightforward process since textual data also derives properties of language. *Synonymy,* expressing a single concept in a number of ways (i.e., car and automobile) and *polysemy,* using the same term to refer to multiple concepts (i.e., jaguar which can mean a special car or an animal, as well), are two major obstacles in IE since in reality there is often no one-to-one correspondence between concepts and textual terms [1]. That word-sense ambiguity could utterly fool algorithms, which search terms only as a sequence of characters [2]. Lexical co-occurrence that is determined on the basis of statistical significances is an important indicator for term associations. According to this approach, two terms or a sequence of terms (*n-gram*) are associated when a presented term triggers the mental activation of another one. However, lexical co-occurrence cannot handle the above described ambiguity because it is not only invalid from a linguistic-semantical point of view but also prone to overestimate the semantic similarity [2][3]. On the other hand, incorporating knowledge in the form of an ontology bridging the conceptual and real world [2][4][5] can help to overcome challenges in text mining. Ontologies allow storing domain knowledge in a more sophisticated form, conceptualizing a domain [6]. By using ontologies, text terms could be indexed by ontology concepts, which reflect terms' meaning rather than words considered as lists with all the ambiguity they convey.

The main goal of this study is to contextualize semantically enriched text-based discourses to gain information from the scope of a specific domain eliminating the ambiguity of the discussion. After that, the next step is to enhance the discussion by supplying it with connected wiki pages. For this purpose, an ontology is used as a representation of the domain knowledge to match concepts with terms in the discussion. In the literature, the most common method applied in such cases is to map concepts on text. At the same time, this paper suggests two different approaches for tackling the above-described issues. Both of our approaches make use of topic models to discover the hidden semantic structure of the text-based discourse. The discourse may concern one or multiple topics in different proportions. After that, text mining methods are used to measure the similarity between the discourse and concepts belonging to the concerned topics.

Section II provides specific details about the case study. In Section III, we describe in detail the clustering topic model approach to contextualize and enhance the text-based discourse developing by that way a public policy. Section IV presents a probabilistic topic model approach to tackle the same issue. At the end, conclusions are drawn in Section V.

II. THE CASE

The textual data to be analyzed is collected from forum discussions, which collect conversations in the form of posted messages. On the investigated forum, people having ideas regarding eco-friendliness, and experts from the field of waste management can leave comments to provide help and enhance problem-solving. A domain ontology of waste management [7], holding knowledge about ten subdomains, is used to contextualize and enhance text-based discourses. Each concept in the domain ontology includes a label, which consists of one up to five terms, a set of synonyms, and a wiki page describing in detail the given concept. WordNet [8] – a language engineering tool – has been used to extract the set of synonyms for each concept label.

III. THE CLUSTERING TOPIC MODEL APPROACH

A. *Methodology*

In the current study, the first aforementioned approach tries to match concepts from an assigned subdomain to a text-based discourse. The process is broken down into three tasks. In the first step, a clustering topic model is applied on the domain ontology to verify that it is well-structured and there is no noise. The clustering algorithm automatically identifies subdomains in a group of concepts (Figure 1). Despite the fact, that the ontology structure will finally be used, the clustering algorithm is also used for extracting labels for each subdomain. Actually, the resulting centroids are being viewed as the resulting labels. In the second step, once a new text-based discourse comes out, it is assigned to one of the subdomains (Figure 2). In the last phase, the text-based discourse has to be associated with the concepts of the assigned subdomain. There are different methods to do that, however in this case we calculate the distance between the discussion and each concept in the assigned subdomain (Figure 3). Concepts with short distances are dominantly presented in the discussion while the ones with long distances are either weakly associated or not at all. After that, concepts with the shortest distances are chosen as predominant in the discussion, returning back a wikipage describing in detail the given ontology concept to enhance the discourse.

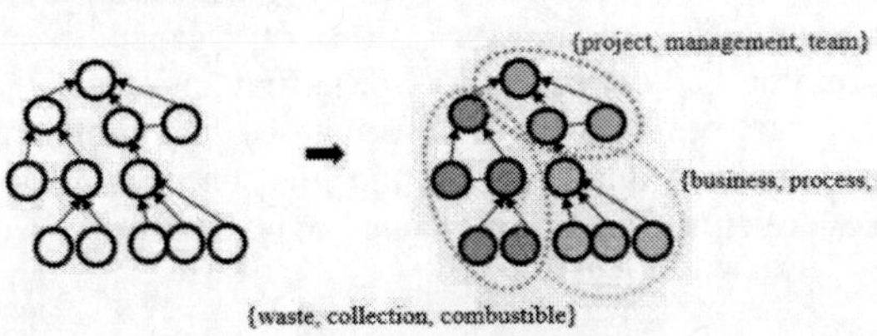

Figure 1. Automatic subdomain identification throughout the ontology and topic label extraction.

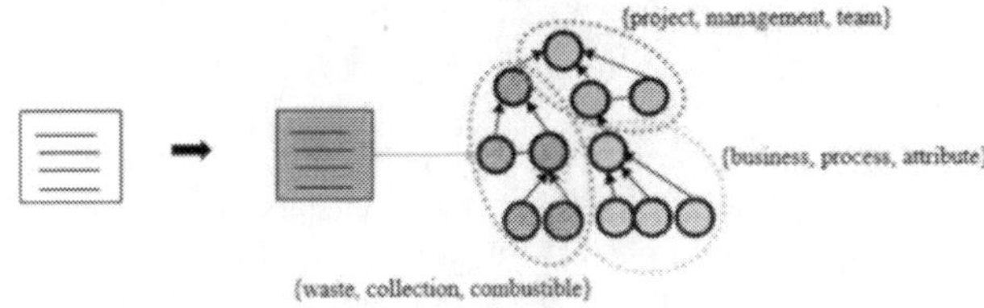

Figure 2. A text-based discourse is assigned to a subdomain.

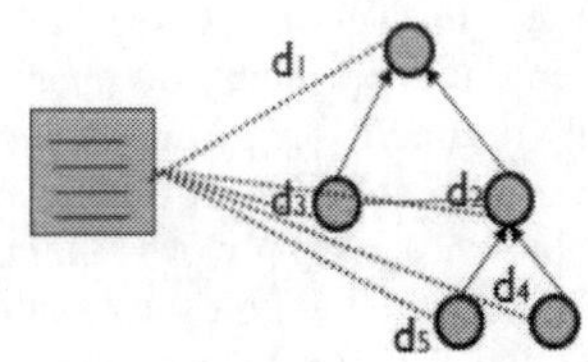

Figure 3. Distance calculation between text of discussion and concepts in the assigned subdomain.

B. *Implementation*

This section describes in detail the text preprocessing, the clustering topic model and the matching process to contextualize and enhance a text-based discourse.

1) Text preprocessing

At first, ontology concepts are extracted and saved into a text file. After the cleaning of the extracted concepts the most crucial part, the preprocessing of the extracted concepts, starts. In this phase, some basic techniques [9] are applied starting from *tokenization*. In this process, the text is split into a stream of words by removing all non-alphanumeric characters, such as punctuation and mathematical symbols, and then it is normalized to lowercase. This tokenized representation is then used for further processing, applying some filtering methods. Thus, words that bear little or no content information are removed. Initially, a stop-word filter removes high-frequency words, such as "the", "a", "or", with no content information. Then, a stemming or lemmatization filter is applied in order to reduce further the number of the words. At the end, one stemmed and only one tokenized vocabulary are created.

2) Clustering topic model in the domain ontology

Transformation is the next step after preprocessing. In the current approach, a vector space model is used to transform the textual data in a data structure before data mining techniques are applied. In order to assign a weight to each term or continuous sequence of n terms (n-grams) to a concept within a group of concepts, the *term frequency-inverse document frequency* (tf-idf) measure is applied looking at unigrams, bigrams, and trigrams. After that, the similarity between concepts in the domain ontology can be measured based on cosine similarity [10]. In reality, cosine similarity is a length-agnostic metric and measures the cosine of the angle between two text vector representations (formula (1)). Subtracting cosine similarity from one provides cosine distance, as it is seen in formula (2).

$$\text{similarity} = \cos(\theta) = A*B/ \|A\|*\|B\| \quad (1)$$

$$d = 1 - \cos(\theta) \quad (2)$$

After having computed cosine distances between each concept and all the rest of the concepts in the domain ontology, a hierarchical clustering is performed on the concepts to find out the optimum number of clusters. In that case, we chose the agglomerative Ward clustering algorithm.

At the last step, the vector space model enclosing tf-idf measurements and the optimum number of clusters, that Ward clustering returned, are used as input to a k-mean clustering to assign each concept to a cluster with the nearest mean. Finally, the top n words that are nearest to the cluster centroids are sorted to be used as labels. The result is a set of important words for each cluster giving a sense of what a subdomain is about.

3) The matching process

As it has been already mentioned, the matching process consists of two levels. In the first one, the text-based discourse is matched to a subdomain in the ontology to enable a general contextualization, while in the second step, it has to be calculated which subdomain concepts are the nearest to the discussion, not only to contextualize the discussion in a deeper semantic level but also to enhance it by returning a list of indexes, which point to the aforementioned wiki pages.

Once a new text-based discourse appears on the forum, we extract the textual data, filter the words based on the mentioned above vocabulary, and transform it to a space vector using tf-idf measure to assign weights to the terms. Then, the existing k-mean clustering model assigns the discussion to a subdomain. In the second phase, we define the nearest concepts of the discourse by running a k-nearest neighbor algorithm. The word tf-idf vectors are used to represent the concepts and the discussion, and cosine distance to measure distance.

IV. THE PROBABILISTIC TOPIC MODEL APPROACH

A. *Methodology*

In the previous approach, every cluster includes a prevalent topic and once a new text-based discourse comes out, it is assigned to a subdomain of the ontology. The question is what shall we do if a discussion covers more than one topic? In reality, a discussion can enclose many topics in different proportions. Even in the current case study, where only domain experts took part in the discourse about a quite specific topic, there is a high possibility that a variance of topics will come up in the discussion. In order to address this issue, the second approach makes use of latent Dirichlet allocation (LDA) model [11] - a probabilistic topic model - to be able to learn even about hidden topics in a discussion [12].

LDA is a probabilistic extension of latent semantic analysis (LSA) [13] assuming that each term is a mixture of topics and it is attributable to the LDA's topics. In general, a bag-of-words model – disregarding grammar and even word order – and the number of topics – given by an expert or applying a trial and error method – are used as input to the LDA model. After that, the model outputs a) topic vocabulary distributions b) topic assignments per term and c) topic proportion per text. Such a probabilistic approach not only has both favorable semantical and statistical quality [14] but also offers a dampening of synonymy [15].

In the current study, the concept labels are used as a domain corpus to train the LDA model to provide topic vocabulary distributions (TABLE I). In this case, once a text-based discourse appears, each term in the text is assigned to a topic. However, the goal of the mixed assignment is not only to associate the discourse with a collection of topics but also to calculate the relative proportion. The latter, besides a broader understanding of the text, could be leveraged to enhance a discussion and develop a public policy in a broader way. In order to calculate the topic proportion in the text, each assigned term is scored under the probabilistic topic vocabulary distributions (TABLE I). For instance, if the domain ontology includes three topics, the result will be a normal distribution over the prevalence of topics (π) in the discussion, as it is seen in formula (3).

$$\pi = [0.1*\pi1,\ 0.4*\pi2,\ 0.5*\pi3] \quad (3)$$

TABLE I. TOPIC VOCABULARY DISTRIBUTIONS

Topic 1		**Topic 2**		**Topic 3**	
Waste Management		***Business Process***		***Project Management***	
waste	0.1	business	0.18	project	0.15
collection	0.08	process	0.09	management	0.07
combustible	0.05	attribute	0.03	team	0.07
...	...	...	...	...	...

At this point, we have acquired a broader but quite general idea what the text-based discourse is about. In order to contextualize the discourse in a semantic level, it has to be associated with the concepts of the ontology. The main difference between the first and the second approach is that in the second case we match concepts from many subdomains that are presented in the discussion. However, subdomains with a low prevalence in the discussion are not taken into consideration. In order to match concepts to the discussion, we firstly compute the topic distribution for each concept, and then compute some sort of divergence between the discussion and concepts. As in the first approach, short distances between two topic distributions are dominantly presented in the discussion while the ones with long distances are either weakly associated or not at all.

B. Implementation

The same process is followed in the text preprocessing, that has been described in Section III./B. The main difference compared to the previous approach is that instead of a vector space model with tf-idf measures, we use a document-term (DT) matrix. LDA model is actually looking for repeating term patterns in the entire DT matrix. The optimum number of topics is equal to the number of the subdomains in the domain ontology while the number of terms composed in a single topic is chosen to a high number as we want to extract themes and concepts. Closing, we take 100 iterations to allow LDA algorithm for convergence.

The LDA model outputs topic- and weight terms. After that, we score all of the words in the text-based discourse under the above described probabilistic topic distributions to track the distribution of prevalent topics over the discussion. In the second phase, we calculate the distribution of topics for each concept belonging to prevalent subdomain. Finally, we compare the topic distributions between the text-based discourse and concepts using the Kullback–Leibler (KL) divergence measure [16].

V. CONCLUSION

Word-sense disambiguation (WSD) is an important and challenging process of determining which sense of a word is used in a given context. There are hundreds of WSD algorithms for bespoke applications. However, in this paper we follow another way. A domain ontology is used as a dictionary to specify the senses which are to be disambiguated and text-based discourses to be disambiguated. Actually, we propose two different topic models – a clustering and a probabilistic one – to contextualize text-based discourses. In the first case, cosine similarity is used to measure the similarity between the text-based discourse and concepts, while in the second one, KL-divergence measure is used to compare topic distributions between the discussion and concepts belonging to prevalent topics. On one hand, since cosine similarity is a length-agnostic metric, it lets us compare word distributions between texts of varying lengths. Thus, it seems to be a good metric to compare discussions with concepts consisting of one up to five words. On the other hand, measuring distances directly using vector representations may not be reliable because, in very high dimensions, a distance between any two points starts to look the same. An LSA faces efficiently the issue since it reduces the data dimensionality.

Even these methods have already been implemented, they have not been evaluated by a domain expert as they are part of an ongoing research project. However, we expect for the clustering approach to perform better in cases when discourses are strictly domain specific, framed in well-defined borders, and they have a low deviation from the discussed topic. The latter situation seems to be ideal or at least scarce. In reality, there is always a topic deviation in a discussion, as humans tend to integrate concepts from different domains when they are critically thinking. For this purpose, a probabilistic model seems to tackle the contextualization issue better.

There are also two important points, which deserve further investigation. It has been mentioned that the discourse is enhanced by adding wikitext describing an ontology concept in detail. However, what shall we do if people omit important topics and the quality of the discussion is not desirable? In that case, the ontology structure could be used to identify any of the important and omitted concepts. In the opposite case, it should be investigated what to do if people mention concepts that do not exist in the ontology? It is obvious there is a need for a two-way interaction. In that case, new concepts from the discussion should be extracted to enrich the domain ontology. Thus, the latter could process similar future discussions more efficiently.

Nevertheless, the two approaches look quite promising. These approaches just need to be experimented under different circumstances followed by an evaluation process to confirm or reject the aforementioned assumptions.

REFERENCES

[1] I. Spasic, S. Ananiadou, J. Mcnaught, and A. Kumar, "Text mining and ontologies in biomedicine: making sense of raw text," Briefings in Bioinformatics, vol. 6, no. 3, Sep. 2005, pp. 239–251.

[2] G. Nagypál, "Improving Information Retrieval Effectiveness by Using Domain Knowledge Stored in Ontologies," in On the Move to Meaningful Internet Systems 2005: OTM 2005 Workshops, R. Meersman, Z. Tari, and P. Herrero, Eds. Springer Berlin Heidelberg, 2005, pp. 780–789.

[3] B. Lemaire and G. Denhière, "Effects of High-Order Co-occurrences on Word Semantic Similarities," ArXiv08040143 Cs, Apr. 2008.

[4] N. Aussenac-Gilles and J. Mothe, "Ontologies As Background Knowledge to Explore Document Collections," in Coupling Approaches, Coupling Media and Coupling Languages for Information Retrieval, Paris, France, 2004, pp. 129–142.

[5] G. Solskinnsbakk and J. A. Gulla, "Ontological Profiles As Semantic Domain Representations," in Proceedings of the 13th International Conference on Natural Language and Information Systems: Applications of Natural Language to Information Systems, Berlin, Heidelberg, 2008, pp. 67–78.

[6] B. Chandrasekaran, J. R. Josephson, and V. R. Benjamins, "What Are Ontologies, and Why Do We Need Them?," IEEE Intell. Syst., vol. 14, no. 1, pp. 20–26, Jan. 1999.

[7] R. Vas, "STUDIO – Ontology-Centric Knowledge-Based System," in Corporate Knowledge Discovery and Organizational Learning, A. Gabor and A. Ko, Eds. Springer International Publishing, 2016, pp.33-58.

[8] C. Fellbaum, "WordNet: An Electronic Lexical Database," Cambridge, MA: MIT Press, 1998

[9] A. Hotho, A. Nürnberger, and G. Paaß, "A Brief Survey of Text Mining," LDV Forum, vol. 20, no. 1, May 2005, pp. 19–62.

[10] A. Huang, "Similarity measures for text document clustering," in Proceedings of the sixth new Zealand computer science research student conference (NZCSRSC2008), Christchurch, New Zealand, Apr. 2008, pp.49-56.

[11] D. M. Blei, A. Y. Ng, and M. I. Jordan, "Latent dirichlet allocation," Journal of machine Learning research, Jan. 2003, pp.993-1022.

[12] D. M. Blei, "Probabilistic Topic Models," Communications of the ACM, vol. 55, no. 4, Apr. 2012, pp. 77–84.

[13] S.T. Dumais, "Latent semantic analysis," Annual review of information science and technology, vol. 38, no.1, Jan. 2004, pp.188-230.

[14] W. Zhang, T. Yoshida, and X. Tang, "A comparative study of TF*IDF, LSI and multi-words for text classification," Expert Systems with Applications, vol. 38, no. 3, Mar. 2011, pp. 2758–2765.
[15] S. Deerwester, S. T. Dumais, G. W. Furnas, T. K. Landauer, and R. Harshman, "Indexing by latent semantic analysis," Journal of the American society for information science, vol. 41, no. 6, Sep. 1990, pp. 391–407.
[16] S. Kullback, and R.A. Leibler, "On information and sufficiency," Annals of Mathematical Statistics, vol. 22, no. 1, Mar. 1951, pp. 79–86.

AUTHOR INDEX

International Academy, Research, and Industry Association (IARIA)
412 Derby Way
Wilmington, DE 19810

ISBN 978-1-5108-4322-6
9 781510 843226

CURRAN ASSOCIATES INC.
proceedings.com

Nineteenth International Conference on Networks (ICN 2020)

Held at NexComm 2020

Lisbon, Portugal
23 - 27 February 2020

IARIA